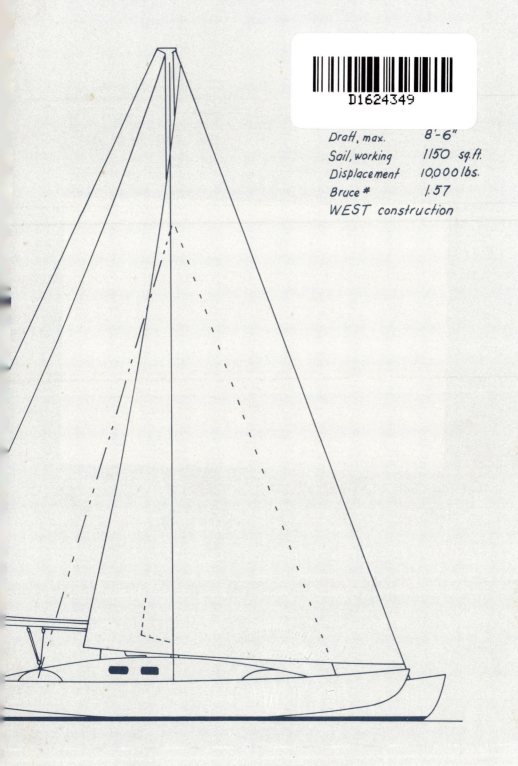

Draft, max.   8'-6"
Sail, working   1150 sq.ft.
Displacement   10,000 lbs.
Bruce #   1.57
WEST construction

MOXIE
1980 OSTAR entry for
Philip S. Weld

RICHARD C. NEWICK
R.F.D., Vineyard Haven
Mass. 02568 , U.S.A.

design #48
sheet # 7
8 Sept. '80

$\mathcal{M}$OXIE

The American Challenge

Foreword by
WILLIAM F. BUCKLEY, Jr.

MOXIE

The American Challenge

By Philip S. Weld

An Atlantic Monthly Press Book
Little, Brown and Company   Boston/Toronto

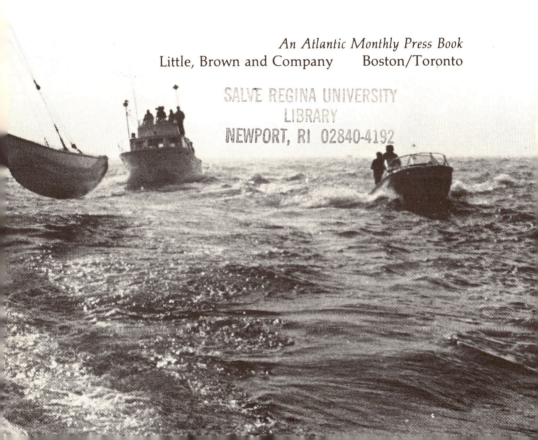

To Anne

FIRST EDITION

Portions of this book appeared in different form in *Sail, Multihulls,* and *Harvard Magazine.*

Lines from Homer, *The Odyssey,* translated by Robert Fitzgerald. Copyright © 1961 by Robert Fitzgerald. Reprinted by permission of Doubleday & Company, Inc.

Photo on page 222-223 by Christian Février; photos on pages 224-225, 227, 229 and 230-231 courtesy of the *Boston Globe;* photo on page 228 by World Wide Photos.

Chapter opening race charts drawn by George W. Ward, based on computer printouts copyrighted by Richard Boehmer.

Library of Congress Cataloging in Publication Data

Weld, Philip S.
  Moxie, the American challenge.

  "An Atlantic Monthly Press book."
  1. Moxie (Sailing yacht) 2. Observer Transatlantic
Singlehanded Sailing Race. I. Title.
GV822.M64W44   797.1′24′0924   [B]   81-15566
ISBN 0-316-92929-8   AACR2

ATLANTIC–LITTLE, BROWN BOOKS
ARE PUBLISHED BY
LITTLE, BROWN AND COMPANY
IN ASSOCIATION WITH
THE ATLANTIC MONTHLY PRESS

VB

Designed by Janis Capone

*Published simultaneously in Canada
by Little, Brown & Company (Canada) Limited*

PRINTED IN THE UNITED STATES OF AMERICA

Contents.

Contents

Foreword.

BY WILLIAM F. BUCKLEY, JR.

I don't know for sure why, but I tend to resist sailing books about solo passages. Joshua Slocum is everybody's exception, and justly so. But Slocum was obstinately healthy. Most such stories, one suspects early on, are written (though this too is a problem, since the prose is more often long entries under traction) by dead souls, driven by misanthropic winds. The desire, never adequately excogitated, is to get "away." Anyone whose life is hectic can understand such an impulse, but then anyone who knows anything at all about life aboard a small boat knows also that there are times at sea when one envies the serenity of the traffic cop at Times Square. Life at sea is most fearfully demanding, and that probably is why its measured joys are so distinctive. But these pleasures — the obliging winds, the beneficent sky, the sweetly composed set of sail, the fleeted speed — are building blocks for the supreme pleasure of camaraderie. I have always thought it impossible, and if possible abominable, to harbor it all to oneself. It is as if, coming on the lone copy of an unknown sonnet by Shakespeare, one were to read and then toss it away; internalizing the pleasure, but only for the finite length of time the lines stay vivid in the memory. There is no witness. You cannot prove it existed. There is, then, none of that enduring satisfaction of shared pleasure.

I confess I have been jarred by this extraordinary book. The stereotype of the neurotic loner is, quite simply, shattered. I am not so affected by this volume as to change my own predilection for gregariousness at sea, but I am moved to acknowledge its pleasures. Now since this book includes a compliment paid to me, I am impelled to shield the author, as also I suppose myself, from the suspicion that I am motivated in my enthusiasm by personal bonds. I have met Mr. Weld on a single occasion, and have no ties to him save a common devotion to a friend. There now. I am free to proceed to say that much of this book's success lies in the revelation of a wholesomely remarkable man. Here is no fugitive from anything at all. His life at home reminds me (the highest compliment) of that of my parents. In his profession (as newspaper publisher) he was successful. His boyhood was privileged. As a soldier during the Second World War (and he lets us learn this with singular becoming grace) he evidently exhibited those virtues we dare still to call manly, and when they would locate his ragged column of soldiers, on those desultory missions in Burma, and airdrop relief to them, the mail drops brought him from his wife one letter for every day since the last he had received.

He had sailed, as yachtclub-oriented boys and girls on the eastern seaboard almost necessarily sail; but it was some time well after he had returned from the war and raised a family that something happened that arrested his imagination. And from the imagination of a Yankee engaged comes something very like monogamous union. A Yankee of the best kind is what Philip Weld plainly is. He is the reassuring reproach to Ortega's mass-man, who drifts parasitically through life, without any sense of reciprocal obligation to his patrimony. When the author got caught up in sailing, and more particularly in multihulled sailing; when he discovered his hunger for solo sailing, he realized intuitively that he could justify his self-indulgence only by enhancing the sport (though what he enhanced was more merely than that). Accordingly he spent thousands of hours, and uncounted thousands of dollars, striving to develop new skills, new contrivances, fresh knowledge; and then to advertise these, so that all who cared to sail would benefit from his own thought and adventures.

And these they surely were. He combines here, as well as anyone whose writings necessarily describe his own exploits, a quality of self-deprecation with a lucidity of detail, and the result is the emergence of a truly endurable, endearing, winner. Lindbergh captured all of Gaul when, after landing and being asked why he had twice circled the field where half of Paris had assembled, agitated, to wait for him, he replied that he suddenly remembered that he had forgotten to bring his passport. There are such lines in this book, and none synthetic. Some, even, are just over there on the side of otherworldliness, as when, to guard instinctively against lionization, Mr. Weld says that such a solo passage as he undertook (in which he broke a world record) was anything but an ordeal. "A long voyage refreshes, rather than tires, me." Then, "Every healthy person ought to try it to see how it tones the skin and sharpens the senses." Right. And everyone should fly to the moon. The view from there is incomparable.

Students of technique should study not only what the author tells us about such subjects as how to behave when capsized at sea, how to prevent this from happening, what is useful to take along on an ocean passage. There is all that and more. But there is also much here for students of narrative prose. It is an unusual tribute to this volume that there isn't a line of it an editor would want to cut, nor (I can think of only one or two exceptions) passages one feels should have been extended. It is a perfect mix, the flashbacks, the autobiographical details, the technical descriptions, the flashes of sheer excitement, the narrative tension. And yet one has the feeling that he wrote it all not by the kind of laborious planning he invested in the devising of his beloved (and mortal) trimarans, but that he wrote it exactly in the way we read it; started with the first sentence, and ended with the last, and then sent off the whole to whomever he had agreed to send it off to. When he wrote (high tribute) it was because he needed to tell us what he had to tell us; and when he stopped (high tribute) it was because, for the nonce, he had nothing to add.

I say for the nonce because I hope that Philip Weld will not deny us, when he is ready, a second book; and, as someone who hasn't won a sailboat race since age fifteen, I wish him to know that it matters not at all to me whether the next time out he wins or loses; the book's success will not hang on his competitive supremacy. But having said as much, I fervently hope he wins that other struggle, which here he more nearly adumbrates than expostulates on, in the closing passages, fearful as he is — so doggedly courteous — of being pedantic, or evangelistic. He is strategically concerned not so much to win races as to harness the wind, and he sees a nexus in what he did with *Moxie*, and what others might do, without *Moxie*. But here I turn to the text, because I can't in paraphrase render authoritatively the kind of charged simplicity with which this self-effacing man communicates what he feels so deeply:

"On *Moxie*'s eighteen-day sprint to victory in the OSTAR, I savored my investments in Windpower and Windship. I seemed to be getting one good break after another from the weather. I convinced myself that by making these commitments, I had gained special favor with Aeolus. I also reflected that here I was, at sixty-five, making a record westbound passage with no great demand for physical effort. Modern gear, such as my roll-into-the-mast Stoway mainsail and my autopilot powered by batteries charged by photovoltaic displays, provided a metaphor for modern seafaring that should be inspirational, or so I thought."

"Or so I thought." Philip Weld doesn't want to be carried away, or make you think him importunate. It is by such graces that he achieves in this book so much more than the tribute due him as the fastest sailor in the history of the world.

MOXIE

The American Challenge

Prologue.

NEWPORT, RHODE ISLAND, JUNE 25, 1980

WHY I TOOK UP SOLO OCEAN-RACING AND WHY I'VE WRITTEN A BOOK ABOUT IT

Clipped to the pulpit by the tether of my safety harness, I penciled into my notebook in big, triumphant figures "0812," the moment of *Moxie's* finish. To windward and to port, the orange oblong of Brenton Reef Tower showed through the early morning mist. The wakes of twenty powerboats churned the water on all sides.

To starboard, *Rogue Wave*, the 60-foot sister to *Moxie*, glided along under full sail. With her engine on, she had the power to stay ahead and she did so to clear the way. Bright with orange T-shirts, she bore my wife, Anne, and a fair sample of our family.

Close astern followed Arthur Choate's big powerboat, *Red Rover*, with Cousin Eloise Choate and more family and friends. Horns bleated and blared. Cries of "Well done, Moxie!" and "Yea, Phil!" from outboards and the flying bridges of sports fishermen, chartered as press boats, punctuated the thrum of the mini-armada.

I felt myself to be the luckiest man in all the world. *Moxie*, my 50-foot trimaran, built to win the Observer Single-handed Transatlantic Race, the OSTAR, had won in record time — 17 days, 23 hours, and 12 minutes, cutting 2 days and 13 hours off the previous record. A playwright taking a standing ovation on opening night, a scientist awakened to news of his Nobel Prize, could not have been more filled with utter joy.

How had I managed to finish first in a fleet in which almost all the skippers were much younger than I? As a newspaperman, I knew the answer to this question had news value. Too much reticence could be a bore. Perhaps at last I had a point for the book I'd so long postponed. I would try to splice three stories; the race day by day; my ten-year cram course in ocean sailing; the influences in my life that made this a sport to suit my tastes.

On December 1, 1970, I sailed from Plymouth, England, for St. Croix on Trumpeter, *the first of nine and a third crossings.* (J. S. Biscoe)

Before the race, "My Atlantic, My Walden" had been my working title. I made a sketch of the tracks of voyages from 1970 to 1980, first in *Trumpeter*, then in *Gulf Streamer* and *Rogue Wave*, finally in *Moxie*; they form a dense cat's cradle, from which a triangle emerges. England, the West Indies, and New England lie at the corners. The total distance sailed comes to more than 80,000 nautical miles. They have accumulated far faster than they ever could in coastal cruising. Nearly half came on nine and one-third Atlantic crossings. It's all been on fast trimarans. My time at sea has accounted for about twenty-four months of the past ten years.

Solo ocean-racing first caught my fancy at age forty-five after reading of fifty-eight-year-old Francis Chichester's 1960 victory in the first single-handed race from Plymouth to New York sponsored by the London *Observer*. Here was a sport in which enlarging experience could offset diminishing vigor. I found out, eighteen years later, that a 4,000-

4

mile race at sixty-four tired me less than a 3,000-mile race at fifty-six because I'd become wiser in choice of boat and gear and in the husbanding of my energies.

But it wasn't until June 1970 that I actually sailed on an ocean race. To look back on my ignorance then still makes me blush. On the first night of a race from Cowes to Plymouth, Bob Harris had to tell me to keep my eyes on the compass to steer at night. I'd never before been at the helm in the dark. Crossing from America to England for three two-handed Round Britain races, the 1972 OSTAR, the 1978 Route du Rhum, four Bermuda races, and half a dozen delivery trips from home base in Gloucester to the Caribbean and back had corrected that.

The satisfaction of getting to know a body of water had seemed to justify my Walden title. On night watches I often found myself humming Frank Hatch Sr.'s merry ballad telling how "Henry Thoreau, Harvard man, fell in love with a pond." My pond forms a quadrangle with corners at Newfoundland, the Shetland Isles, the Canaries, and the Panama Canal. If it is laid on the pilot chart of the North Atlantic, its sides measure only twelve inches. Compared to that 70 percent of the planet's surface we call the Seven Seas, it's no more than New England is to the other forty-four states. But it has seen more history than all the rest combined. Record the tracks of all the ships that ever entered it,

T-R-U-M-P . . . spells Trumpeter. Grandchildren and friends welcome Welds home from the 1970 Round Britain. (Arthur Hodges)

starting with the Phoenicians' first trip from Gibraltar to Cornwall; summon onto a video screen from the memory banks of three millennia the passages made by Norse marauders, British fishermen, Spanish plunderers, Nelson's frigates, German U-boats, and Allied convoys, and they will glow as a solid band of light. No other ocean has carried as much traffic. Yet crossing it today, out of the shipping lanes, for days on end you won't see a living soul.

My voyaging has introduced me to people, to concepts, to adventures, to raptures, and to demands on physical and emotional reserves. It has made this the happiest period in my happy life. A century ago, the magic of the Atlantic touched most seaboard Americans. My parents knew saltwater travel from the deck of a ten-day Cunarder. People spoke jocularly of crossing "The Big Pond." When, in 1932, I made my first transatlantic voyage aboard the *Europa*, it took four and a half days. It was far more enriching than the scores of 747 flights I've taken since.

How the Gulf Stream, first mapped by Ben Franklin on his missions to Europe, shaped the history of our continent will not be sensed from the cabin of a jumbo jet. In a ship, or better yet alone in a small, fast sailing yacht, one can experience the ocean's vitality in the ever-changing colors of the sky and textures of the water. The tug of the current beneath the hull; the varying skew of the magnetic pole's pull on the compass card; the transits of the sun north and south through the seasons that affect wind strength and direction — because these forces bear upon a lone voyager's personal well-being, they focus his mind. Like a whispered scheme for making an easy million.

People are forever asking: "Why do you like sailing alone?" There's no quick answer for someone as gregarious as I am. Back in 1972, on the nineteenth day of *Trumpeter's* OSTAR, I sat on the forward hatch, ghosting northward under the spanker to escape the Azorean calm, and set down nine reasons. Eight years later, they're still valid.

1. Voyaging provides the sense of adventure that animates youthful souls. It nourishes the explorer instinct.

2. Voyaging hardens the physique. New sleep patterns, enforced low alcohol intake, unsullied air, no disagreeable sounds or smells — these influences combine to stimulate and cleanse the senses. The hands toughen, leg and back muscles become more flexible from moving about in close quarters. One loses weight. It's a low-cost health cure.

3. Solo voyaging sharpens perceptions. The lone sailor must develop an animal cunning to avoid hurt. Forethought can prevent the cuff on

Phil Weld earns his letter

By Jack Thomas
Globe Staff

"Don't quote me on this," said a North Shore man, "but Phil Weld's social position in this state couldn't be higher. His middle name is Saltonstall, his wife is from the very distinguished Warren family of Boston, and one of his ancestors was the sheriff who took Anne Hutchinson into custody in the 1600s."

So here, then, is Phil Weld: Milton Academy, Harvard College and the Tavern Club of Boston, a retired 65-year-old newspaper publisher from Dolliver's Neck, Gloucester, healthy and wealthy, with ties to Brahmin Boston that would have drawn a harrumph from old John Winthrop himself.

Then how come Phil Weld is endangering his life in a madcap solo sail across the Atlantic Ocean in a race against scores of men half his age for . . . what? Honor? Glory? To prove himself? To be known as a man willing to risk everything, even his life, to be better than anyone else at one thing – transocenic solo sailing?

Ironically, to find out what makes Phil Weld run; to find out why he is so competitive – no, compulsive about proving his stamina, his athletic prowess, and his physical courage – you have to go back 50 years to his days as a student at Milton Academy, when he wasn't good enough to win a football letter.

In the interim, the theory goes, he has been like Hemingway, driven constantly to prove himself.

"In those days," explained Herb Stokinger, his coach at Milton Academy, "we were niggardly with letters, giving only as many as there were positions, and while Phil was on the football squad and ran track he didn't get a letter because there were boys ahead of him who were better athletes."

Milton Academy now distributes letters more liberally. But Weld has told friends that his failure to win a letter so many years ago is part of what drives him to competitive sailing today.

A few years ago, in honor of his success as a sailor, Milton Academy awarded him an honorary sweater of burned orange and navy blue, not, as a school official explained, "to make up for past deficiencies, but rather because here was someone who had really done more than the average person, certainly demonstrating more courage than is required on a football field."

Weld, in turn, by the way, has been most generous to Milton Academy, having endowed a teaching chair in 1978 in memory of his father.

For all his Brahmin credentials, though, Weld delights in tweaking the establishment, in needling Elliot Richardson, for example, at Tavern Club discussions, or chastising his banker friends for their conservative ways. Even his choice of a multihulled boat like the trimaran Moxie is a way of twitting traditional sailors who are contemptuous of multihulled boats.

"Weld is a rebel," said a friend. "That's why he developed a taste for multihull sailing. When the monohulled people disdained multihulled sailing, not permitting them to race and all, well, that was just the kind of challenge Phil needed to get into catamarans."

Let no one underestimate Weld's accomplishment.

A solo sail across the Atlantic is not for the faint of heart.

Like auto racing, mountain climbing or skydiving, solo oceanic sailing is a lonely, dangerous business, yet another bizarre challenge for men and women who must test themselves relentlessly to find the limits of their courage, skill and derring do.

People wish sailors fair winds and seas. But when the sailor is crossing the Atlantic alone, they add their prayers.

Listen, for example, as Herbert Kenny 3d, a sculptor from Nantucket, describes a crisis several years ago as Weld's boat crossed the Atlantic:

"We'd come into a heavy gale one night, and our rudder, a swing rudder, became useless because a cotter pin had snapped, and it had to be replaced. It was treacherous, and the water was cold, very cold, 39 degrees, but Phil went to work, hanging over the stern, his hands in and out of that water for four hours, trying to free that rudder.

"He didn't succeed until the next morning, and when it was over, he couldn't move his hands because of the cold. They were stiff, and we had to unzipper his jacket for him, but never a word of complaint. It was a tremendous act of physical courage."

It's not easy to find a bad word about Weld. His friends praise his humor and fellowship. His employees laud his skill as a publisher. The men he commanded in Burma in World War II talk about his courage behind the Japanese lines, and fellow sailors describe his seamanship with awe.

In scores of interviews over several days, the most severe criticism came from a few friends who complained that Weld talks so much about sailing that his listeners become bored.

"Sometimes he just goes on and on," said an acquaintance, "and I don't listen, really. I just say, 'Yes, Phil,' and 'No, Phil,' just agreeing with whatever he says."

Weld, who disdains golf as an old man's game, is a lean 6 feet 2, with ears so prominent that friends on his boat joke that he ought to wiggle them to pick up speed. He is physically strong, though, and enormously capable at sea, they say. "He knows every minute detail of his boat," said a fellow sailor. "He's totally in command, even on a leisure sail."

But Weld's boat is for racing, not leisure, and as his guests have pointed out, for speed, not comfort.

"It's a hell of a meal when you get a canned tuna fish sandwich," said a friend.

Once he took a Gloucester reporter out for a sail.

"Phil was a perfect gentleman," said the reporter. "He asked me where I wanted to sail to, and told me to relax and enjoy myself. But the damn boat was going so fast and rocking back and forth, and even though I'm an ex-Navy man, I got seasick and threw up in Gloucester Harbor. I wouldn't go out again on that boat for a farm Down East."

Following graduation from Harvard in 1936, Weld went to work for the Chicago Daily News. He bridled at the affectation of the word "journalist," and, although the pay was small, he said he enjoyed the business.

While in Chicago, Weld became friend and apprentice to Edwin A. Lahey, the colorful labor reporter for the Chicago Daily News, who said he had learned journalism himself, not in classrooms, but in barrooms.

In 1942, when he reported for induction into the Army, the doctor tried to reject him because of hypertension, but as Weld later wrote in his Harvard report: "Sure my pressure was high. While strapping on the sphygmometer, the churl made remarks about 'you Harvard jerks.' "

Weld parachuted into Burma and won the Silver Star fighting with Merrill's Marauders. A few years ago, at a reunion on the North Shore, the men in his unit praised him as a superb commander, and one of them told a reporter, "He never asked anybody to do anything he wouldn't do himself."

After the war, he worked first at the Boston Herald, then the Boston Post, and in January 1952, with the help of Roger Babson, he became owner and publisher of the Gloucester Times and the Newburyport News.

"Because Babson had helped Weld financially," said a reporter for the Gloucester paper, "we had to write a feature story every year in recognition of Babson's birthday."

In the early 1960s Weld spent 18 homesick months in Paris as publisher of the European edition of the Herald Tribune, and as he noted in his 25th report to Harvard:

"Nothing like a gray Christmas in the Paris suburbs to convince a man on which side of the ocean he belongs. There's a point after which one does not transplant successfully, especially if the home soil remains utterly congenial. So what am I doing here?"

Increasingly, as he grew older, sailing and the sea became more a part of his consciousness.

In January 1964, for example, when he expanded his newspaper chain to three, he described the addition of the Beverly Times as the third hull to the other papers in his daily trimaran.

A highlight of each summer was the sail to New London for races with a merry crew of males. "Martinis and sea water," said Weld, "definitely do mix."

Weld was a hard-working publisher, say friends and employees. "He didn't run the place from a broker's office. He was in the composing room or in the editorial office. And he'd kill stories for nobody."

Some years ago, one of Weld's senior editors lost out on a promotion, and quit, but then couldn't find a job for nine months. "Phil kept paying the guy until he found another job," said a long-time employee.

"I'll tell you about Phil Weld," said Bill Cahill, a reporter for Weld's newspapers for 25 years. "I swear by him personally and professionally."

When Cahill suffered a slipped disc in 1965, Weld comforted him by providing the services of his own doctor and by promising Cahill a paycheck every week until he was well enough to return to work. "The paper was not a union shop, and I was out of work more than seven months, but I didn't lose a dime," said Cahill.

"He's a great guy to work for," said Marty Horgan, the mechanical superintendent at the Gloucester Daily Times. "He'll listen to you. He's the kind of guy the employees look up to. He lives in a different world than we do, but he gets along with both sides."

Among small daily newspapers, Weld pioneered in the endorsement of poltical candidates, and in 1958 his Gloucester paper became the first small afternoon daily to print the Saturday edition in the morning so the employees could work a five-day week. "Now," said Cahill, "everybody does it."

Although he and Gloucester Mayor Leo Alper have disagreed often, the mayor conceded his respect for Weld.

By 1971 the three daily newspapers were shifted to photoset composition and offset presswork, and as Weld said, "The operation runs so smoothly that I can indulge my lust for high-speed sailing."

"He would never interfere with the writing in the newspaper," said Alper. "It didn't matter who you were. If you were going to get banged in the newspaper, you were going to get banged. If you had a friend who was involved in drunken driving, and asked Phil to muffle it in the newspaper, he wouldn't do it. He treated everyone alike."

Last year Weld sold the newspapers for $10 million to the Ottoway Newspapers Group. "He sold primarily because of inheritance tax problems," said a friend. "He figured also that at age 65 he had earned retirement and the pleasure to do what he goddamn well pleased."

What pleased him, even before his retirement, was sailing, and he was such a dedicated student that in 10 years he became one of the world's outstanding trimaran sailors.

Multihulled sailing is a passion with the French, said a friend of Weld, because "they beat the bejesus out of the British at it, but now here is Phil beating the French at their own game."

For a transoceanic race a few years ago, the French issued television cameras to four boats, asking the skippers to photograph their own voyage. "Phil took a lot of pictures inside and out of his cabin," said a friend, "including one of himself in the shower with shampoo in his hair, and when it appeared on television, the French loved it, and they called him 'Monsieur Shampoo.' "

Weld's worst sailing crisis came two years ago on a four-week voyage to England when a 40-foot rogue wave roared out of the Atlantic and capsized his 60-foot trimaran Gulf Streamer 325 miles south of Nantucket. For nearly five days Weld and his crewman, William Stephens, 21, of Birmingham, Mich., lived atop the hull until they were rescued by a British cargo ship. The $150,000 boat, not insured, was salvaged by the Russians.

As Weld described the incident: "One minute I was lying comfortably in my bunk reading a novel by Anthony Trollope. The next, the boat had flipped upside down, and I was standing on the cabin ceiling up to my waist in water."

Later Weld joked with a reporter that he might abandon sailing and take up horseback riding, but he never seriously considered quitting sailing.

"He seemed to want to get right back at it," said Bill Ellis, a neighbor. "But then, anything he goes into, he goes wholeheartedly."

Another Weld passion is tennis.

"In 30 years of playing tennis with Phil," said Herb Kenny, the writer, "I have never seen him for one minute display irritation, let alone anger. You might also be interested to know that Phil is the inventor of a stroke called the 'Hindu Squat,' which is when he leaps into the air to hit an overhead and falls on his ass."

Colleagues at the Tavern Club describe Weld as a faithful member. "He's certainly not the type to boast about his exploits," said one. "To hear him describe one of his Atlantic crossings, you'd think he'd just sailed across the Frog Pond."

Other members point out that in matters of food, Weld is anything but a gourmet. "His favorite food may be chocolate ice cream," said a member. Before dinner he enjoys a martini or a Jack Daniels, and with dinner, a glass or two of white wine. As one Tavern Club member said: "We have a pretty good Montrachet."

Weld seems to move as easily among blue-collar workers as he does among his social peers. "He could be a great snob if he wanted to be," said a Tavern Club member, "and I'm sure some people think of him that way. But he's only a snob about subjects that have no interest to him."

"Nope," said Cahill. "No snobbery at all. He can walk into a neighborhood pub like Kelleher's, and drink a beer with you and you'd never know that he's a Yankee, a Brahmin and a WASP. And if you play tennis with him in his back yard, he's very graceful, not snooty at all. That doesn't mean he's going to invite me to his daughter's wedding, though."

Weld lives in a concrete block home overlooking the entrance to Gloucester Harbor. "Some think it resembles the Peruvian Embassy," he jokes. "Others say a giant Exxon Station."

Weld has been married to Anne Warren for 44 years. They have a son, Philip, a reporter, and four daughters, Eloise Hodges, Katharine, Anne and Helen.

A neighbor said that Weld is sometimes criticized for not participating enough in community affairs.

"A lot of people in Phil's financial class think he should be on the board of this or that or the trustee of this or that," he said. "But he's not the type to be on the board of the Red Cross or the YMCA. He's very devoted to Harvard, though, and was director of the alumni magazine."

Weld's doctor has urged friends to try to get Weld to take life easier, but that does not appear likely.

He's talked recently about heading to the Pacific to help improve wind power transportation among the islands.

That fits with one of three convictions he expressed a few years ago: "That William Shakespeare, the Stratfordian, did not write the plays; that Columbus did not discover America, and that the wind is the most neglected source of useful energy."

In his 40th report to Harvard, though, Weld let slip a remark that suggests there are values in life beyond sailing and racing and winning.

"Ocean voyaging," he wrote, "leaves time to contemplate the verities – first among them that after 60, friendships count beyond all else."

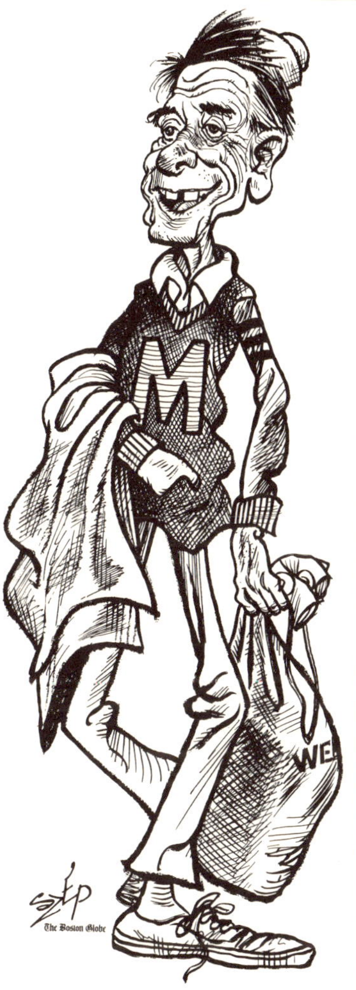

'Martinis and sea water definitely do mix'

Paul Szep, the Boston Globe*'s Pulitzer-prize-winning cartoonist, records my honorary letter from Milton Academy, awarded for sailing forty years after graduation.* (Boston Globe)

the ear from a flailing genoa sheet. By rehearsing his moves out loud, he can exercise his voice muscles and avoid a balls-up on a spinnaker jibe.

4. Voyaging requires learning new skills: pilotage, celestial navigation, meteorology, the use of tools, some understanding of radio. Such schooling stimulates the brain, particularly if the subjects concern survival.

5. Solo racing brings one together with new acquaintances from many countries, all total individualists worth discovering. The three Round Britain races have given Anne and me a chance to make real friends among the British. The Route du Rhum brought me closer to the French than I could ever get during my eighteen months in Paris as publisher of the *New York Herald Tribune*'s European edition. On short-handed passages with crew younger than my own children, we've had cockpit cocktail hours that loosened the tongue and made for frank exchanges such as one hadn't had since college.

6. Risking the "hazards of the sea" all alone, because so few do it, commands recognition. Phil Hersh, *Gloucester Times* sports editor, asked before the 1972 OSTAR, "Why do you do this?" "Because I've always been a frustrated jock," I answered. "How else can a man my age get his name on the sports page?" No matter how hard I'd tried, I'd never won a letter in track or football at Milton or in rowing at Harvard.

7. One achieves a sense of Earth's rotundity, of the planet's fragility.

8. One gets some hints of The Scheme. On deck alone at dawn, there's time and quiet to ponder the verities.

9. One finds a purpose in retirement, an aim for that period in a man's life when he can call himself semi-retired, or "semi-working," as I preferred to call it. Edward Bellamy in his utopian novel *Looking Backward* divided the populace into these age groups: five to twenty-five, study; twenty-five to forty-five, full-time work; forty-five to fifty-five, part-time work. Over fifty-five, instead of a period to dread, becomes the time for pleasures, among which sailing short-handed should surely be included.

Time and again during the last eighteen days, I've said to myself, "There's nothing in the world I'd rather be doing than what I'm doing right now." This race, as fifty super-8 film cassettes from the on-deck sound camera will testify, has been, not an ordeal, but a joyful experience. It helped to know right from the start that *Moxie* was fast enough to win. Midway across, when victory seemed possible, I anticipated a Newport press conference. I wrote out questions and answers, among them: "To what do you attribute your win?" Answer "Three P's — Perseverance — Preparation — Pocketbook."

This book will tell why I persisted, how I got ready, and how I could afford it. These may seem unlikely themes for an admirer of Henry David Thoreau. But right now, in my view, the Atlantic doesn't appear much like Walden Pond.

1.

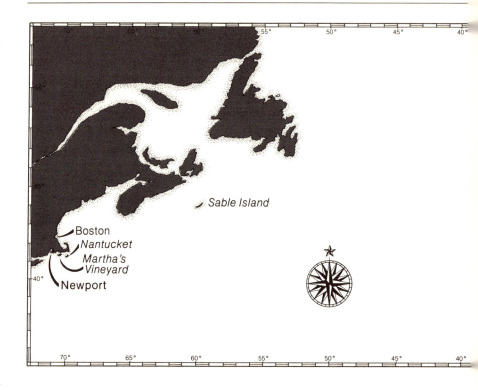

Sable Island

Boston
Nantucket
Martha's
Vineyard
Newport

STATING THE CONTEXT

I'm a sixty-five-year-old, retired American publisher of small-city daily newspapers. After forty-three years of marriage, I'm still in love with my boyhood "dream girl." We have a son, four daughters, nine sturdy grandchildren, and three dogs. We own two beautiful places, one on Gloucester harbor from whose terrace on a clear day you can look south and see Boston's skyline. The other overlooks Saltmarsh Cove in Edgecomb, Maine, on the Damariscotta River.

We have good health; old friends and new friends; dozens of cousins; plenty of money, people would say; and concern for public causes to which we can contribute. Life has been so kind to me I'd turn down any offer of a substitution no matter how many throws of the dice I might be allowed. This might sound smug but it means I'm grateful. One chapter after another has turned out well — boarding schools, Harvard College, first newspaper jobs in Chicago, three years in the infantry, four years' postwar frustration, then a chance to follow my

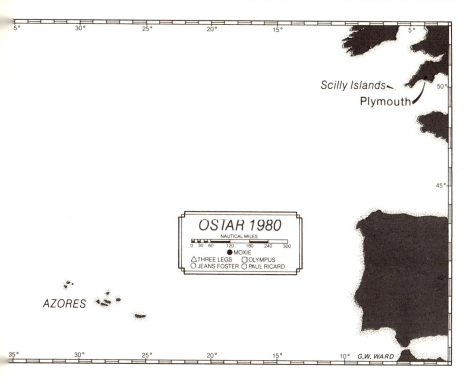

bent — ownership of a business suited to my tastes. Newspaper publishing combines the literary and entrepreneurial urges.

I stand just over six feet two. My weight varies from 185 to 200 pounds. Since my hair has only just begun to gray, some people take me for a bit younger than I am. Because I understand the newsman's problem, finding something fun to write about, I get along easily with the press and so have been treated well beyond my deserts in pre-race coverage of this yachting event that I have embarked upon for the third time.

Most of the stories mention that I'm the oldest competitor in this, the sixth running of the London *Observer*'s Single-handed Transatlantic Race (the OSTAR), a contest for sailing yachts over a 2,810-mile course from here to Newport, Rhode Island. But I don't feel any older than the others, no doubt because getting ready to compete has forced me to stay spry and flexible. The 1960 race involved four Englishmen and one Frenchman. This year we have ninety official starters from eighteen countries and two "unofficial," both French.

The family gathers on Dolliver's Neck for the wedding, August 18, 1979, of daughter Annie and Mac Bell, farthest to the right. (Goodwin Harding)

The international, polyglot flavor of the yachts rafted five abreast along the sides of the Milbay Dock adds interest for the many Devon and Cornish folk who make it a practice every four years to give the fleet a warm send-off. The three lady skippers — France's Florence Arthaud, New Zealand's Dame Naomi James, and America's Judy Lawson — are all sailing single-hulled keel boats, as are the great majority of the men. But the savvy yachting writers say one of the eighteen trimarans will win.

Such was not the case at the start in 1972, when the favorite was the three-masted, 128-foot French schooner *Vendredi Treize;* nor again in 1976 when the odds-makers picked *Club Mediterranée,* a French four-master, 236 feet long. Neither of these giants won, but the fears of catastrophic collisions engendered by their presence resulted in a limit on length for 1980 of 46 feet on the waterline, 56 feet overall, too small to give the monohulls a chance against tris of this size.

In 1972, I raced a British-built, 44-foot trimaran, *Trumpeter.* Beginner's problems dogged us. We finished twenty-seventh in 39 days, 13 hours, nearly twice the time it took Alain Colas to win and set the record that year of 20 days and 13 hours, which still stands. In 1976, I sailed from Florida for the start in a new 60-foot trimaran, *Gulf Streamer*, designed by Dick Newick; she capsized north of Bermuda. In her replacement, *Rogue Wave*, I finished third in the 1978 Route du Rhum, a French solo race from Saint-Malo to Guadeloupe. But the new rule excludes her for 1980, so I'm here in *Moxie*, launched only last August, designed by Dick for one purpose, to see if I can win this race.

This experience has put enough lead in my pencil to make my forecast heeded. "Mike Birch, Eric Loizeau, Walter Greene — one, two, three," I rattle off when queried. "Then you have to reckon with three more tris, any one of whom could win: Nick Keig, Tom Grossman, and Phil Steggall."

"What about Eugene Riguidel in *VSD?*"

"Alone, he'll push the boat too hard and get in trouble."

"You've only mentioned trimarans. Doesn't any mono have a chance?"

"If it blows hard on the nose for days on end, Jaworski or de Kersauson might fool us. Warren Luhrs could do well, too. But I don't know all that much about the monohulls."

"How about *Moxie?*"

"I'll be happy to finish in the top ten." Lying hypocrite!

To concentrate my race preparation, I have resorted to several devices. I carry in my wallet a list I made up last November of twenty-one skippers I consider threats. Sadly, two can already be scratched: Rory Nugent and Yves Le Cornec, both of whom lost their boats in capsizes en route to England from America. Last summer I wrote three scenarios: The Start, The Middle of the Race, The Approach to the Finish. They avoid giving *Moxie's* exact standing but all include her among the leaders whom I name.

(*Sail* magazine couldn't accept these because they were "fiction." *The Atlantic*, quite understandably, found them "too specialized." But, by submitting them, I gained an introduction to Upton B. Brady, Director of the Atlantic Monthly Press, who has encouraged me to write a book.)

I typed out a daily check sheet I call my *"Moxie* Prod." It reminds me constantly to recalculate the shortest compass course to Newport from the ship's latest position; to analyze the latest forecast for the most likely wind shift; and to consider what change in sail trim would improve our average speed. On the chart of the North Atlantic, I ruled a line joining Plymouth and Newport. Using dividers, I stepped off seventeen segments of 168 nautical miles, the distance traveled in twenty-four hours at an average 7 knots "made good over the bottom," par for the course. I labeled this "Ideal Passage." Since "ideals" rarely materialize, I added a day for good measure.

On August 3, 1979, three days before *Moxie*'s launching, I wrote an article for *Sail*, "How to win the 1980 OSTAR." It opens with the prediction that the winning time would be "less than 18 days — say 425 hours." Runners aspiring to a four-minute mile time their laps in seconds; marathon racers measure progress against 120 minutes; a competitive transatlantic sailor, or so it seemed to me, had to condition himself to think in hours rather than days. My piece was held back for the June issue so I have only a Xerox of the typescript aboard. Let's check what I wrote:

> A skipper who can't say: "I have no boat worries" doesn't belong on the bookies' list. But what of his other concerns: mental and physical fitness; flawless self-steering capability; understanding of the weather patterns for each of the three 1,000-mile segments into which the course naturally divides; navigation technique to take advantage of what may be rare sights on sun and stars; knowledge of the boat's best performance under different sail combinations.
>
> Fitness — ... The readiness to change sail — up or down — will separate the pros from the amateurs toward the end of the race when light airs will prevail. Changing from a working jib to a bigger, lighter-weight genoa may require exertion every bit as strenuous as a set of tennis singles. For these stresses, one must have nourished the will to win — an attitude that comes naturally to most serious international athletes, but not necessarily to solo sailors who are often philosophic types quite simply rewarded by having made a fast passage against odds. It's impossible to engender the killer instinct against your friends, all of whom are, like yourself, contending against the true adversary — the wind, or the lack of it.
>
> Like infantrymen in opposing fox-holes, opponents share bonds of common discomfort and frustration that make adrenalin-pumping hatreds difficult to summon. And yet the ambitious skipper must somehow sharpen his appetite for victory if he hopes to get the most from the sudden wind shift no matter how exhausted he may be. For example, my competitive effort was heightened during the 1978 Route du Rhum by going to the pulpit each morning and shouting toward the west, where I fancied Michel Malinovsky in his beautiful big sloop might lie, "One of us multihullers will git you yet."

Thanks to the trip across, the racing in France and down the Channel, I feel as fit and race-ready as my boat. My hands have been toughened and my sleep habits disciplined. Tom Perkins, my shipmate all through *Moxie*'s tuning, has goaded me to go through the main hull from bow to stern taking off for shipment home every surplus piece of cordage, any needless tool, the anchor and chain, the outboard motor, one bunk cushion, any bit of weight not deemed useful to the race. We're riding high on our lines for the first time since loading up in Fort Lauderdale. I'm heavy only in backup for that most precious of devices, the self-steerer. I'm carrying three complete spare Autohelm kits.

No skipper has prepared more elaborately than I to get weather information. In combination with Bob Rice of Weather Services Corp., Bedford, Massachusetts, and Art Zolot of Aeromarine, Inc., Beverly, Massachusetts, a radio expert and skilled ham, I have a plan for special forecasts tailor-made for whatever might be my current position. While the first edition of the rules barred private advisories, the Royal West-

Tom Perkins prepares to strip Moxie *of all surplus weight, such as the outboard engine, at Plymouth's Milbay Dock.* (Philip S. Weld)

ern Yacht Club of England, the race organizers, later lifted the ban. Such a regulation seemed no longer practicable when competitors were being encouraged, for reasons of safety, to communicate on amateur-band radio. Not wishing to seem selfish about my arrangement, I've given any skipper who cared a sheet detailing the times and frequencies of Art's daily broadcasts together with the form that the spoken forecasts would follow.

The best of all worry-erasers has been bolted to the afterdeck — an Argos transponder. It will remove my worry that Anne is worried. Better than I can, let's hear Frank Page explain it to *Observer* readers:

> The best news of all for the newsmen came in November 1979, when the Observer announced that it had arranged for every yacht to be fitted with an Argos system transponder, so that everyone following the race would know exactly where each boat was all the way across the ocean. The Argos system is a world-wide operation weather data collection satellite system which has evolved out of the co-operative space program developed by the United States and France. The transponders would send automatic signals 500 miles into space, to be collected and stored by the Tiros-N and NOAA-6 satellites, circling the globe on polar orbits.
>
> The messages would be "read out" once each orbit to three ground telemetry stations — one in France and two in the United States. The information would then be sent to a processing center in Washington, from there to Toulouse for decoding, and on to race information centers in Britain, France and America. The computer print-out would show the exact location of each yacht, the direction it was sailing and the progress made since the last "sighting." . . . The British Meteorological Office was to receive some of the data, which could help it to make more accurate weather forecasts during the race, and in turn the BBC's World Service was to broadcast a weather bulletin specially prepared for the singlehanders at 3:30 A.M. Greenwich time each day.
>
> In emergency, the Argos system can be a vital aid to search and rescue. If any yacht gets into trouble, the rescue services will know where to look for her. If the singlehanded skipper should be forced to abandon ship, he can unhook the Argos transmitter from its deck position and carry it into the life-raft with him. Operating a special switch on the transmitter will change the regular message from "routine" to "emergency."

The expectation of continuous coverage of the race, both in Europe and the United States, gave me the final shove I needed to underwrite a risky venture, a documentary movie for TV showing called "American Challenge." Chris Knight, Boston filmmaker, has installed cameras on four tris and four keel boats. My on-deck sound unit, inside a waterproof case, has been set to roll with the crack of the 2:00 P.M. starting cannon. One more prod to make me competitive.

2

THE START FROM PLYMOUTH

The gates to the Milbay Dock swung open about ten in the morning to permit a procession of launches to take in tow those competitors without engines. A smart crew aboard a navy vessel took *Moxie*'s line. On both sides of the lock, I could pick out the smiling faces of the many British friends we'd made over the past ten years of racing from this historic port. As we passed into the harbor, the volume of hand-clapping and decorous cheers gave clear recognition that the beauty of *Moxie*'s three slender hulls made her a favorite.

Something about the proportion of her overall length, 50 feet, to her overall beam, 33 feet, gave her a grace that brought gasps of delight even to the least knowing observer. She looked at once dainty and spare, strong and sea-kindly. "Like a great gull on the wing," became the cliché.

Her 50-foot mast seemed short beside those of *Three Legs of Mann* and *Kriter VII.* But to those who know trimarans, its modesty bespoke safety and freedom from "hobbyhorsing," that is to say, tiresome pitching up and down of the whole boat in rough head seas. Her three tip-tilted

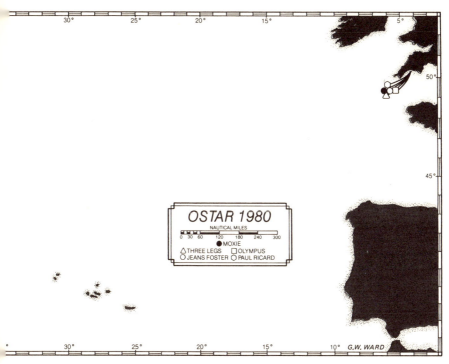

OSTAR 1980
NAUTICAL MILES
0 30 60   120   180   240   300
● MOXIE
△ THREE LEGS   □ OLYMPUS
○ JEANS FOSTER ○ PAUL RICARD

G.W. WARD

prows gave her profile a saucy air while the three slender sterns made her look fast even alongside a wharf.

"Tell me where I'm most likely to goof?" I asked Tom Perkins, my steadfast friend, who through months of building and shakedown had come to know every last reinforcing batten in the wing connections, each bolt holding rig to deck.

"The runners," he said. "Don't forget to take up the running back-stays when you're using the staysail."

As if to accent his warning, there ahead of us lay Florence Arthaud's sloop, *Miss Dubonnet,* with her mast crumpled halfway up. Press boats swarmed around, filming Arthaud's tears and the limp sails. Just two hours before the gun, some nightmarish rig failure had caused the first calamity.

"Oh, Tom, I feel so sorry for that nice girl."

"Goes to show," said Tom. "Until late last night there was a gang aboard changing her rig."

We, thank heaven, had stuck to our rule of letting nothing new come aboard in the way of rig and gear once we got to Plymouth.

The inner harbor was rapidly filling with competitors and spectator

Moxie - OSTAR START
Plymouth, England - June 7, 1980

Moxie *seen from a helicopter at the start.* (Daniel Gilles)

craft when we cast off our tow. We agreed to roll out only the staysail and a third of the main to hold us down to a sedate pace. When it became frenetically crowded, we sailed out past the breakwater, checked the angle of the starting line to the wind to see if there were any grave disadvantage to making a cautious start somewhere in the middle. We hove to about half a mile from the navy ship anchored at the westerly end.

"Collision. That's what scares me most," I said. "From now on until I'm clear of the land, I'm playing old Mr. Cautious."

Two pretty girls came alongside in a whaler and handed us two splits of Kriter wine, nicely chilled. We popped the corks and toasted one another. Then it was time to hail Chris Knight in his filming runabout to ferry Tom to the fifty-passenger boat Dick Newick had chartered. *Moxie* and I were on our own.

I had the advantage of having been here several times before. In the 1970 Round Britain, *Trumpeter's* rudder blade had slipped out of its housing just after the start. Recovering it among the swarms of press and spectator craft had been awkward. Always at these highly publicized races, the helicopters thrumming overhead and the light planes buzzing the masthead make it hard to concentrate. But the 1972

OSTAR, two more Round Britain races, and the Route du Rhum at Saint-Malo in 1978 had helped accustom me to the frenzy.

I tuned the VHF to Channel 68 over which Commander Lloyd Foster, sailing secretary of the Royal Western, had told us at the skippers' meeting he would call the countdown. No need for a stopwatch.

Now all but competitors were barred from the starting area. I kept my eye on Walter Greene and Mike Birch. They, too, were planning conservative starts at the middle of the line. At the ten-minute gun, I rolled out the full main and reached back from the outer harbor, where I'd been lurking safe from the mob, to a point where I judged I'd have about a three-minute dash to the line.

As I jibed, I rolled up the staysail and rolled out the genoa. It took slightly longer than I'd planned because an out-of-bounds spectator yawl suddenly emerged from nowhere to delay my coming hard on the wind. But no matter. With two minutes to the gun, *Moxie* was moving in clear air at 9 knots in the 12-knot southwesterly. I crossed about a minute late.

I could hear the camera whirring under the dodger. Chris had set its automatic timer to start filming with the gun.

(In the film sound track, you can hear my voice over the choppers saying, "We're off and running. One minute late but we beat Mike and Walter. Phil Steggall in *Jeans Foster* got the best start among the tris. Even so we'll catch him in a minute.")

Chris came alongside in his speedy outboard. I pointed to the camera and gave him a thumbs-up. Per plan, it had shut down after thirty seconds and would not resume its programmed duty for four hours unless I threw a switch to override the automatic shutoff. Already I felt kindly toward it. Its microphone provided a sympathetic ear for my hopes and fears.

Within minutes *Moxie* had sailed through Phil Steggall's lee. It was the first time our two tris had been pitted against one another. Though *Moxie* was longer, she carried less sail area for her weight. In theory, in the moderate seas of the moment, no telling which should be the faster.

The ten miles to the Eddystone Light gave me a great surge of confidence in *Moxie*'s ability to win the race. No boat was footing faster. She was the only boat among the leaders pointing high enough to leave the Eddystone to port. If she could do better than hold her own against the tris of Greene, Birch, Keig, Riguidel, and Loizeau, all of whom had relatively taller rigs, in these conditions — close-hauled into moderate

Nick Keig's **Three Legs of Mann III** *at the start.* (Joyce Zino)

wind with no chop — then she should do even better slugging her way into heavy seas and higher winds. Then everyone would have to shorten sail. Their higher masts, so useful in light air, would become encumbrances. The extra weight aloft would cause the boats to pitch and toss and slow down.

I couldn't resist switching on the camera. Listen to the sound track: ". . . in a moment we'll have the Eddystone Light to leeward and abeam. We seem to be leading. Eric Loizeau is behind me and a bit to windward. Mike Birch and Walter Greene are down to leeward. *Paul Ricard*, the unofficial entry, is falling off well to leeward. He's footing a little faster but now he has tacked and I'm clearly going to take him. Here come the speedboats. All acting as if I'm in the lead. So here we go, *Moxie*."

As the late-setting June sun bathed the Cornish coast in gold, the spectator fleet diminished until finally there was only the big Brittany ferry, chartered by the French press, to keep us company. She came charging up from the south, where five or six tiny sails could be seen, to circle first Eric, then *Moxie*, before speeding a mile to the north for final shots of *Paul Ricard*. As twilight descended, she gave us four blasts on her horn and took off at 20 knots for Plymouth.

To my relief, the wind backed into the south as we approached the Lizard. We three leaders — by now I felt confident that's what we were — would no longer be able to point high enough to pass between Land's End and the Scilly Isles. This shortcut to Newport involves crossing busy sea-lanes. No fun for the solo sailor, especially if the fog should roll in.

Only now, seven hours from the start, did I dare to leave the helm and put *Moxie* under the care of the autopilot. The breeze dropped to a gentle 5 knots. In trying to haul the daggerboard down to its fullest extremity, its tip nine feet below the waterline, one of the secrets of *Moxie*'s astonishingly good windward performance, I got in irons (boat going backward, nose in the wind). In the minute it took me to get moving again, Eric Loizeau reduced my lead by half with frightening rapidity. In the dark I could see him shining his flashlight on his telltales to check the set of his jib.

Ah, the intensity of Youth.

"Eric, me lad," I said out loud. "You'll never be able to maintain that pace all the way to Newport."

For myself, I was content to keep an eye on the wind-angle and boat-speed indicators to satisfy myself that *Moxie* was performing well on her own. Slight wind shifts required no more than a tweak left or right on the autopilot steering knob. I was at last free to slice some cheese, heat water for coffee, and pour myself a small whiskey and water. The midnight shipping forecast promised light and variable westerlies for the Scillies.

One mile astern and slightly to windward, Eric's tricolor masthead light shone red, but Marc Pajot in *Paul Ricard,* somewhere to the north, had evidently not switched his on.

In the moonless starshine, the lights of a tanker parade plodding eastward from the entrance to the Channel were all that showed we were not a thousand miles from shore. At 2:00 A.M. the log said we'd made 116 miles through the water in the first half-day of the race. One couldn't have asked for a happier send-off.

THE COMPETITORS MOST TO BE FEARED

My competition was formidable. While almost everyone of the serious contenders among the bigger boats in the Pen Duick class had become a good friend, I knew each to be a skilled sailor with a savage desire to win.

Nick Keig, on *Three Legs of Mann III,* represented the British threat. Slight, fortyish, he's a master of the soft-spoken, deadpan gag. He runs his own photo business on that feisty little island in the Irish Sea where birching schoolboys is legal and the national motto, "However you throw us we land on our feet," is symbolized by three legs joined at the thigh, pinwheel fashion.

I first met Nick the day before the 1972 OSTAR. He'd recently capsized his Iroquois catamaran racing in a gale. He wanted to check out Derek Kelsall as a designer by having a look at *Trumpeter.* In his first tri, *Three Legs of Mann,* he won the under-35-foot class in the 1974 Round Britain by finishing fourth to *Gulf Streamer's* third. On the last afternoon of the 1978 Round Britain, when the wind had dropped to near zero, his new *Three Legs II* snatched second place from *Rogue Wave.* With his taller mast, 70 feet as compared with 56 feet, Nick was able to catch up and ghost past us over an agonizing seven hours.

The following October Nick joined me in Scotland to sail *Rogue* to Plymouth. As we sailed past his home shore, I asked, "Nick, how long has your family lived there?" Pause. "About twelve hundred and fifty years."

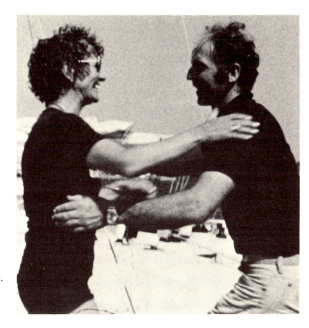

Mo and Nick Keig reunited at Newport. (Christopher Knight)

Because he actually enjoys building boats, he sold *Three Legs II* and built *III* for the OSTAR. Some said she was too much the heavy family cruiser to be competitive. But one look at her tall rig and I knew better.

Walter Greene, off the water, gives no hint that he'd be first choice as sailing master for every ocean-racing owner with whom he's ever sailed, and they are many. His slight frame, his loping, stoop-shouldered gait, his horn-rims suggest an overscheduled engineering-school instructor who is moonlighting as a consultant. Until his hands give him away. Large, nicked, and spotted with patches from the last resin batch, his fingers tell you this man doesn't work at a desk.

After the University of Vermont, he married Joan, a biochemistry major, whom he'd met skiing. Together they've made high-performance ocean-racing boats their life. When he and I first met, he was working for Alan Vaitses at Mattapoisett. The bold competence with which he attacked *Trumpeter*'s broken cross arms impressed me. Owner of a traditional schooner, watch captain for Ted Hood on the Florida racing circuit, Walter then regarded trimarans with skepticism.

But helping me to win the 1973 Multihull Bermuda Race by a wide margin in *Trumpeter* changed his mind. He learned to loft a hull by taking a correspondence course in naval architecture. Working days for

Walter Greene at the christening, July 30, 1979, in Falmouth Foreside, Maine. (Christopher Knight)

Ted Hood, he and Joan slaved nights and weekends to build a 31-foot tri, based on Dick Newick's design for the 1976 OSTAR. They named her *Friends* "for all the people who helped" and in her Walter finished eighth overall.

The Greenes then moved to Maine to work for Handy Boats in Falmouth Foreside. They sold *Friends* and commenced another year of eighty-hour weeks, building in their spare time a larger tri of Walter's own design, named by Joan *A Capella*. In this they finished fourth in the 1978 Round Britain, winning the under-35-foot class. After that, they chartered her to Mike Birch, who sailed her to victory in the Route du Rhum. Walter became an instant guru among French multihullers.

Shortly after contracting to build *Moxie*, Walter called to ask if I objected to his designing and building simultaneously a second OSTAR tri, *Gauloises*, for Eric Loizeau.

"I must warn you," said Walter, "if I do this for Eric, I won't have time this fall to help you shake down *Moxie*."

Naturally, I wasn't about to stand between Walter and his first client. Besides, I figured the more he was working with other competitors, the more knowledge he'd gain to pass along to me.

Walter likes to be as familiar with a new boat as a good chef with his new kitchen. Boarding for the first time, preparatory, say, to co-skippering a race with the owner, Walter roves the deck like a bird dog in a quail cover. With a Magic Marker in his teeth and a small Vise Grip in hand, he sets about checking shroud tension, identifying halyards and examining sheet leads with the intensity of guitarist Andrés Segovia tuning up.

"This winch could stand cleaning," he'll announce. In no time he'll have it disassembled and will be rinsing away the salt, all the while scrutinizing the cockpit and environs for the undersized block or the unwired shackle pin that could bring on trouble. Once under way, if not at the helm, he begins a continuous routine of small sheet adjustments to which the boat responds either by pointing a degree higher or footing a tenth of a knot faster. He's never satisfied. He has been my best tutor.

Walter's sister, Esther, and Joan worked eighty-hour weeks last summer to build *Chaussettes Olympia* for him under his direction. He wanted a bigger boat that could win the Gypsy Moth, or intermediate class, prize. Its near-twin, *Jeans Foster*, designed by Walter, will be sailed by his friend, Phil Steggall.

Phil, a New Zealander by birth, settled with his American wife, Beth, in Marblehead, where he works for Hood Sails. He's the man sent to check out new sails for the maxi-ocean racers like *Kialoa* and *Ondine*. Sailing to England in 1976 with Walter in fifteen days converted him to fast, short-handed passage-making in a trimaran. Despite the pressure of a travel schedule that had him flying from Florida to Cowes to Honolulu advising clients, he still found time to worry about *Moxie's* shortened rig. He insisted I needed a larger working jib to remain competitive and took personal charge of its design. While he's the next to youngest skipper in the fleet, he's probably had more racing experience on hot boats than any of us.

Mike Birch, a Canadian, was working fourteen-hour days to finish *Third Turtle* for the 1976 OSTAR when I first met him on Martha's Vineyard. His spare frame and tidy ways exuded competence as he went about readying his tiny tri. He got to Newport in her faster than anyone but the two Frenchmen, Eric Tabarly and Alain Colas, in their much bigger boats. This won him renown all over France and sponsorship for the Route du Rhum. He chartered *A Capella* from Walter, sailed her to victory by 98 seconds, and won the $50,000 first prize. His new tri, *Olympus Photo*, had been my selection to win this year's race because I agree with Dick Newick, "Mike is one of those sailors who does everything right instinctively."

Tom Grossman bought his first trimaran, *Cap 33*, at a bargain just

27

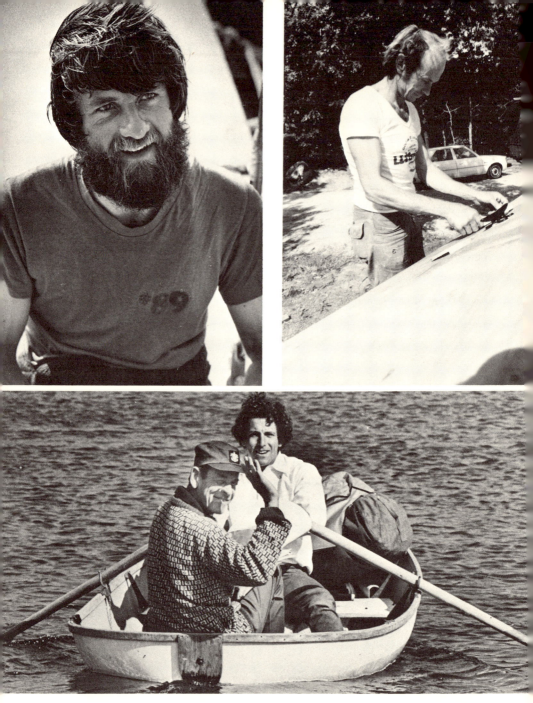

Above left, Phil Steggall, *sail designer and skipper of* Jeans Foster, *fastest light-air boat in the race.* (Kirk R. Williamson) **Above right,** *Canadian Mike Birch, the contestants' pick to win, skipper of* Olympus Photo II. (Christopher Knight) **Below,** *Tom Grossman, the bookmakers' choice, ferries us to* Gulf Streamer *for her May 1974 Atlantic crossing.* (Ulrike Welsch)

after she had finished third in the 1972 OSTAR. He sailed her to fifth place four years later, the first American to finish. He then began a campaign to find a sponsor for the new tri he had Newick design him for 1980. She was launched as *Sponsor Chaser*, but before he sailed for England from Florida, he renamed her *Kriter VII*, for the French white wine whose makers believe in the publicity value of a favored entry in this race. While she's the same 46 feet on the waterline as *Moxie*, she's 6 feet longer overall. This makes her appear much bigger.

The two French trimarans I most fear are Eric Loizeau's *Gauloises IV* and Eugene Riguidel's *VSD*. These young Bretons make ocean-racing their career. They have enthusiastic sponsors, a cigarette company and a weekly news magazine, *Vendredi Samedi Dimanche*. They will be bold and highly competitive.

There are half a dozen keel boats demanding attention, especially if the race is dogged by strong headwinds as in 1976. The skippers provided quite an international mix: Olivier de Kersauson, France; Kazimierz Jaworski, Poland; Edoardo Austoni, Italy; Warren Luhrs, USA; Bertie Reed, South Africa; and Richard Konkolski, Czechoslovakia. Olivier's boat, now named *Kriter VI*, raced as *Bestavaer* in 1976 with Gerry Dijkstra at the helm. He crossed in twenty-days after being forced back to Plymouth with rigging problems. Jaworski's new *Spaniel II* looks even more impressively rigged than his boat of the same name in which he finished right behind Mike Birch in 1976 to win the Gypsy Moth trophy.

The fortnight at Plymouth allowed me to meet almost every entrant but the late arrivals. But always one wishes there had been more time to get to know them better. The groups that coalesced in Milbay Dock did not form by virtue of any ties of nationality, but more from the way we'd been rafted together — a multihull group over here, a clutch of very small keel boats, Jester Class rivals, over there. Excellent lunch and supper, served cafeteria-style, made the Royal Western the best place to eat in Plymouth and to talk with the competition.

There's no question that racing alone across the Atlantic is a far less lonely business than simply sailing alone. The ninety-two skippers who set out across the Atlantic this afternoon will soon scatter so widely they'll be most unlikely to see another competitor until they reach Newport. But there'll be the Argos system, the BBC broadcasts, the ham radio net, and the shared adventure to make it all seem more like a community spree than tight-lipped competition. But . . . it is still *Moxie* and me against them.

3.

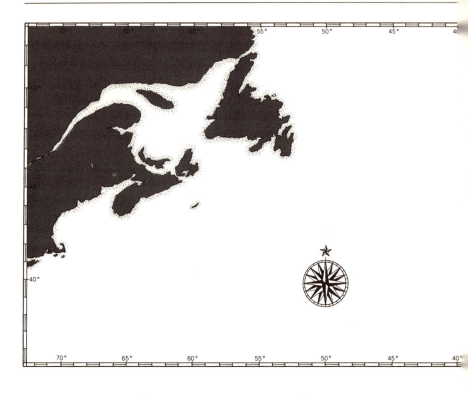

(FROM THE FILM SOUND TRACK)

8:00 A.M. *There's a sail down to leeward on port tack. It must be a noncompetitor. I don't know what the hell anybody'd be doing on port tack going off to Greenland. There's not that much advantage to northing.*

Then there's a guy back there, you can't see him on camera but I can just pick him up. Eric Loizeau was right up close all through the night and I only lost him at dawn. So it's a mystery. All pretty exciting.

The camera switched off automatically. I went below to call up Chris aboard *Fathomer II*, the British research vessel out of Falmouth that he had chartered to film as many entries as he could find far offshore this first morning of the race. He sounded exultant. He'd been threading his way through the fleet since dawn at 20 knots filming nearly everyone. He was down to the southeast, with Mike, Walter, Nick Keig, and Riguidel all within sight.

He appeared just in time to film *Paul Ricard*, the mysterious sail I'd

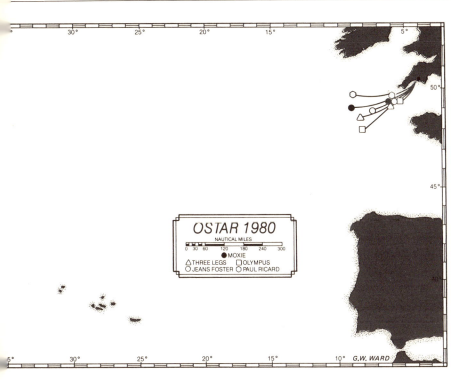

reported to leeward, crossing my bow. We passed close enough for Marc Pajot to hear my hail and to respond with a friendly wave. I felt profoundly grateful that I'd had the temerity to lobby the race committee to permit his entry.

Keith Taylor, editor of *Sail*, had joined Chris, and he and I chatted on the VHF about Tom Grossman's collision. While ducking below for his stopwatch, he had hit a Spaniard on the port tack and holed his bow. When they circled me for about the fifth time, I protested that they should not waste so much film on a "house account" — a reference to my being the financial backer. Chris retorted: "Never mind. Right now it looks as if *Moxie* is leading the fleet."

Then off they went to film the boat astern, which proved to be Eric Loizeau's. Their faces were to be the last I'd see until Nantucket Shoals.

L'AFFAIRE PAJOT

All during the spring, my faith in *Moxie* as the best boat for the race had been blossoming. There were skippers aplenty to fear — Birch,

Christopher Knight, Producer of "American Challenge." (The New Film Company)

Loizeau, Greene, Keig, Steggall, Jaworski. Such was the litany I'd spin off when asked who were my favorites. But among the boats there was one unknown, the reconstituted *Paul Ricard*, the foil-assisted tri of Eric Tabarly, OSTAR winner in 1964 and 1976, undoubtedly the world's greatest sailor.

Built of aluminum to the legal length limit of 56 feet, and 56 feet also from outer hull to outer hull, she had reached Bermuda first in the June 1979, two-handed Le Point race. But on the nonstop return to France, Eric and his shipmate, Olympic medalist Marc Pajot, lost the wind. They were nipped by just five minutes at the finish by Eugène Rigui-del's *VSD*.

I admired Tabarly for daring to pioneer on three fronts at once — with hydrofoils (they looked like big belly fins, angled inboard) on the outriggers; with jointed, articulating cross arms; and with a wing mast. None of the three innovations had been ventured on a transatlantic race before. After being caught on the run from Bermuda, Tabarly decided the boat was too complicated, too heavy, and ordered her into the yard for a total refit. Our French friend, Christian Février, the most thorough reporter among all the yachting writers covering the OSTAR, had told us in Florida before our departure that except for the main hull it would really be *Paul Ricard II* that Eric was sailing.

Aware that labor trouble had bedeviled his shipyard, I couldn't imagine how Eric would have her ready in time. We hoped for the chance to see for ourselves at the La Trinité-sur-mer multihull regatta. Came our first daybreak in French waters. Who should appear for the three days of round-the-buoy racing but the great Eric and his man-eating aluminum shark.

I invited myself aboard. To my surprise, everything was shipshape and navy fashion, not in the post-refit clutter I'd expected on a first passage following a nine months' lay-up. The gear seemed massive compared with mine. Her sail-handling layout would surely demand more exertion. The cabin had no headroom. When a launch took her in tow to the mooring area, I felt the foils dig into the water in a way that caused severe strain on the tow line.

"That boat's gotta be a monster for one man," I reported to Tom Perkins. "With anyone but Tabarly she shouldn't be a threat."

She had jib problems the first two days that prevented fair comparisons between her and *Moxie* and *Gauloises.* But on the last day, in light airs that should have given us the edge, she caught a turn of the tide neatly and left us both far behind.

On the beat around Ushant and up the Channel to Cowes, Tom and I discussed the French favorite by the hour. We agreed she was the most gutsy entry in the race, living proof of what the OSTAR was all about, a possible breakthrough in man's continued effort to cross the ocean ever faster under sail.

Our first night on British soil reminded us that the Hundred Years' War between the French and British had not ended. The *Daily Telegraph* reported that the race committee had disqualified *Paul Ricard.* Tabarly, the item read, had been grounded by his doctor for a shoulder injury suffered while skiing earlier in the year. Marc Pajot had not properly qualified as his substitute. I was utterly dismayed. A race without the most interesting entry would be like the Moscow Olympics without the Americans.

Almost as soon as *Moxie* had crossed the finish line at Plymouth, first in the Crystal Trophy Race, an easy victor since none of the other serious OSTAR contenders had seen fit to enter, I began to lobby for reconsideration of the Pajot ban. I wrote the following letter to the Royal Western Yacht Club of England Race Committee:

Paul Ricard, *the French favorite, albeit an unofficial entry, in a cut-away drawing as originally designed.*

Gentlemen:

We, the undersigned, competitors in the 1980 OSTAR, respectfully appeal to the Committee for further consideration of the *Paul Ricard* entry, unfortunately placed in doubt by the injury to her qualified skipper, Eric Tabarly.

In the circumstances it seems to us that Marc Pajot, co-skipper with Tabarly aboard *Paul Ricard* in the June '79 "Le Point" race around Bermuda, could be considered to have qualified under the substitution rule in fact and in spirit even if not to the strict letter of the rule. Pajot is wholly familiar with the vessel. He is an experienced solo sailor having qualified the 70-foot catamaran *Ppalu* for the Route du Rhum in 1978 and then sailed it from St. Martin to St. Malo with his ladyfriend as sole crew.

To us the OSTAR with one of the most imaginative new boats of the fleet excluded would seem seriously diminished in competitive interest. While several boats could probably beat *Paul Ricard* to Newport, her exclusion would always leave a lurking doubt and a dilution of the victor's satisfaction. . . .

With full understanding of the committee's effort to administer the rules fairly to all, we urge the exercise of their prerogative to change a decision.

Respectfully submitted . . .

Not a skipper of whatever nationality hesitated to sign it. I took pains to gather by phone the proxies of all the serious contenders who had not yet appeared, such as Mike Birch, Walter Greene, Nick Keig, and Phil Steggall. It all seemed to me to be in the proper OSTAR spirit. Nevertheless, it made for a couple of uncomfortable days. I seemed to be challenging my good friends in authority at the Royal Western who had always been so courteous and kind through ten years' racing and who had elected me a nonresident member in 1974.

Happily, a compromise was reached. Pajot, by sailing solo from La Trinité to Plymouth, won the right to be fitted with an Argos satellite transmitter and permission to start along with the rest of us as an unofficial entry. The Argos concession was crucial. The Paul Ricard Company, makers of a popular aperitif, had put up close to a million dollars toward the Tabarly effort. They were hesitant to risk their investment on a passage holding no possibility of any publicity for their sponsored craft.

The day before the race, Marc came around to Milbay Dock to thank me for my effort. "Sorry I couldn't have done better," I told him. "But if you get to Newport first, even if I'm right behind you, you've won the OSTAR and I'm only second."

Thanks be to Aeolus, the Wind God of the Greeks, my bluff wasn't called. It would have embarrassed everyone. A problem with his jib furler, installed only the day before the start, probably cost Marc his victory. He finished fifth, just fourteen hours behind me.

On July 24, Eric Tabarly, with three shipmates sailed *Paul Ricard* from Sandy Hook for the Lizard in an effort to set a new transatlantic sailing record. They made it in 10 days and 7 hours, taking nearly two days off the 75-year record set by Charlie Barr in the schooner *Atlantic* in 1905. For the first eight days, before the wind died, the four Frenchmen, shielding their eyes from stinging spray by wearing snorkeling masks whenever at the helm, averaged 13.66 knots. Yet the wind never blew more than 25 knots. A true midsummer crossing and proof that Tabarly had been right to put his faith in foils.

EVER AN INTERVENER

In getting embroiled in the Pajot affair, I suppose I was exhibiting an hereditary trait. My father used often to chide my mother for being what he called a "Citizen Fixit."

In July 1936, just out of Harvard, I went to work on the *Chicago Daily News.* Dempster MacMurphy, who hired me, told me: "You'll love the newspaper business. It allows you to make everybody's business your business."

He'd sized me up quickly. It must have been my mother's example that encouraged me to intervene at the age of seven in what seemed to me to be an injustice. Michael Quinn, the coachman on my grandfather's place in Dedham, Massachusetts, where we'd moved from Long Island in 1920, had become my closest friend. I loved horses. Every afternoon I'd help him to currycomb and brush the pair of chestnuts that drew the carriage in which we rode two miles to school.

In the tack room, redolent of horse sweat and saddle soap, Quinn's copy of the *Boston Post* introduced me to the "funnies" and the delights of newspaper reading. The big story one Friday that autumn was the match race to be run the next day at Jamaica between the British horse Papyrus and the American champion, Zev.

"If you care so much about it, why don't you go?" I asked.

"Agh, sure, I could never get away so long."

"Why not? Don't you ever get a day off?"

"Day off! I haven't had a day off in twenty-one years."

I stood on a box to reach the hand-crank phone that connected the stable to the pantry and summoned my mother. She listened to the case carefully, then agreed that George, the chauffeur, should drive Quinn to the midnight train for New York. I promised to help George feed the horses over the weekend. Quinn was ecstatic. He chortled, danced a little jig, kissed me on the head, and scampered home to change into his Sunday best.

He promised to bet on Zev. Zev won. Except for the day he walked off the ship from Ireland, he said, it had been the high point of his life. Intervention had paid off. Thereafter Quinn worked only a six-day week. He'd been the victim of inadvertence on my parents' part. Having just moved into Rockweld, my grandfather's place, they were still new to managing a payroll.

A later intervention was less successful and could have gotten me court-martialed. My infantry outfit, for various exploits in North Burma during early 1944, had earned, at least in newspaper stories, the sobriquet "Merrill's Marauders."

Most of the regiment had been evacuated from the recaptured airstrip at Myitkyina during late June. One battalion, recruited from volunteers on Guadalcanal, had been promised home leave "after one dangerous mission." Its gaunt and weary riflemen erupted in angry revolt over the broken promise when the rear-echelon types at Stilwell's headquarters ordered them back to battle against counterattacking Japanese. *Time* carried a story of "mutiny."

It so happened that my constitution resisted malaria longer than most so that I'd been the last platoon leader flown out to hospital and recuperative leave in Kashmir. When I returned to duty with my unit in Assam, it was late August and the eyes of the world were on the fighting in Normandy. Higher echelons had decided to forgive the soldiers but to take it out on our gallant field commander, Colonel Charles Hunter, the man for whom the regiment should have been named.

Lieutenant Sam Wilson, later to become a three-star general, then the most decorated American infantryman on the Asian mainland, rallied· us junior officers somehow to express our indignation over the fact that Colonel Hunter was being sent home by slow boat while privates had orders to go by plane. It was clearly a plot to hush up the man who had gone to bat for all of us. Never in my life have I felt more angry. Before the colonel embarked for the States I offered to intervene on his behalf with my mother's first cousin, Senator Leverett Saltonstall from Massachusetts, a member of the Armed Services Committee. In the body of a discursive letter to my wife, I outlined the Hunter case. She passed it along verbally to Cousin Lev. But by then events in France and the Pacific had reduced the Burma campaign to a paragraph. Colonel Hunter languished in limbo, back in Washington, a great warrior discarded.

But I guess I was lucky. Another lieutenant, loyal to the colonel, wrote directly to his congressman and wound up before a court-martial.

A newspaper publisher worth his salt should find at least one event a day to rouse his indignation. Soon after my purchase in January 1952 of the *Gloucester Daily Times* and the *Newburyport Daily News*, I had my first run-in with the Port's blustery mayor, Andrew J. "Bossy" Gillis. His antics as "the boy mayor" years back had made him a favorite in the Boston papers. Frequent reelections had not diminished his ego.

My first visit to Bossy's filling station had been intended as propitiatory. The staff had told me of the feud the previous owner of the *News* had had with Gillis and it seemed wise for me to try to bury the hatchet. Alas. "And how's the new owner of the Dirty News?" was Bossy's opener, as he finished gassing up a customer. "Come on in and I'll fill you in on your Jew boy," referring to our most trusted reporter. That was too much. I threatened to punch him in the nose. The paper's feud resumed.

Ten years later, Bill Plante, editor of the *News*, persuaded Washington to install a bronze plaque on the banks of the Merrimac River registering Newburyport as the birthplace of the Coast Guard. A bandstand with bunting, an unveiling, a nice little speech by the Undersecretary of the Treasury, signalized the Port's big day. Because he regarded the whole business as a promotion stunt likely to reflect more credit on the *Daily News* than on himself, Mayor Gillis sulked inside his gas station throughout the event.

A short editorial by me next day, titled "Bossy's Boffola," chided him for having lost his showman's touch. He'd once appeared on the vaudeville circuit in recognition of his municipal clowning. I suggested that by missing the previous day's platform opportunity he was showing his age. This maddened him.

I've saved the longhand letter, addressed to "Penis Saltonstall Weld," which he stuck that night through the slot in the newsroom door. We photographed it and ran it on page one, misspellings and all. Among my many weaknesses, it alleged I kept a lady in Seabrook whom I visited Thursday afternoons. It confused poor Bossy that I'd print such slanders. He never again caused me trouble.

Essex County newspapers got sued for libel many times before I sold to the Ottaways in 1978. We never settled, preferring to have our lawyer, Phil Cronin, fight every case before a jury. While it cost us legal fees, we never lost a big one and it was good for the staff's adrenals to have a few battles.

4.

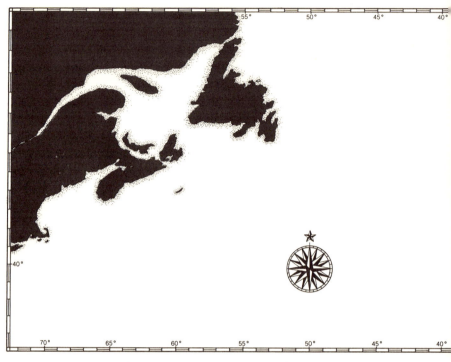

(FROM THE FILM SOUND TRACK)

1:00 P.M. *Well, here we are winding up the second day of the 1980 OSTAR. It's more than twenty-four hours since Chris Knight took shots of* Moxie *from* Fathomer II. *Then I'd just completed my first daily report on deck, where he prefers we do it. But it has been so wet and rough ever since that I've had to come below to use the chart table camera.*

The water has been coming over the deck like crazy. It seems a little low developed west of Ireland yesterday afternoon and moved to France right across our track. This meant we had two wind shifts: west to southwest, then southwest to northwest. In the middle of the night, it blew hard on the nose up to 30 knots.

Boy, did that Stoway main ever come into its own. I kept rolling it up until I had about four reefs in it, then I even rolled in some of the staysail. We went jogging along due west at 6 knots. Nothing great but at least we're keeping going.

According to Radio Europe 1 yesterday afternoon, Moxie

40

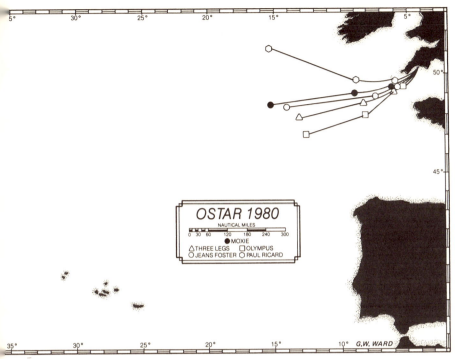

is second to Pajot, whom the French continue to treat as a contestant. The British, if they mention him, call him the "irregular entry" and continue to place me in the lead. According to the French version, it then goes: Eric Loizeau, third; Mike Birch, fourth; Nick Keig, fifth; Eugene Riguidel, sixth; Phil Steggall, seventh; Walter Greene, eighth; and one monohull, Olivier de Kersauson, ninth.

It's uncannily close to the imaginary account of the start of the race that I wrote up in Maine last August for **Sail**. So far it's a trimarans' race.

I've had four hours' sleep in forty-eight. Not too sharp, but everything's going great. No problems. So far!

MASTING MOXIE

As we approached the gap in the bridge across the mouth of Chesapeake Bay, Tom Perkins and I had debated whether to put into Norfolk to replace the broken odometer-speedometer through-hull impeller.

That morning we had resumed the delivery of *Moxie* to Florida for her winter shakedown.

"It will probably take us two days to find a spare," Tom said.

"What's more, it's good drill for the navigator to do without the log now and then," I rationalized. So we took off for the Bahamas into a southwesterly chop without a speedometer. The next sixty hours were as physically fatiguing for me as any I'd ever sailed, even though the wind was rarely more than 20 knots. *Moxie,* jaunty with her 54-foot-high mast, pranced like a skittish pony fed too generously on oats. She'd be trotting along at 8 to 10 knots on the Autohelm when a gust would set her cantering at 12–14–17.

If you sat in the cockpit as she accelerated, it felt the same as being pressed against the back of the seat of a fast car leaving a traffic light. Once out in the ocean, we could only guess true speed. We consistently underestimated. Later experience aboard her showed us that she was bounding into the chop at 12 knots when we judged her speed at less than 10. Dawn of the third day found me just coming off watch and grumpy. I was trying to get breakfast while being tossed about the cabin as if I were in the back of a truck on a badly rutted road. It was blowing only 15 knots, nowhere near hard enough to have required a reef in *Rogue Wave,* but the bouncing made me wish Tom would slow her down.

Black thoughts plunged me in gloom. Am I getting too old for this? This hobbyhorsing has me exhausted. I'll be forever reefing and unreefing. If I'm thrown to the deck and break an arm, then what good will I be? In a tone that must have revealed my despair, I announced three decisions: "I'm going to get the mast shortened. We've got to make the luff slides move easier for reefing. The staysail, like the jib, should roller-reef."

Tom agreed but allowed that he hated to see me slow her down too much. As the breeze picked up, we discussed the alternatives. We came off one wave with such a shuddering slap that Tom reached for the furling line to roll up some jib. Then I heard a metallic ping like one I'd heard more than eight years before.

Sailing up from Florida in April 1971 on *Trumpeter,* Tom's father, Forbes Perkins, and I had been interrupted by the same sound while taking a late afternoon cup of tea. A shroud tang, a tongue-shaped piece of stainless steel joining the backstay to the mast, had broken. I looked out the cabin window just as the mast gently descended into the water.

The spread sail, acting like a parachute, checked the speed of the falling rig so that it caused only minor scars on the deck. Over our emergency radio, we asked a passing merchant ship, just out of Norfolk, to notify the Coast Guard. The next morning, though we were actually sailing nicely under jury rig, a 40-foot cutter appeared to take us in tow for the sixty miles into harbor. I regret having needlessly bothered them.

When a mast collapses on a racing trimaran, it's not as if a tree had crashed in the forest. It's more as if a wild goose circling a blind had been brought down by a gunner. One moment the boat has been bouncing along at 10 knots into the seas, the next her hulls lie dead in the water like a great bird's carcass. Sails and shrouds are heaped every which way; all is silence.

Now I came on deck and looked about with a sense of déjà vu. Like a beer can crimped under the pressure of two thumbs, the mast — without the stiffening effect of the shrouds, no more than a wobbly, oval tube, eleven inches across — had buckled halfway up, just above the spreaders. Tom's check of the deck quickly ascertained that the ping we'd heard had been caused by the inner forestay's wrenching off the tang that held it to the front of the mast.

Neither of us felt the slightest alarm. Tom expressed annoyance that a failure could occur in such comparatively light air, barely more than 20 knots. I concealed my pleasure that the decision to go to a smaller mast had been made easier. We were both nonplussed as to why it had happened.

The expert diagnosticians at Hood Yacht Systems told us later "the mast got out of column and failed in compression." Two miscalculations, it seemed, had fatefully combined — the upper shrouds were one size too thin, therefore stretchable; the lower shrouds led sideways to their fastenings at deck level instead of angling aft by 15 degrees. A racing mast, it seems, can be as injury-prone as a star quarterback's knee. If the ligaments don't support it just right, expect it to kink.

Tom and I surveyed the wreckage. We resolved to try to make it to Florida without calling for help until we were really hungry. Tom dealt masterfully with the tidying up, but I gave myself such a bruising kidney punch falling on a winch that I could give him little help. By dawn the next day, he had stepped the boom as a mast. He hoisted the staysail upside down to give us a mainsail and, after taking a tuck in the storm jib, used it for a headsail. Soon, thanks to one of those wind shifts awarded by Aeolus for good behavior, we were reaching for the

Abacos before a northerly breeze. Our 17-foot-tall jury rig pushed us through the northern Bahamas without a pause and across the Gulf Stream to Fort Lauderdale.

"We're going faster than the one-tonners through here last winter in the SORC," Tom noted with glee as a puff lifted us above 8 knots, a prodigious pace with makeshift sails.

Once home in the North, I huddled with the Hood team in Marblehead. Defying the disapproval of most of my young friends, I chose to replace the lost rig with a 50-foot Stoway mast. This Hood development, conceived for big cruising boats, and by now tested in about 200 of them, provided for the mainsail to be rolled up around a rod inside a tube welded inside the back of the mast. As the wind strengthened, I had only to rotate a winch from the cockpit to make the triangle of the main disappear. As the wind dropped, I winched in the other direction. The sail would reappear as its aft corner was hauled out along the boom.

"Say it isn't so," pleaded Damian Laughlin, builder of Mike Birch's new tri, when I told him my decision. "That's awful. You'll ruin her performance." I might as well have told him I was divorcing Anne.

To the young, I decided, mast height must express machismo: the taller, the more virile. Even at the ratio of 54 feet of mast to 50 feet of overall boat length, my rig had been senior-set conservative.

However, the longer I weighed the advantages of "going geriatric" with a Stoway, the more sense it made. The first two thirds of the race would be against winds from 15 to 30 knots that would require frequent diminutions and expansions of sail area. If this cruiser's rig could save time and effort over the twenty-minute struggles I usually had with a fully battened main, then I'd be less inhibited about increasing sail when the wind lightened.

Every solo racer concedes that miles can be lost by succumbing to the temptation to "leave the reef in . . . it's sure to breeze up soon," and then to have it go lighter. Ted Hood himself supported my reasoning, and where could I have found a wiser counselor? He said a reefed Stoway made for a better-shaped sail than a mainsail reefed in the customary way, gathered in folds where the boom meets the mast. What I gained in the early stages of the race, I might well lose in the light airs at the end. But, wishing to husband my energies, I felt I had to take this gamble.

We partially compensated for the sail area lost from shortening the

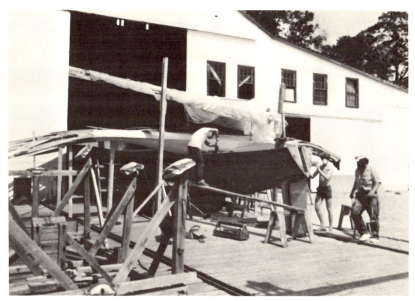

Moxie *ready for outriggers at Handy Boats Inc., Falmouth Foreside.* (Philip S. Weld)

mast four feet by adding four feet to the boom. But a square foot of Dacron near the deck is much less effective than one aloft where the zephyrs exert more force on a balmy day. Now that I've invested in U.S. Windpower, Inc., I'm forever seeking analogies between windmills for making electricity and racing trimarans. I see the mast as a tower; the sails as blades; the hulls as the magnetic fields of the generator, which, if moving with minimum loss from friction in the gears, will convert the Wind King's gusts to kilowatts.

Moxie's hulls and cross arms had been designed by Dick Newick to move through that level where air and ocean meet with minimum friction. "My boats don't make waves," is one of his better slogans. We delayed freezing the new design until after I'd finished the Route du Rhum. Happy that I found myself so fit after twenty-three days of solo racing, I brashly told Dick: "Give me a boat to win the OSTAR. Forget about my age."

Stamped on the lower right corner of the drawings for *Moxie's* construction, beside Dick's Vineyard Haven address, there appears "design #48." Except for a few monohulls, the previous forty-seven were trimarans, catamarans, or proas, a full spectrum of multihulls more diverse than those from the board of any other designer in the history of naval architecture. They share qualities of strength, simplicity, and grace that give them a family resemblance from a mile away. Dick discourages clients who come to him for a "room-aran," an overloaded luxury home afloat, weighed down by what he terms "all the modern inconveniences." He fosters monastic austerity below deck because excess comfort means weight and that spoils the Bruce Number, that most significant figure to the multihull racer. It is derived from the ratio of a boat's "all-up," ready-for-ocean-racing, weight to her working sail area.

Moxie's wood and glue come to about 8,000 pounds. Add 2,000 for rig, hardware, sails, and stores for a three-week passage. Her working sails measure 1,150 square feet. These figures give a Bruce of 1.57, not the highest, but well up there. Her waterline length of 45 feet 10 inches falls just inside the 46-foot limit set by the rules for the 1980 race. Her overall beam of 33 feet 3 inches is as great as *Rogue Wave's*, although her overall length, at 50 feet, is 10 feet less. Making her proportionately broader evolved partly in response to the capsize threat. Working together now for the third time, we could quickly agree on such changes as adding a foot in depth to the daggerboard to improve light-air windward performance.

Dick's art, to my mind, represents a marriage of sculpture and engineering that da Vinci would have applauded. In Walter Greene, Dick had a weight-watcher every bit as zealous as himself. Walter drilled his Handy Boats team in Falmouth Foreside, Maine, never to use an ounce more of glue or a pound more of wood than was needed to make a strong boat.

"Remember, with this big daggerboard, you're going to have to be careful," Walter warned me several times during the building. "If you leave it way down except in light airs, you could break the box."

"You're not going to have a small *Rogue Wave*," Dick kept reminding me. "She's a big Val." He referred to his 31-foot design of which there'd be four in the race. I regarded them as great day sailers but far too small to take a man of my years across the ocean with any dignity.

To locate the fifteen winches, the traveler, sheet leads, turning blocks and cleats, the wheel, the compass, the hydraulic backstay pump, the door to the cabin, and the calamity locker, we built a plywood mockup

Dick Newick,
Moxie's *designer.*
(Christian Février)

Moxie's *winch layout*
avoids awkward chore-
ography. (Chris-
topher Knight)

of the cockpit and cabin top up in the yard's sail loft. We would climb inside to try make-believe tacks and jibes with different arrangements to test which best avoided awkward choreography. Below deck was so Spartan it presented few choices. On either side of the single cabin, a shelf projected over the water for bunks. Forward on the port side, I put a roomy chart table; aft and to starboard, a small galley with a shelf for two dozen cans, a dish rack, and a hanging one-burner stove. The nearest thing to plumbing was a hand pump in a rubber collar thrust into the fill-up hole of a 2½-gallon plastic water jug.

In the wings on either side of the daggerboard box and in the space beneath the cockpit, we had room to store food for two on an Atlantic crossing. Extra sails — two spinnakers, a big reacher, a lightweight genoa, and backup main, staysail, and jib — filled the forepeak, to which one had access through a hatch in the deck, although, with great effort, I could crawl through to it from the cabin. I was under strict orders to leave the aft compartment empty to avoid drag from an over-laden stern. Both Dick and Walter classed me as a sybarite who bore watching.

Before embarking on my 500-mile qualifying solo the first weekend in September, I had sailed only once aboard *Moxie.* So on the eastward reach to Nova Scotia from Handy Boats, I cautiously carried a reef in the main and never rolled out the full jib until I headed home for Gloucester. I thrilled at the way she ghosted through the fog. With a main hull waterline beam of 3 feet 6 inches — no wider than the dis-tance a tall man spreads his feet to hit a golf ball — she made such a trivial wave that her wake disappeared in a boat length.

The next weekend, Eric Loizeau and Walter interrupted their rush to launch *Gauloises* long enough to sail with me on the Cruising Club's New Jeffreys Ledge Race, an overnight circuit of Massachusetts Bay. On the beat from Boston to Gloucester, as we passed Lynn in the dark heading into a fresh northwester, Walter's professional reserve melted. The apparent wind angle showed 33 degrees on the Signet readout. Boat speed 12 plus. Walter at the helm. "I'm telling you I've built you one fast boat." It's the nearest to self-praise I've ever heard from him.

When Anne and I sailed from home on the first half of the delivery to Florida, we put into Jim Brown's in North, Virginia, thirty miles from the entrance to Chesapeake Bay, without ever having been in more than 10 knots of wind. That's how it came about that just before the dismast, Tom and I found ourselves in the most wind the new rig had ever expe-rienced.

That it chose to topple in such a convenient place, with the right crew aboard, in plenty of time to rig and install a substitute before sailing for France adds up to good fortune typical of that which seemed to follow *Moxie* all the way to the OSTAR finish. Like her skipper, she was born lucky.

5.

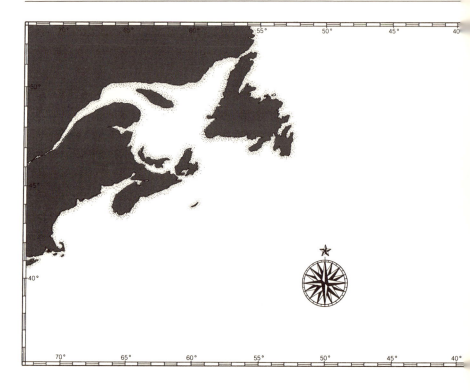

REACHER IN THE DAWN

1:00 A.M. The sound of water burbling by my ear had diminished enough so that the strange silence the other side of the half-inch-thick wooden hull wakened me. By the lowered wick of the kerosene lamp, I could just read my watch. I'd slept nearly an hour.

The pipe berth, slung like a first-aid stretcher from the cabin ladder steps to the bulkhead beneath the mast, carries my body below the waterline. Here I bounce far less than in my wing bunk with its mattress. Resting here, I remain in harmony with the motion of the boat even in sleep.

Swinging my rubber-booted legs to the cabin floor, I beat my arms across my chest to stir the blood against the chill damp. I need to jostle my wits into focus. Plainly the wind has all but vanished. *Moxie's* pace falters.

I haul myself up to the chart table, rotate the wall-mounted directional light to the bright position, and open the loose-leaf binder that

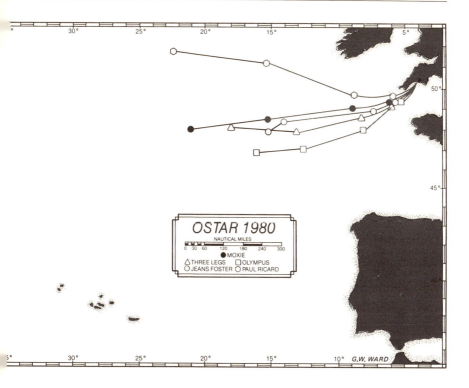

OSTAR 1980
NAUTICAL MILES
0 30 60   120   180   240   300
● MOXIE
△ THREE LEGS   □ OLYMPUS
○ JEANS FOSTER ○ PAUL RICARD

serves as my log book to the fresh pages of a new day. I shine a flash-light on the mileage gauge, a window in the Signet control box above the table, then go to the cabin entrance for a glance at the winking or-ange digits in the on-deck instrument display. Now I'm ready to make an entry:

HOUR	MILES	COURSE	SPEED	TACK	WIND	REMARKS
0100	527	282	1–2 k	Stbd	3-North	Reacher?

I check the barometer, 29.9 and steady, the thermometer, 56° Fahren-heit, enter the figures, and repair to the cockpit for a look around. No ship's lights on the horizon. Just enough breeze to flutter the telltales affixed to the shrouds. Flecks of phosphorescence pass sluggishly be-neath the wing nets, slung between the main hull and the outriggers.

"Something must be done about this, Mox, ol' girl," I say aloud. "Dare we raise the reacher while it's still dark?"

I munch saltines, swig orange juice, while I wait for the special OSTAR weather forecast on the BBC. Scheduled daily for 3:30 A.M. Greenwich Mean Time, it will come on an hour earlier by ship's time for every 650 miles of westing. Now that we're in a new time zone, it will come on at 2:30. After two confusing bouts, I'm at last familiar with the format. It divides the eastern North Atlantic into six rectangles, three tiers high, two blocks across. The announcer reads the forecast first at dictating speed, then conversationally. Most helpful. Good show.

I transfer the centers of the low pressure areas and the wind direction arrows with their estimated strengths to the transparent, erasable Mylar sheet with which I've covered an overall chart of the Atlantic. It lies on the starboard bunk from which the mattress was removed in Plymouth to give me a generous ancillary chart table. Here I can also spread out the chart on which I plot the positions of the leading competitors that will come over the BBC thrice daily.

"Light northerly winds, freshening" would seem to be *Moxie*'s diet for today.

Now I've no further excuse to delay raising the reacher. Other than rolling in the mainsail and the jib, this will be my first sail change of the race. I'm apprehensive about embarking on it in the dark with no Tom to bail me out if I blunder. It will be strenuous, so I shed my oilskins and heavy sweater. The synthetic nap of my blue Helly-Hansen undershirt and pants will make me sweat quite enough. For quicker footwork, I change my boots for low, nonskid Top-Sider moccasins. For security, I buckle on my safety harness and twist through the hatch to the cockpit.

Clipping the harness's safety strap to one of the two plastic-coated wires that run over either side of the main deck from the aft end of the cabin top right up to the bow, I keep a strain on it as I stride forward. Without this mobile handrail I could easily be thrown to the deck by *Moxie*'s liking for sudden heaves upon the swells. I pause in the pulpit to shine a pocket light on the reflective arrow at the masthead. It points at an angle to our course of more than 45 degrees, perfect for the reacher.

Unclip. Cross to the port net. Clip to the shroud at the outer hull. Kneel to relax tension on the block and tackle holding the alternate headstay in its idle position. Unclip. Grasping the stay in my left hand, I scramble forward on all fours to the tip of the bow. There a wire with a loop in the end passes through an upright pulley. I shackle the headstay to this loop, then tauten the assembly with another block and tackle leading to a cockpit winch.

Now I'm ready to manhandle the 1,000 square feet of light Dacron that I call our secret weapon. It comes easily through the hatch to the foredeck because Tom has folded it into a compact sausage. I clip the stainless steel hanks along its leading edge to the alternate headstay. To avoid snapping one on upside down, I squeeze each of them deliberately.

The chore's nearly done. Now to knot the blue spinnaker sheet to the stainless steel circlet in the sail's rear corner, the clew, and snap on the spinnaker halyard to the thimble at the top. Ready to hoist.

Fast as I can, hand over hand, I haul on the halyard with one turn around the deck-mounted winch near the base of the mast, all the time watching that the white triangle of sail rises smoothly. When the wire portion of the halyard reaches the deck, I take five turns, then with the winch handle give it a final tautening to bring the head of the sail snug to the top of the mast. It begins to shake and rustle.

I jump into the cockpit and haul rapidly on the blue sheet. The bottom edge of the sail becomes a hard white line against the dark of the glassy sea. Next I roll up the working jib so nothing can interfere with the mere breath of air passing over the silken curvature of the reacher's mighty foil. It's an expanse of cloth to dwarf the ship and it brings *Moxie* to life again. In the little windows of the instrument panel, the orange figures indicating boat and wind speed climb by tenths of a knot as fast as the indicators on a gasoline pump.

Now to enjoy it. Shutting off the Autohelm, I take over the wheel. We'll indulge in a bit of "scalloping," the multihuller's most thrilling drill, an experience no obdurate keel boat sailor can ever know. The helmsman sneaks the bow of the ship high of the course to reduce the wind angle. The boat speed picks up, the wind angle narrows, the wind speed over the deck goes up and up. We're making our own wind. Like an iceboat.

Soon I have her moving at 5 knots in 3 knots of true wind. In the 6-knot puffs that can now be seen in the first light of dawn ruffling the sea's glassy surface, my glorious craft sprints ahead at 7, 8, 9 knots. So delicately do we glide over the water that the bubbles of our wake endure for no more than a boat-length in the sheen of the rising sun. The hulls greet the dawn with the traditional, good-natured hiss that a Harvard professor can raise from his class with a scholarly pun.

Let's take a break for breakfast

MY FIRST SOLO RACE, THE 1972 OSTAR

Looking back eight years to my first OSTAR in *Trumpeter*, I realize how handicapped I was by, among other things, not having a reacher. I had no functioning self-steering either, nor a good radio for weather forecasts.

The only thing I did right in 1972 was to predict the winner. A week before the June 17 start, at the bar of the Royal Western, I told Frank Page, the *Observer*'s yachting editor, that *Pen Duick IV* — a 70-foot trimaran skippered by Alain Colas, a twenty-eight-year-old Frenchman — would win the race in less than 500 hours. Colas crossed the line in 493 hours and 15 minutes, or 20 days, 13 hours, beating the 128-foot schooner *Vendredi Treize*, the single-hull favorite, by nearly a day.

My prediction for *Trumpeter* had been cautious: "Anything under thirty days will please me. I'll be satisfied to place in the top third."

Alas, it took me thirty-nine days and I finished twenty-seventh out of fifty-five starters, barely in the upper half. Considering our preliminary passage from Gloucester to Plymouth, May 2 to May 21 (18 days and 15 hours, with three aboard), the performance was acutely disappointing.

But so it goes, heading westward in the North Atlantic in midsummer. It's a wonder the Europeans ever settled New England before the steamboat was discovered. Light westerly winds, Long Island Sound strength, frustrated *Trumpeter* and me on most days. On a dozen days we were dead in the water for more than six hours. The wind came from behind for altogether fewer than twenty-four hours while we were logging 4,700 miles to cover a great-circle route of 2,810 miles.

Enough for the complaints. The whole experience was joyful, from the April launching in a snowstorm to the landing July 26 at the Port O'Call Marina in Newport. Solo voyaging has to be the healthiest of all pursuits.

After the race, so many people asked pretty much the same questions that I included the answers in a piece I wrote for John Bethell's *Harvard Bulletin*.

"Weren't you bothered being alone so long?"

What with navigation by sextant, changing sails, cooking, mending gear, studying pilot charts, watching for ships, tuning in for the weather forecast, it was busy, busy day after day, with just enough space in the twenty-four to get five to six hours' sleep. Since it was a light-air race, on the wind, there simply was no time for boredom or loneliness.

Trumpeter gets a tow into Newport after finishing twenty-seventh in the 1972 OSTAR. (Phil Hersh Photo)

"Were you ever scared you wouldn't make it?"

Never. A thoroughly tested boat with backup for every mishap provides peace of mind. My one fidgety moment came on the eighth day when I hoisted myself up the mast in a calm to replace a frayed shroud. The dangling end of the hoist line cleated itself at deck level, requiring me to wriggle out of the bosun chair and slither 40 feet down the mast. (Next time I'll be careful to keep the tail of the hoist up there with me in a sail bag.)

"Did you see other boats?"

No other competitors after the first afternoon until I sighted *Mex*, a West German entry, two miles from the Nantucket Light vessel. But I saw many steamers, three of which reported my position to Lloyd's of London: a German freighter in the Bay of Biscay, a Turkish tanker in mid-passage, and an American container ship off Newfoundland.

Only the Turks stopped to socialize. They bade me circle under their stern for photos. I complied. Most un-racy.

"Did your supplies hold out?"

Food enough for another ten days. Water for a month. But liquor ran out the thirty-fourth evening. Canned orange juice sipped in the dark simulates sauterne if you work at it.

"Any major gear failures?"

The secret weapon against the westerlies, a mainsail with full-length battens, ripped beyond repair the first night. The less efficient, substitute "soft" main slowed me at least 15 percent. Just 300 miles from the finish, the centerboard broke at the slot. I limped in with a spare rudder blade jury-rigged down the back of the box to check the leeway a little. This mishap cost me three days.

"Why did you sail way south to the Azores?"

When we sailed the great-circle course to England in 1972, the temperature dropped to 34 degrees. Icebergs had drifted farther south than in any June for years. Two fast-reaching boats finished well in the 1968 race taking the Azores route. This year the sixth and ninth boats sailed even farther south than I and found wind. Either I guessed wrong or I failed properly to propitiate Aeolus, the Wind King.

"Did you have much time for reading?"

No. But I read Robert Fitzgerald's glorious translation of *The Odyssey* as if it were a cruising guide. Difficulties with calms outnumber those with gales two to one. Aeolus appears as a testy character no sailor wishes to offend so I made it a point never to complain about the wind, or lack thereof.

"Did you get anything special out of the trip?"

In Book Five, Odysseus, clinging to the rugged shore after his raft has been wrecked, faces drowning unless he can swim to a more sheltered landing spot. "Grey-eyed Athena" rescues him with the gift of "epiphrosyne" ($\epsilon\pi\iota\phi\rho o\sigma\acute{v}\nu\eta$), translated as "prudence" in the Loeb Classical Library, but as "self-possession" by Fitzgerald. I think every skipper in the race would prefer the second meaning, and would like to think his supply of this elixir had been enlarged by the endeavor.

Those answers sounded braver than I felt. On a September day following the race, I took Ray Hunt, the famous yacht designer, out in a brisk northwesterly to show him the charms of a trimaran. A mile from the house, an ugly sound from one of the armpits sent us scurrying for home. One of the aluminum tubes in the cross arms had finally succumbed to metal fatigue, cracked right across. It was the first real breeze I'd been out in since the day on the race when the board broke.

But my dander was up. Within a few months I'd commissioned Dick Newick to design me a trimaran that could win the 1976 race. By January 1973 *Gulf Streamer* was under construction at Vaitses' yard in Mattapoisett.

Gulf Streamer *before her starboard outrigger was jacked into position, November 1973.*

CAPSIZE!
How I Lost *Gulf Streamer* . . .

The irony of losing *Gulf Streamer* in the Gulf Stream still makes me wince. It had been in a mood of celebration racing to Bermuda that I'd chosen the name. To pay tribute to this elemental force had seemed the friendly thing to do.

When planning the voyage to England for the 1976 OSTAR, it never occurred to me to regard the Stream as anything but a beneficent force that would hasten us on our way. It would sweep us past Florida, once we'd made our way from St. Petersburg to Key West, at 4 knots. From Cape Canaveral, we'd follow a great circle to the Scilly Isles. This track would cut northeast inside the Stream's curve. We'd rejoin it east of New Jersey, somewhere north of Bermuda, to allow it to keep us warm and boost us on our way to Plymouth.

The low coast of America disappeared in the sunset the afternoon of Tuesday, April 20, 1976, as *Streamer* cantered along at 10 knots in a light southeasterly. The stern, relieved of the weight of the diesel engine, had risen two inches to give her a new lightness of foot. In light air, it could mean 8 knots instead of 7. Both the boat and I felt up for the race.

A new antenna rigged from the port spreader captured the Coast Guard's new sequence of voice broadcasts of North Atlantic weather. All through Sunday, April 25, as we ran almost dead before a freshening southwesterly, it warned of a new gale center over Cape Sable, Nova Scotia. It forecast winds from 25 to 35 knots and waves to 20 feet as far as 450 miles from the center. Our position midway between Cape Hatteras and Bermuda came within that circle.

Bill Stephens, my twenty-one-year-old shipmate from Birmingham, Michigan, helped me to tie in a second reef before it got dark. By Monday's dawn, continuous streaks of foam were showing in the wave troughs. Time to drop the main. Under staysail only, it required constant attention at the wheel to hold the course without flogging its 300 square feet in accidental jibes. All through the day, the seas built up. Between wave crests, the surface took on that creamy look that indicates Force 9 — over 47 knots.

"I'm rapidly gaining respect for the power of the Atlantic," Bill remarked in mid-morning. His offshore sailing had heretofore been in the Great Lakes.

Frequent checks on WWV, the government station broadcasting from Fort Collins, Colorado, at eight minutes past the hour, indicated that the gale center, per the prediction, was moving northeast, as were we, but much faster. As it outdistanced us, conditions would steadily improve.

"Bet on the wind's veering northwest tomorrow," I said. "Then look for six days of perfect reaching to England."

So dawned the fateful morning of Tuesday, April 27. The wind had veered. We'd come over to the port jibe. During my watch from 5:00 A.M. to 9:00 A.M., the seas had notably decreased. It seemed prudent to put the helm under the control of the electric autopilot, a Tillermaster, while I took a sun sight through the patchy clouds and plotted our position.

I was using an old small-scale chart that showed this was the sixth time in two years that *Gulf Streamer* had been within 300 miles or less of this intersection of latitude and longitude, 38° north by 64° west: eastward from Gloucester to England, May 1974; St. Martin to Gloucester,

Gulf Streamer *off Cowes in June 1974 before winning the Crystal Trophy.* (Beken of Cowes Ltd.)

April 1975; back and forth on the Bermuda race, June 1975; Gloucester to Puerto Rico, December 1975. Like Old Home Week!

When Bill came on deck to take over the watch, we remarked upon the abating seas and noted that our speed had dropped to 8 knots. "If we were racing," I said, "we'd be putting up the main." But we agreed in the interest of rest and comfort to postpone this until I came on watch again at 1:00 P.M.

I went below and kicked off my boots for the first time in thirty-six hours, hung up my harness and oilies, and prepared for a nap. My bare feet tucked into the sleeping bag, my head pillowed in the outer corner of my berth, my knees wedged against the canvas bunk board, I felt utterly content. I munched a RyKrisp.

Bill had impressed me as an alert helmsman more than once in the past ten days. I could see him through the companionway checking the Tillermaster. I hadn't the slightest worry, only a small guilt that, had I been solo racing, my lot would have been less easy. I took out *Can You Forgive Her?*, the first volume in an Anthony Trollope six-pack that my mother had given me for Christmas, and was in the middle of the first sentence when I heard Bill shout, "Look out!"

A second to rise up. Another to swing my legs off the bunk. Four seconds. Bill's next agonized cry coincided with the cracking, slapping sound of flat surface slamming water with maximum impact. Cracker boxes, dishes, cups, books, came tumbling about my ears. Water, sunlit and foam-flecked, poured through the companionway.

Even as the mast must have struck the water, and *Streamer* lay like a wing-clipped swan on her side, I still felt confident that the immense strength and buoyancy of her outrigger would be able to heave her upright.

"This just can't be," I thought.

A second shattering smack. Then gently, as the mast subsided below the surface, the bunk revolved upward above my head. I stood calf-deep in water on the cabin ceiling. All was suddenly quiet except for the water gushing through from the cockpit.

Panic for Bill seized me. The trapped air was being compressed upward against the bilge by the rising water which had yet to reach the level of the cockpit sole. I wanted him clear of the cockpit. He put his head into the rising water to swim down beside me but had to withdraw to unhook his safety harness. Then he swam down inside.

Ten, twelve, fifteen seconds might have passed since his shouted warning, surely less than thirty.

I remember the smell of damp Naugahyde, the plastic fabric sheathing the underside of the bunk cushions. As the outstretched arms of the outriggers assumed their upside-down position, their buoyancy took over part of the support of the main hull now resting on the flat surface of the main cabin top. The water level had stopped rising at about our belt line. The last temperature reading had shown 68 degrees. As the sea surged both fore and aft and crosswise inside the hull, the sun shone through the fiberglass, causing the interior wavelets to twinkle merrily.

Bill and I discussed the air supply and agreed it was adequate. We both seemed gripped in the same icy calm. "Well, I'm sorry if I dumped your boat," said Bill. "But I don't feel guilty because I know I did the right thing."

"I know you did," I said.

"I'd been looking ahead. I turned around. This wall. Forty feet high. It had two crests just off the stern. I kicked Tilly clear. Grabbed the wheel and pulled her off with all my weight. Three spokes. I thought she'd come back until I saw the mast hit the water. Then the second crest hit us."

"I could see you hauling on the helm," I said. And with few more words we got down to the business of survival.

Multihull designer and sailor Jim Brown, who had questioned the survivors of *Meridian*, a trimaran that had capsized off Virginia in June 1975, had told me the key: "The hulls will float high. Don't rush the vital items into the vulnerable life raft. Save your energy to live aboard upside down."

From the welter of objects surging in the waist-deep water we grabbed first for the three radio beacons. We tucked them with the two sextants, the almanac, the navigation tables, a pair of pilot charts, the first-aid chest, the waterproof metal box of flares, into the shelves and corners most nearly high and dry, in this topsy-turvy world. The crown-jewel safekeeping spots were the underside of the chart table and the two bins for cleaning materials beneath the stove and galley table. Here, safely wedged, we found the two-gallon jerry can of emergency water.

Now came the urge to communicate with fellow men. As I'd planned with Jim Brown, I unscrewed, from what was now "the overhead," the through-hull fitting for the log propeller, just forward of the mast and of the midships bulkhead. Through the two-inch hole I could see blue sky. I'd punctured the seal of our air cushion. Would the escaping air cause the water to rise? We thought not and it did not. The craft's inherent buoyancy from her Airex sandwich construction, together with the four airtight compartments in each of the outriggers, provided us with what would prove to be raft status of indefinite duration.

Into the little window on the world, I thrust the rubberized antenna of the oldest of the three beacons and set it to pulsing.

Next we had to cut a hatch through the keel to the outdoors. It took three hours to complete the fourteen-by-eighteen-inch aperture. First a drilled hole. Then enlargement with hammer and chisel to make a slit admitting a hacksaw blade. Then a pruning saw with a curved, coarse blade to lengthen the slit on one side. My talk with Jim had prompted me to tuck these tools for safekeeping beneath the chart table. We repeated the process at three subsequent corners. It was tiring, this reaching overhead to saw. Glass dust got in our eyes. Mounting claustrophobia kept us hard at it until finally we'd hammered the rectangular panel free.

Once again we could look out into the real world, and a somber sight it presented: gray sky, gray water; squall clouds all about on the horizon, but nary a ship. Here and there bits of Sargasso weed.

"We're in or near the Gulf Stream," I said.

"The nearest shipping lane?" Bill asked.

"About thirty miles southwest of here the pilot chart shows a junction point. But I think we shouldn't plan on a quick pickup. Let's think in weeks. Not hours or days."

Looking out of our hole in the hull, I saw the big red spinnaker clinging to the aft end of an outrigger. However did it get there? It takes the weight of a man to force it bagged through the forward hatch. Only then did we note how empty the cabin had become of floating debris. Investigating the head, we saw that the hinged hatch cover had opened under the pressure of water on its "inside" surface. Through that two-foot-square opening the hungry sea had sucked seven-by-three foot cushions, sail bags bulky as barrels, boots, clothing, pillows, bottles, cans, fruit, anything that floated.

We began then to retrieve whatever we could grab and to dive for heavier items lying on the cabin's former ceiling, now its floor, or caught in bunk or locker corners. I dove five times to grope for and find the pistol-grip hacksaw and extra blades that I'd taped inside three waterproof bags and secreted in the aft starboard locker where it could have been reached from outside after capsize. Triumph!

I'd bought three extra sets of these to present as boat-warming presents to the skippers of the three 31-foot Newick trimarans fitting out at Vineyard Haven, Massachusetts, before their 500-mile qualifying solos for the OSTAR. All during Monday's gale, I'd worried about them and thanked my stars that I had more boat under me than they. As it turned out, all made uneventful fast passages to England.

Outside, the sea remained too rough for us to want to venture out onto the keel to commence cutting through to the aft cabin where we knew we'd eventually find food aplenty. Both encased raft and deflated dinghy remained beneath the cockpit seat, now upside down.

First night adrift. Bill waded to the forepeak to fashion us a dry lair on the underside of the bow deck. Though it was dark and narrow, with the one remaining bunk cushion as a base, and the new staysail and light spinnaker to use as coverlets, he made us a bed just clear of the water.

"The first night will be the worst," I said. We discussed strategy. Protection against cold and wet came first. We calculated that we had a liquid supply for three to four weeks. Juice in cans of fruit and vegetables to be salvaged later would stretch it out.

The underside of the chart table formed a mini-quarter-berth, more nearly high and dry than any other place inside. I stuck it out there for two hours, then gave up when a cramp knotted my thigh. Sucking wind as I lowered myself into the waist-deep water, I lunged forward to join Bill. Flecks of phosphorescence gave our cabin the eerie glow of a darkened discotheque, "Davy Jones's Hideaway." My left leg went down through the hatch to the open sea. I checked my descent by clutching the toilet seat dangling overhead. I muttered an oath.

"You all right?" from Bill, deep back in his den.

"Yes, but I just lost the bottle of bourbon," I had to confess. My lurch had dumped it from my oilskin pocket. It was a dreary moment.

I crawled inside beside the daggerboard trunk and stretched out on the bunk cushion. As the hulls pitched slowly to the ocean's rhythm, the water ebbed and flowed up my trouser legs. My shoulders, resting against Bill's knees, felt him shivering.

"Tomorrow we make a hammock," he said.

Second day adrift. At first light we shared a can of orange juice. Even if we'd had food, I doubt we'd have eaten anything.

From its bag came the never-used staysail, reserved for the race. Neither of us could bear to hack at the pristine Dacron so we gathered it at the corners — as one would knot a handkerchief headdress — and hoped for the best. Every twenty minutes one of us would squirm shoulders through the lookout for a scan. We agreed that the wind and sea had dropped. From a skein of wires suspended from the chart table's instrument panel, we retrieved the bubble compass from the RDF set and established that the hulls lay on a north-south axis athwart the wind with waves still coming from the west.

Gingerly, I folded back the sodden pages of the Nautical Almanac, noted the declination of the sun for 4:00 P.M. GMT, Wednesday, April 28, mentally calculated the sextant setting for a meridian crossing of the sun at latitude 38° 30′, and settled down to pounce on "noon" like a duck hunter awaiting dawn in his sneak box.

Squall clouds rimmed the north horizon. Sargasso weed floated in the cabin. A Portuguese man-of-war had hung itself up in one of the wing nets. The water felt warmer than the air. The sea was smooth enough to go "on deck."

"Time to tackle that hole to the aft cabin," Bill said. He wriggled out, humped himself aft along the keel to a point we'd agreed on over the engine bed, and set to with a will to saw slots through the inch-thick keel, laid up of layers of solid fiberglass, hard as steel.

Bill kept at it for two hours. Two slits athwartship, through the tough spine of the keel down to the foam sandwich, testified to his zeal. Having earned a rest, he took to the hammock and I took his place astride the keel. It was slippery and sloped down toward the stern. I had to grip with my knees as if riding bareback on a horse that's stopped suddenly to crop grass. At a millimeter a minute, the slit lengthened. I drilled, chiseled, and hacksawed four corners. When it was almost too dark to see, I knocked off. Only one side of the rectangle remained to be cut in the morning.

Second night. I tried to leave the hammock to Bill and stretched out in the forepeak. More water had settled way up in the bow so that it continually rinsed me, first down the collar, then up the crotch. Bill insisted I join him. We lay head to feet. I actually slept fitfully, despite the frequent splashes from below. But at Bill's expense, I fear. The bulk of the sail had bunched up on my side, leaving him slung lower and less protected. He didn't sleep until daybreak when I returned to my hacksaw.

Third day adrift. The sea was down. Only a gentle westerly riffled the surface. Pink in the east. Blue sky above. Using a fresh blade, I attacked the last eighteen inches with vim. A final hammer-whack broke out the V-shaped segment. Bill heard my gleeful call and stood in the lookout prepared to receive each recovered item. We'd rehearsed the priorities.

Four cases of tins had stacked themselves on the underside of the bunk projection — high and dry as if placed there by a grocery clerk.

Then through the hole to Bill's outstretched arms went a five-gallon jerry can of water, three life jackets, two radar reflectors, a horseshoe life ring, floor boards, strips of batten, the rubber survivial suit, a sleeping bag, a tool box. I emerged with a can of chicken stew and a can of corn. We breakfasted astride the hull. The roofs of our mouths were unaccountably tender.

Refreshed, Bill took charge of rehanging the hammock. Working down from the head of the sail to a point where its breadth would then span the gap between the bunks, we measured off a further seven feet, and sliced through the Dacron. We cut more lanyards, drilled more holes. Stretched taut by the bolt rope on one side, by rolled cloth on the other, at last there was a proper litter. A length of anchor warp, pulled tight beneath, provided a fore-and-aft dividing ridge and extra security. So absorbed were we that I missed my noon sight.

We rested in the late afternoon sun, squeezing water from the down in a sleeping bag, scanning the horizon, and planning for the morrow.

"We need a way to get from the hammock to the lookout without getting soaked," Bill said. "And tomorrow I'll unscrew the big cabin mirror, break it up and glue pieces with epoxy to the hull. We need more ways to attract attention."

He had stuck a six-foot aluminum extrusion, a spare for the jib-furling system, into the daggerboard slot and had wired the metal reflector to its peak. But the first of three beeping beacons had exhausted its battery some time the night before. We agreed to husband the expensive unit with the capacity to receive and transmit voice as well as beep, for moments when planes might appear overhead.

"Every helicopter in Vietnam carries one," the boatshow salesman told me. Pilots with whom I'd checked it at both Boston and Beverly airports considered it good. We even had an extra battery for it. The less costly beeper-only beacon would remain in reserve. Its test light failed to blink but because it was brand new, we had a right to think it would work.

Third night. The hammock, though vastly improved, lacked room for two to sleep. Inadvertent jostling kept one or the other awake. Wavelets from below splashed up water that pooled in the hollows. By using my end of the damp down bag to cover my nose, and exhaling forcibly, I generated enough heat to forestall shivering.

At dawn we agreed hereafter to split the dark hours into two five-hour shifts, sundown to midnight, midnight to light. Off watch in the hammock, on watch in the survival suit.

Fourth day adrift, Friday, April 30. I rose first, made a bad guess on an unlabeled can: cold watercress and lentil soup. Bill began to make a crawlway to get from the hammock to the lookout without getting wet.

Soon we'd unscrewed the seven-foot mahogany planks that served as the outer edges of the forward bunks. We cut one into two-foot lengths. Into one end of each we drilled a hole. We screwed down the outboard ends to the hull, then lashed the inboard ends with wire to holes drilled in the reinforcing of the daggerboard trunk. Thus they served as the trestles in a swinging bridge. Twisting the drill chuck a quarter turn at a time by hand (the rusting handle turned hard) had chafed the soaked skin of our fingers so they were painfully raw.

While I took the noon sight, Bill tackled the adhesion of the broken mirror shards to the flanks of the main hull, well forward, and aft by the rudder.

About 3:00 P.M., basking in the sunshine and holding damp sweaters to the light westerly, Bill spotted a ship's bridge just appearing from the northeast.

The flare sequence was an orange, a big parachute rocket, then the small rocket and the cartridges for the signal pistol. Our logic: first an attention-getter, then the big one to mark us by, then the smaller ones for follow-up.

"Perfect angle for visibility."

"Let's hold back till they're within two miles."

We each took a sizable hunk of broken mirror and practiced bouncing the focus of the sun in the west toward the approaching vessel whose white bridge and three buff cranes were now visible.

Now the orange flare was stripped of its protecting tapes, the "scratch-to-light" directions reviewed.

"Two miles? Okay. Now."

The hot magnesium sputtered. It was plausible that the torch, held high for nearly a minute, could have been seen by an alert lookout.

"I believe they've altered course."

"Now for a rocket."

First I tried one dated 1971, expecting a dud, and it was; then one of the five fresh ones.

"Point downwind . . . press the lever firmly." Up, up, 300 feet. High in the sky burst a pinky-orange ember that floated slowly down, in perfect view of any watcher on the bridge, now well within a mile.

"They've slowed down." We fired the small rocket with the pistol.

"They've got to see this mirror. See it bounce on the bridge."

We called "Mayday!" on the beacon that had a voice transmitter. There was the odd chance that the ship might monitor its aircraft frequency. We waved orange towels. Now she was broadside.

"She's going to drift down on us."

"She's going away." The last of the three cartridge flares in the pistol packet proved a dud. What a fraud.

"They just had to have seen us," said Bill, momentarily enraged.

"Maybe we only thought they slowed down," I said. Disappointment engulfed us. We shared an inch of bourbon from the remaining half-bottle and a can of stew.

Fourth night. A coin toss gave me first watch. At sunset I pulled on the survival suit over oilskins and sat snug where I could catnap and peer around the horizon every twenty minutes. It was comforting to hear Bill snore. Solo, the hammock worked.

I reviewed our state. My reading had buffered the impact of the ship's failure to see us. Dougal Robertson, the Baileys, *Meridian* — all had shot flares for several ships that didn't stop before at last one did. By the law of averages, over a period of weeks in this busy area east of Norfolk and New York, we were sure to be sighted. We had food and water to wait it out for at least five weeks. We could now manage to stay dry and out of the wind. There were no signs of the hull connections weakening. We'd ration our flares, watch for planes on which to use the beacon.

My only haunting worry: my wife, Anne, had a ticket for the plane to England on May 16. By then we'd be overdue. We just had to be picked up in the next two weeks. But until then, it was comforting to know that no one was worried. When the handle of the Big Dipper stood erect, I swapped places with Bill and slept like a felled ox till dawn.

Fifth day. A half-can of juice, a can of stew. The warming sun had Bill down to bathing trunks and safety harness while he stood barefoot on the underside of the bunks with a screwdriver, scratching "SOS" in four-foot-high letters into the bottom paint.

We'd agreed on today's goal: rest the hands, dry out the clothes, settle in for a long siege. But the ship-miss had Bill restless.

I tore some pages from the back of a used notebook to make a log.

Artist Jeremy Ross evokes life upside down. (Courtesy Sail)

On one sheet I mapped our position showing Bermuda 325 miles south; the Azores, 1,700 miles downwind, downstream to the east; Nova Scotia, 300 miles north; Nantucket, 350 miles to the west.

"I'd vote to head for the coast and lots of ships," said Bill. "If we had a stretch of good weather, we could make it in nine days rowing in the dinghy."

We exhausted the possibility of sawing off an outrigger and, with the raft and the dinghy to support the arms, converting it into a proa. At the rate our saw blades and other tools were turning to rust, we'd have lacked the equipment. Besides, to have violated the integrity of our raft would have been an act of desperation.

We agreed to forgo as futile further discussion of leaving the ship for at least another week.

We decided to use up the canned and bottled liquids before calling on the seven gallons of water, our most easily managed drinking supply in case we took to the dinghy.

"Look, jet," Bill said, grabbing for the transmitter, and pointing to a contrail traveling toward New York.

"And there's another," I said, pointing southeast at one homing on Washington.

Two planes at once after four blank days. Unnerving. We fumbled with the antenna before extending it all the way for a sure transmit. The encounter with fellow man, even 35,000 feet away, left me tingling. Petrels dabbling their feet in water, dolphins bounding, small fish swimming about in the cabin, all represented planetary life. None set the pulse pounding like that white trail in the sky saying People.

"Well, now we've had a practice run with a ship and planes," said Bill. "Maybe we score next time."

"It'll not be till the seventh ship," I said.

He retired for a nap while I, in the late afternoon sun, tackled the pulpy wad representing the complete plays of Shakespeare. Whole folios of the least-read chronicle plays remained intact. *The Tempest* had taken a beating. Here was intellectual nourishment for many weeks. Lovingly I pressed pages one by one in the fold of a sun-dried towel. My spirits soared.

"Another jet. Eastbound." On with the beeper. Then: "Mayday, Mayday, Mayday! Capsized trimaran *Gulf Streamer*. Estimated position thirty-nine north by sixty-four west. Please report us. Over."

I paused to listen for a reply and to let the beeper pulse a minute, then repeated the message. There was time for four sequences before the trail vanished on its way to Europe.

At sundown Bill got into the suit and I hit the hammock for four hours' sound sleep.

Fifth night. "Ship's lights. Coming from the south," Bill called. He was astride the keel by the time I'd wormed my way to the lookout. "What luck. I'd just put my head down for a nap when this big wave smacks me in the face. I sat up again to dry off and there she was." Bill was jubilant.

Ship's lights they were. Now we could see red and green running lights as well as the white lights bow and stern.

"First we'll give 'em an orange flare."

It burned hot, glowing much more impressively than in the daytime. Bill held it high in the suit's rubber mitten while I readied the 'chute rocket.

"Now for the big one." It soared magnificently.

"He's blinking. Let's give him a white one to home on."

In close succession, we lit two whites and an orange. Each brightly illuminated the three hulls and the blessedly calm sea surrounding us. Now the ship had halted 100 yards upwind. I scrambled forward for

"Nip up, lads," comes the call from the Federal Bermuda. (Drawing by Jeremy Ross)

Our rescue ship, Captain John Stapleford commanding. (Crescent Shipping)

two life vests hanging from the hammock and urged Bill to get out of the suit, which was too heavy for climbing ladders.

As the ship drifted closer, we could see men readying a cargo net and a figure on the bridge directing a searchlight on our hulls. I had only time to tuck passports, wallet, and letter of credit into a sleeping-bag sack, hang it around my neck, and crawl out.

In big white letters on her lee starboard side, I read *Federal Bermuda.* The rungs of a rope ladder stood out against the mesh of a net as the vessel nestled gently along the outrigger.

"Nip up, lads," a voice called from the deck.

Hand over hand, first Bill, then I, scrambled up the swaying ladder and swung ourselves over the rail onto the steel deck. Concerned British faces came out of shadows created by the glare of a floodlight.

"The master asks do you want to salvage anything?" asked a big blond-bearded man in a heavy white turtleneck sweater.

"No, thanks. Not a thing," I replied.

"Pity we're a container ship," said another voice. "We have no crane."

Anne and daughter Annie greet me at Logan Airport following flight from Halifax, Nova Scotia, where Federal Bermuda *landed me.* (Boston Globe)

From the living quarters in the superstructure at the stern, a bare white deck stretched 250 feet to the stem. We were guided to the bridge, where we shook hands with the skipper standing at the wheel.

Master John "Tony" Stapleford, Norwich, England, shone a floodlight down on *Gulf Streamer*'s upturned hulls. The letters SOS, the orange flag, the radar reflector, the two holes, the rudder aloft like a mizzen sail . . .

"The poor dear," I said aloud, and my eyes filled with tears.

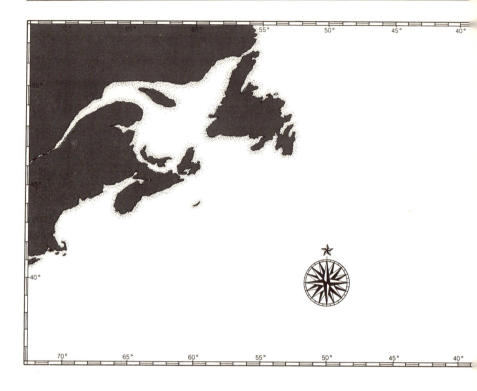

6

1:30 P.M. *Moxie* has just knocked off 295 miles, noon-to-noon. In the 96 hours since the start, we have made good 890 miles at an average speed of 9.16 knots. The odometer shows 909 miles. This would have been a good show for the *Cutty Sark* and a crew of sixty.

The BBC says *Moxie* lies third to *Gauloises IV* and *VSD*, both of whom are up north on the great-circle route. *Moxie* and I are just 200 miles south of them but that doesn't mean we're 200 miles farther from Newport.

Our position lies only 70 miles south of the straight, Mercator rhumb line between Bishop Light and Nantucket. Today's noon position was smack on the track to my point "A," 43° north by 50° west, the southeast corner of the Grand Banks. This bit of ocean with its fog, ice, and fishing boats, is to be avoided by passing it to the south.

We can still stay safely north of the Azores with their enticing warmth and dread calms. So where does the BBC get this stuff about *Moxie* being "way south"? And third to the two Frenchmen? In fact, we're farthest west by 12 miles according to the latest broadcast positions, therefore nearest to the finish according to my little calculator.

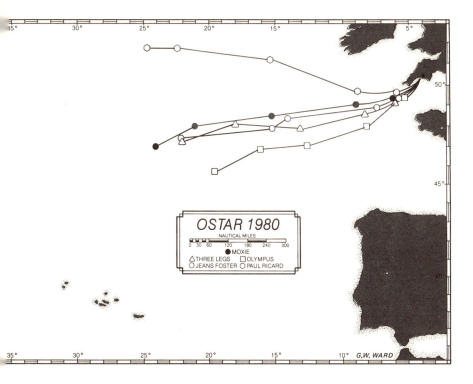

OSTAR 1980
NAUTICAL MILES
0 30 60   120   180   240   300
● MOXIE   □ OLYMPUS
△ THREE LEGS   □ OLYMPUS
○ JEANS FOSTER ○ PAUL RICARD

G.W. WARD

Could the French and the BBC be paying too much heed to the 140 miles overall distance "saved" by following the great circle that fetches one onto the rocks at Newfoundland? Furthermore, by keeping a bit south, I run less risk from being hit by the eastward-moving lows.

The deck officer of the Canadian motor vessel *A. C. Crosbie* agreed with my reasoning when I chatted with him on the VHF this morning. First I asked him to relay two collect calls, one to Anne telling Art Zolot to "keep trying" (I've yet to hear him on our schedule); the second to Frank Page explaining my relatively southerly position and asking him to tell the BBC that I'm not sixty years old, but sixty-five. I don't want my friends to think I'm hiding my age.

Then the kindly voice (I couldn't see his ship) gave me a more detailed forecast for this area than the 3:30 race special. He next volunteered: "This is no place for a fifty-foot boat at this time of year. You'd be better off still further south, given what lies ahead of you." Then, responding to my query as to the wisdom of Eric, Eugene, and Olivier being so far north, he said: "I don't believe the great circle will save them as much time as the bad weather will hold them up."

With these consoling words, he signed off after promising he'd tell his watch officers to keep a lookout for me on their radar screen so they could give me a position. While my dead reckoning showed us to be on the same latitude, steaming toward one another, I was in fact, as the noon line later revealed, some 30 to 40 miles south of him. Could this have been leeway over the last twenty-four hours, slippage caused by my having hoisted the daggerboard all the way up?

If so, it was still a fair trade-off. With the board up as far as the jack-stay permits, it is safely housed. Excess leverage cannot crack its trunk in pounding seas. It was just such pressure that damaged Eric's *Gauloises IV* while he was sailing from La Trinité to Plymouth. With the board out of harm's way, I can let the boat slug along in shudder-making cross-seas at speeds up to 16 knots without fear of damage. Newport lies 540 miles south of Plymouth. So what's wrong with 40 miles of leeway in a day's run of 295 miles?

I'm ecstatic over *Moxie*'s performance. Aeolus has lavished me with kindness. Should I even mention it? Could it be that our decision to invest in windpower has tickled his vanity?

"Nous verrons, Bretons Eric et Eugene, à Breton Reef!"

4:45 P.M. Time Zone 3, already. Well, BBC, you got the word. Now you say *"Moxie* and her sixty-five-year-old skipper down to the south have jumped into second place only five miles behind *VSD,"* then *Gauloises* 53 miles farther back. *Kriter VI*, 118 miles behind *VSD*, incurred a ten-hour penalty for being over the starting line early, it's now reported. Tom Grossman, after losing twenty-five hours for repairs following his prestart collision, has climbed to sixty-fifth place. Daniel Gilard in *Brittany Ferries* leads the Gypsy Moth class.

Has it occurred to Jack Odling-Smee, chairman of the Royal Western Race Committee, that he gives Pajot an advantage? We don't know the position of *Paul Ricard*, but he knows ours. So what that he's "unofficial"! To us racers he's the man to beat. Not knowing his whereabouts will be a disadvantage to us "official" entries as we near Newport.

Next chance I get I'll send this message collect to Angela Green at the *Observer:* "Please persuade BBC or Royal Western to issue *Paul Ricard* position if still leading fleet. Pajot has big advantage in always knowing *Moxie* positions."

After all, the whole of France knows where Pajot lies. Most of the French entries have ham radio links by which they can be informed of his position. But I can no longer find Europe 1 on the dial. Last word I had on Pajot said he was comfortably "en tête."

How We Played the Weather Averages

When I look back to June 1972 and my preparation for *Trumpeter's* OSTAR, I'm aghast at how little I understood the North Atlantic weather pattern. My preoccupation with the problems of bosunry — fixing leaks, replacing broken battens, trying to make the swing-up rudder work — all these concerns must have denied me the time to concentrate on that most crucial problem of all, the wind.

How else could I have sailed so far south? Now I see *Trumpeter* as a small turtle trying to crawl up the inside of a giant soup tureen as we struggled to escape north from Terceira. We lay becalmed for three endless days in sight of those tall mountains. Once out of their shadow, I vowed never again to blunder into the clutches of the Azores High.

For the 1976 OSTAR, I bought a good radio. During the week before the rogue wave capsized *Gulf Streamer*, I was receiving the voice broadcasts from the U.S. Coast Guard in Portsmouth, Virginia, four times a day and plotting the track of the Gulf Stream from the transmitted coordinates every afternoon. In 1978, for the passage to Plymouth and the Round Britain race, *Rogue Wave* carried an Alden facsimile weather-map receiver. It was still illegal for a British race, but the French had sanctioned it for the Route du Rhum coming up in November.

That July, the American balloonists made their record-breaking flight from Cape Cod to France. News stories spoke of the help given the crew by Bob Rice, chief meteorologist for Weather Services Corp., of Bedford, Massachusetts. As soon as I flew home from England, I asked him to analyze the weather patterns for the race from Saint-Malo to Guadeloupe.

His review of the daily maps for the previous twenty Novembers narrowed the problem: how best to duck the eastbound lows which by that late in the year would be crossing the Atlantic as far south as the northerly edge of the Azores; and how to avoid getting becalmed in the Azores High once I got out of the Bay of Biscay.

In a gale, the second night after the start, I lost my radio antenna. This prevented my ever getting a facsimile weather map the rest of the race. But, thanks to Bob's coaching, I was still able to piece together a good enough map using information from passing ships and from voice broadcasts, to plan the right strategy. By hugging the Spanish coast, I managed to sneak past the Azores without once totally running out of wind. By the eighth race day, I was far enough south to pick up a gentle southwesterly that sped me 2,470 miles in ten days. Few solo sailors, before or since, have averaged 247 miles a day for so long.

Naturally I went back to Bob for help in 1980. First we ordered prints made of the daily weather maps for the past twenty Junes.

"This is my ideal," I told Bob. "Never to have to heave to because of too much wind; never so little wind that *Moxie* lies dead in the water."

We began to visualize a corridor that followed a diagonal between Plymouth and Newport. It passed south of the tracks of the most savage eastbound lows that had swept through earlier OSTARs. It stayed north of the seductive ring on the pilot chart indicating the "light and variable air" of the Azores–Bermuda High.

"*Moxie* goes so well to windward," I bragged to Bob, "we don't have to worry so long as it doesn't blow harder than thirty-five or less than three knots. It doesn't matter what direction the wind's blowing. She'll hold her own with anyone so long as she has wind within that range. Especially if it's on the nose."

He gave me one rule of thumb. "Get south of forty-five degrees north latitude before you cross thirty-five degrees west longitude. This way you'll stand a good chance of escaping the worst of the lows. They tend in summer to curve northeast after they pass Newfoundland."

We composed a reporting form to give the centers of the lows, their travel time and direction, and the position of the high. My amateur-radio-band friend, Art Zolot, at the Beverly airport, would relay this to me each afternoon. Race headquarters at Newport could give Bob my latest position. Neat. Alas, the Drake TR-7 radio, no doubt because the solar panels I'd installed on *Moxie* could not keep a strong enough charge in the storage batteries, proved unable to pick up Art's voice after *Moxie* passed the halfway mark on the crossing to France.

By phone from Plymouth, I told Art that while he should try every day to reach me, he should tell Bob not to "turn on the Bedford weather" until I could surely pick it up. It wasn't until Race Day 12 that Art's voice came in loud and clear. He could hear me just well enough to warrant telling Bedford to go to work. On the next two afternoons, I had pinpointed forecasts. For example, Bob warned me to expect a six-hour calm about midnight Friday, June 20. Sure enough, it happened. But it didn't worry me because he also said that a cold front would follow, bringing plenty of wind.

In 1984, all serious OSTAR competitors will have ham radio links on which to receive weather analyses based upon their particular positions. Geoffrey Williams, the OSTAR victor in 1968, pioneered this technique. Then in 1972 and 1976 the rules banned "private advisories." By 1980 all agreed this was silly. Ham radio communication was to be encouraged for the security it provided. How could you stop people talking about the weather?

Moxie's link with Bedford was a luxury. Every night at 3:30 A.M. GMT, the BBC provided a special North Atlantic forecast for the OSTAR. Once we were halfway to Newport, the American High Seas forecast from Portsmouth came into play. By practicing making maps on the way from Florida to France, I developed a certain feel for the way the lows were moving.

I came to envision the race "corridor" as a gigantic bowling alley. Up in Hudson Bay, the playful gods formed cyclones like snowballs, which they then tossed with a twist causing them to curve down through Labrador to Nova Scotia, then northeastward straight for the candlepins in Scotland. If you crouched along the south side of the alley, you could avoid the most severe buffeting. But careful there. If you tumble over the side, you'll be up to your neck in the stagnant muck of the High.

I tried taping the Morse code forecasts from the British Meteorological office broadcast from Portishead, then playing the numbers back slowly. With these a skilled radio operator can construct a weather map. But I soon gave up. Even a professional radio man racing solo would find this too time-consuming. Why don't the British regularly provide voice forecasts for the high seas like the Americans?

After the race, I studied the maps Bob had saved for me. On them he'd put red dots showing my daily positions. The map for Race Day 9 shows the high just below me, a low 400 miles north. It's a classic pattern for June, precisely the condition to have expected if 1980 matched the averages.

So it went for most of *Moxie's* race. Gales for the first third. Headwinds and fog in the middle. Light southwesterlies for the finish. The map for Race Day 15 shows *Moxie* in what Bob describes as "a bubble of a high" surrounded by three lows, clearly slowed to a snail's pace. Right behind her Keig, Steggall, Birch, Greene, and Pajot have plenty of wind to close up her lead.

No amount of science could handle that situation. What the OSTAR skipper needs for that is a private line to Aeolus and that I felt I had.

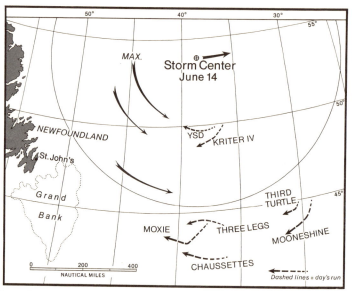

On Saturday, June 14, the BBC warned this storm would hit the OSTAR fleet. Moxie, having heeded the advice given by weathermen before the race, was far enough south to escape the worst of it. (Map by Samuel Bryant)

PRIVATE LINE TO AEOLUS

Ever since I got becalmed in the Azores on the 1972 OSTAR, I've strongly disapproved of crabbing about the wind by anyone aboard my boat. I had turned to Robert Fitzgerald's translation of *The Odyssey* for comfort. I learned that in seagoing matters to do with sailing, Aeolus, even more than Poseidon, is the god to avoid offending. He's the Wind King, who can "rouse or calm at will," and that's a power that can influence a boat race.

So it has become ship routine, early on an offshore passage, to read aloud to new members of the crew the opening eighty-seven lines of Book Ten. It makes a fruitful ceremony of a happy hour to recite the visit of Odysseus and his shipmates to the island domain of Aeolus Hippotades. The tales of the Trojan War enthralled the host. To reward the doughty yarn-spinner, Aeolus provided Odysseus' ship, home-bound for Ithaca, with "a bull's hide sewn from neck to tail into a mighty bag, bottling storm winds ..."

> He wedged this bag under my afterdeck,
> lashing the neck with shining silver wire

so not a breath got through; only the west wind
he lofted for me in a quartering breeze
to take my squadron spanking home.
                                        No luck:
the fair wind failed us when our prudence failed.
Nine days and nights we sailed . . .
but now, being weary to the bone, I fell
into deep slumber . . .

The crew, believing the sack conceals "plunder out of Troy" which the
skipper doesn't intend to share with them, untie the bag.

                                        Then every wind
roared into hurricane; . . .
. . . the rough gale blew the ships
and rueful crews clear back to Aiolia.

This time our hero gets a cool welcome. "Why back again, Odysseus?" "What sea fiend rose in your path? Did we not launch you
well/for home, or for whatever land you chose?" The melancholy
reply: "Mischief aboard and nodding at the tiller — a damned
drowse — did for me." Says Aeolus:

"Take yourself out of this island, creeping thing —
no law, no wisdom, lays it on me now
to help a man the blessed gods detest —
out!" . . .
and comfortless we went again to sea,
days of it, till the men flagged at the oars —
no breeze, no help in sight . . .

Could you ask for a more explicit warning to mariners? Don't take
the Old Boy's bounty for granted. Carelessness will be rewarded with
contempt. Don't expect forgiveness for such a blunder as falling asleep
when you are about to make a landfall.

At the end of the reading, I adjure my shipmates: "Please, aboard this
vessel, never speak ill of the wind, no matter how much or how little.
Aeolus likes a forelock puller, so that's how I behave."

"Yes, sir, thank you, sir. Any breeze you choose to give us is probably too good for us," I'm forever saying in the tone of Uriah Heep,
whether it's Force 9 or Zed. It bothers me on a fluky beat to have someone say: "Now, where's that goddamn air coming from?" Better to
spend your energy figuring what Aeolus will come up with next than to
cuss him. This is the Homeric Code as I read it. It might not win the
America's Cup. But on a long voyage it avoids much frustration.

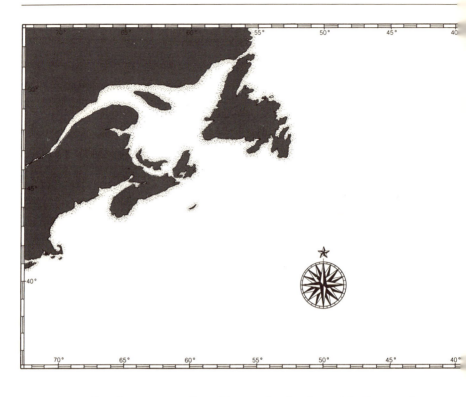

7

8:05 A.M. Sunshine greets Race Day 5. In the last eight hours the northwester has dropped from 30 knots to 10. *Moxie* has been averaging 10. Such speed couldn't last forever. It would have been favoritism from Aeolus beyond justice: 1,022 miles in 111 hours means an average speed of 9.31 knots, according to my trusty calculator. For a westward passage! It has to be historic for all of us front-runners. (I can't help thinking it would have been even faster in *Rogue Wave* considering she's 10 feet longer on the waterline.) If it goes much lighter, I'll have to get out the reacher.

(FROM THE FILM SOUND TRACK)
1:00 P.M. *Well, unless we just lost it in that three-hour calm we've been sitting in, Moxie, according to the BBC, holds the lead over VSD. Pretty exciting, I can tell you. This is turning into a real horse race. The startling news. Eric Loizeau, for reasons not given, has turned back. That's a*

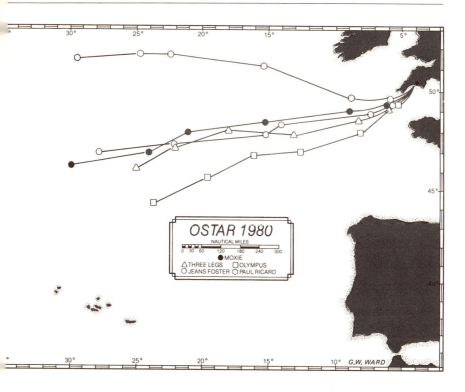

OSTAR 1980
NAUTICAL MILES
0 30 60   120   180   240   300
● MOXIE
△ THREE LEGS   □ OLYMPUS
○ JEANS FOSTER ○ PAUL RICARD

great disappointment. He was my second-place choice, second only to Mike Birch, who has also had his troubles.

Olivier de Kersauson in Kriter VI is third. Sailing a big monohull, he's probably right to stay north where he can buck the gales. He says it's his only chance against us tris. But I think I'm right to keep south, well below the track of the lows. For the moment the wind has shifted from the northwest following this flat calm. It's now filling in nicely from the southwest, so I'm tacking northwest.

My choice is either this or going down toward the Azores. God forbid I get stuck down there in the High. So I'm tacking north into the sector the French will be coming through. Won't know till tomorrow who has lucked out on the wind.

I must say it's pretty heady to find yourself leading after five days. But I really have had extraordinary luck. Averaged over 9 knots and the boat has been just perfect. I'm terribly pleased.

A trimaran at speed: Rogue Wave *making 20 knots off Gloucester.* (Bill Lane)

ELECTRONICS AND SAIL

Electronics has made the lone mariner's life incomparably easier than in the days when an alarm clock served Joshua Slocum as a chronometer. Day or night, I have the voice of station WWV giving a time signal on the minute. With this I can check my digital watch, which loses about a second every three days. To recall the time in numbers after making a sextant sight is ever so much easier than trying to recall the position of a sweep-second hand.

My Tamaya pocket-size calculator for $195 has saved me hours of measuring distances on the chart with straight-edge and dividers. It gives either great-circle or straight-line course and distance answers between two intersections of latitude and longitude. Faster than I can sharpen a pencil, I can check whether I'm on the favored tack for Newport, or whether I'm still ahead of the Frenchmen.

Some of the other gadgets that combine to make this race so pleasant by comparison with 1972:

The Argos satellite transmitter. Screwed to the afterdeck under a translucent bubble the size of a salad bowl sits a transponder on loan to me, as to all contestants, in the interests of safety and journalism. Several times daily it sends a signal, via orbiting Tiros and a computer at Toulouse, giving my location. This is the source of the BBC position reports and such bulletins as that heard last night saying the beacons of Bertie Reed, the South African in *Voortrekker*, and of Phil Steggall had gone off the air.

Phil, who designed my sails, gambled on a tall rig for himself. Did it topple, silencing his Argos? Did he capsize? It's a comfort to know that if he's in real trouble, help will almost surely reach him in time. A search need not start blind as in 1976 with the case of Mike McMullen, who simply disappeared.

The Drake TR-7. This $2,500 transmitter-receiver is a favorite among amateur radio buffs because, with its illuminated frequency figures given to three decimals, it homes precisely. With it I can instantly pick up the BBC race reports, Portsmouth weather, or the scheduled messages from Art Zolot in Beverly without the need to grope about the airways with the dial.

The Autohelm 3000. For this I thank Mike McMullen, a member of the race committee in 1976. He argued for permitting electric autopilots provided the juice used to power them came from battery-charging sources other than petrochemical — *videlicet:* windmills, towed turbo-propellers, or photovoltaic cells. He learned from his experience with *Three Cheers* that trimarans accelerate so rapidly in puffs that they will not hold a course under a wind vane's guidance.

Mike knew that there's no more vulnerable Achilles' heel for the competitive solo sailor than his self-steering mechanism, whether it be an electric autopilot or one of the many versions descended from Chichester's wind vane he named "Miranda." John Letcher's book *Self Steering* gives admirable advice on how to control a boat with sail trim and lines to the tiller. But it doesn't apply at speeds greater than 6 knots unless the boat is dead on the wind.

The quest for reliable self-steering had become an obsession with me. With *Trumpeter*, I tried a simple wind vane. Its rotation activated lines to an auxiliary tiller. Called the QME, it was too feeble. In 1972 I traded up for a Hasler, the invention of the founder of the OSTAR, beautifully engineered but still not powerful enough for a big tri. For *Gulf Streamer's* voyage to Plymouth for the 1974 Round Britain, I installed an Aries, a heavier-duty, British wind vane. But it, too, lacked the muscle to move the rudder quickly enough.

For the 1976 OSTAR, I asked John Ratcliffe, an engineer in Hancock, Massachusetts, to modify the Aries so that its vane activated a trim tab mounted on the transom. This might have answered the problem peculiar to multihulls: how to compensate for the sudden change in the apparent wind angle caused by the boat's surging ahead in a puff. But we'll never know because we hadn't time to test it before the capsize.

Gulf Streamer also carried a Tillermaster, an electric autopilot powered by two solar panels. The same system worked well enough for *Rogue Wave* in the Route du Rhum, but its push-pull thrusting rod, when activating a wheel rather than a tiller, lacked the range to cope with *Moxie*. Her greater sensitivity to puffs that could yank her up into the wind required a different solution. So it was with great relief that I heard from Nick Keig that a British firm had come on the market with a device specially suited to steering with a wheel. The Autohelm 3000 comprises two elements: a compass-sensing unit that one sets to the desired course, and a drive linked by belt to a drum attached to the wheel. A Swiss motor, no bigger than a flashlight battery, designed for the windshield wipers of luxury cars, powers it. We called it "Otto."

To shelter it inside the cabin, safe from salt water, we mounted a second steering wheel for the drum. Even this rig had teething problems.

The second night out from Florida to France, the motor failed and in so doing burned out the compass unit. Since the trip was to be my training exercise for the OSTAR and to train without an autopilot but with Tom aboard would be no training at all, I decided to stop in Bermuda to order two replacements air express.

Even these proved vulnerable. Three days out we noted a weakening in Otto's responses. Suspecting battery depletion as the cause, since there'd been little or no sun for recharging, we steered by hand for twenty-four hours. When we resumed use of Otto, Tom noted that the little motor, a sturdier variety than the original model's, was turning fine. But four plastic tenons that engaged the knurled turning wheel had sheared. He cannibalized a replacement from the burned-out unit and we carried on for nine days. Then the rubber belt wore out.

The spare lasted only to our landfall in Brittany. These omens did nothing for my paranoia. Backup, backup, backup. Of all the departments of bosunry where this must be the watchword, it's self-steering. Without it you spend the off-the-wind hours fighting drowsiness at the helm. Otto steers a better course 90 percent of the time than 90 percent of all helmsmen. Sailing with Tom to France was so relaxed I had time to read 900 pages of the Trollope novel I'd just begun at the moment of capsize four years before. (It made us both a little uneasy to have *Can You Forgive Her?* aboard, but I was determined to lay that particular ghost.)

You can get too dependent on your autopilot. Then if it fails, you're like the mother with three kids under six when the imported English nanny quits. Back to gulped meals, snatched naps, and no time for pondering the weather map. So it pays to learn to balance the helm at speed, close-hauled, using only a length of line and a piece of shock cord to lash the wheel. *Moxie* will sail like this at 10 knots for hours, about 40 degrees to the apparent wind, without my needing to reduce canvas. If I try to point closer, she'll round up in the puffs and find herself in irons. Farther off the wind, both *Moxie* and *Rogue Wave* need a hand to nudge the lashed helm back on course about every five minutes.

At La Trinité, I bought two additional solar panels from Jacques Timsit, an OSTAR entry and a friend from the Route du Rhum. These were fresh from Motorola's Arizona plant, unavailable as yet in America, but supplied to him because he'd renamed his *Arauna*, a fine monohull, *Motorola* for the race. (Alas, she sank after hitting a floating object the second night out of Plymouth.) These panels were touted to be twice as effective as mine, capable of generating at half-speed even when the sun hid behind the clouds. In the self-steering department, anyone can see I'm a belt and braces type.

While *Moxie* waited in the Beaulieu River for the start of the Crystal Trophy, Tom and I visited the factory in Portsmouth where Derek Fawcett assembles Autohelms. We stocked up with four complete units for the race (two were for *Rogue*), plus enough spare belts and rotors to go 'round the Horn. This proved to be absurd redundancy. One unit managed the 432 hours from Plymouth to Newport without a whimper.

The DROM. This is an acronym for "Directional Radar Omega." It's a device perfected by the French in time for the Route du Rhum. Every entry had to carry one to mollify the bureaucrats. The fear that a 126-foot ship like *Vendredi Treize* would run someone down while the skipper napped bothered the French shipping authorities, just as it had the British. But the DROM provided a marvelously Gallic solution.

It has two elements: a four-inch cube mounted on a spreader, which is wired to a small box mounted on a bulkhead below decks. An alarm inside the box beeps when the boat enters the radar scan of an approaching vessel, and a red light flashes on the face of the box to show from which quadrant of the compass the vessel is approaching.

"This electronic watchkeeper will ward off collisions," reasoned the French organizers. "After all, if we protect our West European border from the Russians with electronic surveillance, why not have faith in the DROM?"

This silenced the meddlers. It is, in truth, a most comforting and reliable device.

While I was writing this to pass the time, almost as if to confirm the performance of the DROM, I spotted a ship coming up from the west. I called her on the VHF and recorded the following:

Moxie — Will the orange ship coming up my stern respond, please?

Response — Not to worry. This is the British motor ship *Gannet* just coming over to have a look.

Moxie — May I ask your mission, sir? (He looked research-y.)

Gannet (clipped, educated Brit) — Apples from New Zealand.

Moxie — Did you see me on your radar?

Gannet — Yes, seven miles away.

Moxie — My DROM-radar alert didn't pick you up until you were only a mile away.

Gannet — Suggest you put up a reflector tonight. It may be foggy.

(I discover he knows about the OSTAR. We chat about solo racing, the Argos, the French to the north.)

Moxie — Could you fill me in on what weather to expect?

Gannet — Some rain, light westerlies. A cold front at fifty to fifty-two north.

Moxie — Do you have a north limit on your map showing where the light and variables start around the Azores High?

Gannet — Afraid I don't have a map.

Moxie — Would you think this was the favored tack for Newport?

Gannet — Yes, I would. Well, cheerio, and hope you win.

Back to the DROM. It's still flashing as *Gannet* disappears over the eastern horizon. Oh, shucks, I forgot to ask him to relay my request for Pajot's position.

Signet System 4000. This is the modern supplement to the cheek to the wind, the ear to the sound of the wake, both still important. It comprises two assemblies connected by a cable of many color-coded wires. The deck unit is enclosed in a teak block under the dodger where I can read it from anywhere in the cockpit. Over the chart table hangs a black metal box crammed with circuit boards. These look like toy railroads for a colony of ants. Another cable inside the mast connects them to a wind vane at the masthead.

The panel on the face of the deck unit has four windows surrounding a dial with a needle. These tell me:

TOP LEFT — boat speed to hundredths of a knot;
TOP RIGHT — wind speed over the masthead;
LOWER LEFT — wind angle to the axis of the ship;
LOWER RIGHT — depth of the sea in feet, fathoms, or meters.

The dial has a needle that rotates over the outline of a boat's hull. It shows graphically the apparent wind angle given in figures by the digital readout in the lower left window.

There's also a readout window in the face of the box over the chart table with switches to permit the navigator to summon whichever of the instruments interests him. Here also is a somewhat hard-to-read window giving the miles to the nearest hundredth that the boat has traveled through the water.

The product of El Monte, California, in the heart of "silicone valley," my Signet can claim to be the ultimate in efficiency, for it draws little power. If a circuit board fails, it can be replaced as easily as a cassette in a tape player. I'm already using the second of my two spare wind-point cards so I'm wary.

At night, with the windows glowing orange, I can sit in the hatch and take in at a glance my compass course, boat speed, and wind angle. I steer by twisting the Autohelm's compass dial. It transmits a change of as little as one degree to the wheel. For me, anyway, it's a far more efficient way to go upwind in the dark than trying to hand-steer while shining a flashlight on jib telltales every few minutes.

The VHF 24-channel, two-way radio. The modern substitute for the skipper's brass trumpet of Melville's day. Using it, I can speak not only to ships in sight but to any willing to chat who are within line-of-sight range — that is to say, as far as 75 miles in hours of good reception. If I can raise a friendly deck officer every couple of days, he'll give me a position check and the weather. This way I'd be sending Anne frequent messages by telephone "collect." With the Argos system, however, she gets my daily position. It's the most enormous relief not to be worried that she's worrying.

The Brookes & Gatehouse Homer-Heron. This is the fourth time I've brought along this sturdy, compact, all-purpose radio receiver equipped with a direction-finding antenna and a short-wave converter. It has been a faithful friend on all four of my tris. Powered by four penlight batteries, it pulls in news and music without draining the ship's electrical supply. If it's foggy at the finish, it will pick up radio beacons to guide me past Nantucket, right up to Brenton Reef or the Buzzard's Bay Tower.

I have faith it will work no matter what. There never was a radio so weatherproof, so tolerant of abuse. In the manufacture of such products, we're no match for the British.

So there's the range of *Moxie*'s electronic armament. Such sophisticated aids as facsimile weather-map receivers, loran, and other navigation systems are not allowed for this race. But anything goes in the Route du Rhum and that's bound to be the wave of the future.

8.

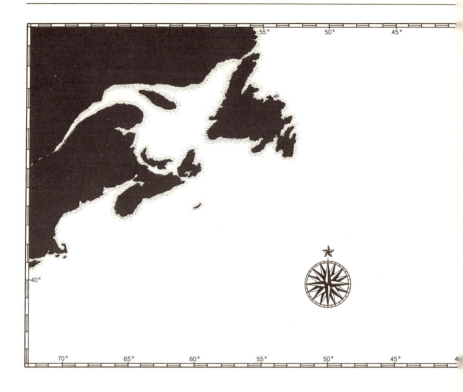

6:00 A.M. Race Day 6, Good Luck Day. The vibrations below brought to mind Dick Newick's "Greed for Speed" paper at the Plymouth Multihull Symposium. He had blamed this propensity among the French sailors for their recent trimaran capsizes. I went on deck to shorten sail. As I luffed to roll in the jib, there, five yards off the starboard bow, floated a lethal metal cylinder with knobs protruding, rusty but sturdy. A World War II mine?

If I'd collided with it at 18 knots, the speed to which we had accelerated after the shift of the apparent wind from 35 to 45 degrees, it could have smashed through the hull and out the other side like a Civil War cannonball.

I've been trying to decide whether it's worth a ten-mile detour to go south of the tip of the Grand Banks to avoid fog and the speed-inhibiting presence of fishing boats. At our weather briefing in Plymouth, the professor told us: "If you stay outside the fifty-nine-fathom line, you'll avoid the fog." But the chart doesn't show a 59-fathom line until we get off Nova Scotia. I suppose he means the shoal shown on

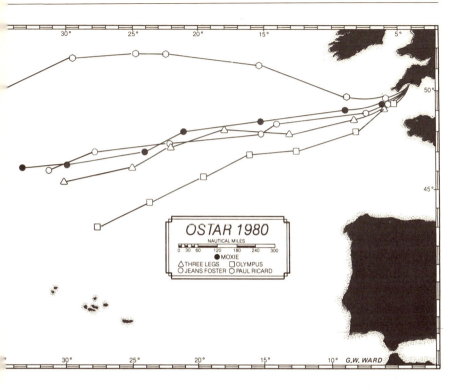

the chart in light blue. The BBC reports icebergs north of 48° north and west of 47° west. I'm well south of there.

9:30. Whoopee. A Norwegian deck officer from the bridge of the Liberian freighter *Freenes* just waked me calling on the VHF. He promised to relay my request for Pajot's positions to Frank Page at the *Observer*. It may stir a tempest in a teapot.

(FROM THE FILM SOUND TRACK)

5:00 P.M. . . . *I'm just about to have the happiest happy hour a man ever had. We're about to pass the race halfway mark and we won't have been out a week until noon tomorrow. Moxie is doing 11 knots, 35 degrees off the apparent wind, 25 knots of wind over the masthead. I don't think that boat of Riguidel's can possibly make this kind of speed dead on the nose into this much wind. I wonder if Olivier de Kersauson on Kriter VI is doing this well.*

Moxie has to be the best little old windward-going boat

93

in the goddamn ocean. . . . She's never going to leave the fam-
ily. I'm telling you, she's staying in the family as our Maine
boat. Moxie *from Maine.*

Sun's about to go down behind a big cloud bank. Wind
shifting from west to southwest. We're going due west. Oh,
man, just der-loverly. There goes the sun back of the clouds. I
think there's a big low up there and I think Riguidel, who's
up to the north, is going to have to beat down here to miss
the Grand Banks, and, bless his heart, we're down here al-
ready. Tomorrow's going to tell a big tale.

BUCKLEY'S "PRACTICAL NAVIGATOR"

What Nathaniel Bowditch's *Practical Navigator* did for clipper captains in 1800, William F. Buckley's *Airborne* (Macmillan, 1976) can do
for yacht skippers. It dispells the mystery shrouding celestial navigation. Buckley, the finest prose stylist writing regularly for American
newspapers, tells in fourteen pages how to get longitude with a pair of sun
sights. I have photocopied these and keep them in a binder on the chart
table. Ambitious shipmates have proved true this claim by Buckley:

"Those curious to know *why* celestial navigation works can consult
the breviaries. . . . Meanwhile — so help me God — they can set out to
sea with *these* pages, and, setting out from anywhere in the world, arrive
anywhere in the world they want to." He then reduces complicated
chapters of other tomes to the navigator's equivalent of a Heathkit
manual.

Lacking this training aid when getting ready for the 1970 Round Britain race, I took a correspondence course. I enjoyed getting my graded
assignments back from Santa Barbara by return mail because
high marks came easy. However, on the crossing in *Trumpeter* from
Plymouth to St. Croix in December 1970, I now confess I never
achieved a proper "fix." Latitude fine. Longitude competence escaped
me until on a trip north from Florida I was able to keep a constant
check on my calculations using bearings from radio beacons along
the coast.

Satellite-linked computer systems may soon be cheap enough for all
oceangoing yachts. But until then, the navigator's kit need not be costly
or complicated. To get his morning sun line, he goes on deck about 8:30
A.M. with his sextant (a plastic job will do), a twenty-five-dollar watch,

and a small notebook in which to pencil the angle of the sun above the horizon in degrees and minutes and the time to the second. No matter how small his boat, his cabin layout should provide him with a chart table at least two feet by three feet on which to spread his plotting sheet, almanac, and sight reduction tables. Using dividers, Weems plotter (a transparent ruler with built-in protractor), a sharp pencil, and a big eraser, he should have laid down his sun line in less than five minutes. A ship's log to show the mileage run since the last sight simplifies the dead reckoning. But don't panic if it fails. Ours packed up on a trip from Plymouth to Madeira. By asking the helmsmen to guess, and record faithfully, the distance made good, hour by hour, I was able to get by fine without the log.

I admire those who find it easy to take star sights. They frustrate me because of clouds, the bouncing ship, and the desperately short period, whether at dawn or at twilight, during which stars and horizon can both be seen through the sextant eyepiece. On a passage in *Rogue Wave* from Gloucester to St. Martin, Ebbe Rosbak, a Danish merchant captain, doubted the accuracy of my plot as we passed close by Bermuda. Because the sun had not shone all day, I was relying for a position on a succession of RDF fixes from the Gibbs Hill beacon.

"We are lost," said Ebbe, a native of Elsinore, in the voice of Hamlet in soliloquy.

"Come off it," I protested. "Kitchen Shoal has to be somewhere about thirty miles to the westward, give or take ten. We'd see the loom of Hamilton long before we'd be in serious trouble."

"Professionally speaking we are lost," he insisted. "On a two-hundred-thousand-ton tanker, we'd be in serious trouble."

His concern impelled him at midnight to go after a five-star fix — Schedar, Sirius, Dubhe, Rigel, and Alpheratz — bolstered by a Polaris latitude. He worked intently under a full moon and a cloudless sky, choosing stars outside the brightest moonshine. Disdaining my offer to slow our 12-knot clip to make it easier to "pull down" the stars, he took twenty-nine minutes to record the sights to his satisfaction and an hour to work them.

"Now I show you where we are," said Ebbe, shining a penlight on the tidiest little cat's cradle of crisscrossing pencil lines. "We passed closer to Bermuda than you thought. About twenty miles."

Not for me to quarrel with such delicate handiwork by asking how come we'd seen no island loom. The bright moonlight could have overlaid it.

"Now, I am happy," said Ebbe, coming into the cockpit for a last smoke before bedding down. "We are no longer lost."

Bill Buckley clearly enjoys as much as I the cozy comfort of a good "fix," one in which the advance of the DR plot comes snug beside the late-afternoon sun line. It sets the right mood for the happy hour and it adds a cerebral side to sailing in which all hands owe it to themselves to share. Accustomed to his beautiful Cyrano's amenities, he might not fancy my notions about boat plumbing. But he knows a good boat when he sees it. Unlike so many members of the yachting establishment, he would not let prejudice close his mind to appreciation of Moxie's graces. He would forgive me for being a speed snob.

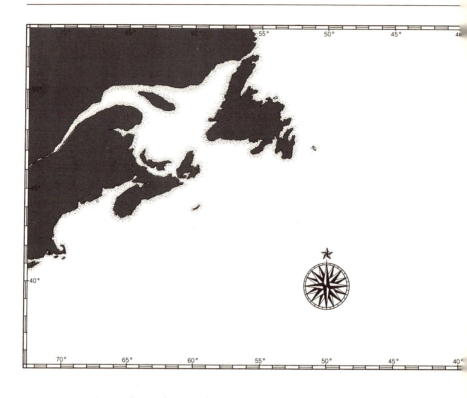

9:15 A.M. Pretty hairy last night. I woke just before midnight to find the wind had veered from southwest to northwest, putting the sails aback. Luckily I'd reefed down when the wind had risen to 20 knots so no damage was done. In tacking over to starboard, the stopper knot in the end of one of the jib sheets shook out, allowing the heavy, one-inch-diameter line to escape through the fair lead on the deck. Writhing like an angry boa constrictor, it wrapped itself thirty times around the other sheet before I could tame it.

It took twenty minutes to unsnarl the mess in the dark holding a flashlight in my teeth. Got soaked. Moral: go back to the old drill of *two* stopper knots in the end of all sheets. Trying to be youthful and care-free, I'd abandoned this old-fogy notion — to my regret.

A low to the north has caused this gale that's now hitting us on the nose. I imagine it's slowing down *VSD* and *Kriter VI* just as much as *Moxie*. Last night's BBC report gave only placings: *VSD, Moxie, Kriter VI*, and (great!) Walter Greene leading the Gypsy Moth (intermediate) class. My message to Frank must have arrived, for they said, "Pajot ahead of them all," giving his position.

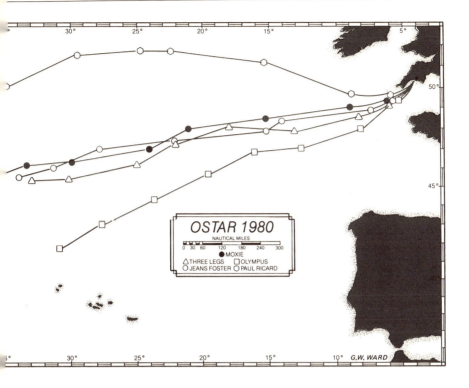

OSTAR 1980

NAUTICAL MILES

0 30 60   120   180   240   300

● MOXIE
△ THREE LEGS   □ OLYMPUS
○ JEANS FOSTER   ○ PAUL RICARD

G.W. WARD

10:45. This is our third gale of the race. Advice to windward-goers in gales. Wear oilies to pour coffee. I just spilled mine all over myself coming off a big wave at 9 knots.

The BBC, if I heard it right, gave Pajot's longitude as 37.65° west. If he's 300 miles north of me, I reckon he's only 31 miles nearer Brenton Reef, not all that much of a lead. My lobbying to have him included seems more than ever justified. Now the race committee seems to agree that it's only fair to let us in the lead know as much about him as he knows about us.

Right now I wouldn't swap positions with Marc. I think I'll be able to fetch the southeast end of the Grand Banks as soon as this low moves farther east. Then I'll have less fog to duck and fewer fishing vessels to dodge than *VSD* and *Paul Ricard*, who'll be approaching the Banks at a more southwesterly angle than my westerly course.

I believe I'm far enough north to avoid the Gulf Stream. I must start plotting the Stream's coordinates given on the afternoon Portsmouth forecast. So far we've adhered to the Bedford advice to avoid the worst of the lows, as they curve northeast after passing Newfoundland by getting south of 45° north before you reach 35° west. We're just about on 45° north and 37.5° west.

To summarize the first week's progress, we've completed 47.3 percent of the course, or 1,358 miles of the total 2,872, leaving 1,514 to go. (To buck morale, I made the map below showing my 1972 position and those of the winning boats in the last four OSTARs at the end of the first week.)

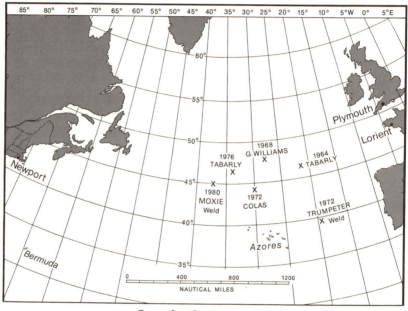

Saturday June 14, 1980.
Moxie's seventh race day position compared.
Lat 45° 07' North Long. 37° 05' West

6:40 P.M. Thought for the day: During a gale, the solo sailor should wear his safety harness even when he's asleep, just as the infantry platoon leader in combat never moves without his carbine slung over his shoulder. Both devices serve as reminders that this is enemy territory.

TESTING WITH HURRICANE AMY

Gulf Streamer had just finished first in the 1975 Bermuda Multihull and it was time to qualify her for the 1976 OSTAR. It was Tuesday, July 1. I had planned to leave for Gloucester Sunday, but Hurricane Amy, first of the season, had just brushed over the British island on her way to the northeast, requiring a delay.

"Amy's now about a hundred fifty miles northwest of Bermuda," said Frank Rogers, secretary of the Royal Hamilton Amateur Dinghy Club, showing us the weather map he'd just sketched from the 0935 off-shore forecast. The group on the club porch included all six of the skippers who'd finished a slow, very light-air race the previous Friday — Larry Bedell, Martin Pollard, Tom Grossman, Manley Williams, Don Karmin, and me.

"She's moving northeast but still at only four miles per hour. One can't be sure she won't turn back south, but it's unlikely," Frank concluded.

Tom had planned to do his qualifying solo in *Cap 33* along with me but decided "to wait another day for Amy to make up her mind." After reviewing the risks and weighing the safety factors of ample sea room and warnings from WWV if Amy should head south, I decided to set sail.

At 11:50 A.M. *Gulf Streamer* had cleared the Hamilton channel. With one reef in the main and the staysail, but no jib unrolled, we were running down the South Channel at 11 knots before a gusty southwester. We kept pace with a seagoing tug on her way to the eastward to tow in *Ajax*, a ketch in distress. She'd been constantly in the newscasts for the last twenty-four hours because of the report that there was an injured woman aboard.

We waved to the crew on the tug's fantail as we rounded the Spit Buoy at 12:25 and set a course of 350 magnetic for Provincetown. I had mounted the servoblade for my Aries self-steering, but I had delayed inserting the plywood wind vane. It was blowing too hard for the gear to steer us with the wind aft. As it was, the gyrations of the blade in the water proved too violent for the coupling. It sheared after two hours, leaving the blade to trail on its wire lanyard until I could recouple it two days later. But no matter. The wind was not so far aft that I couldn't achieve self-steering balance by the time we'd reached Northeast Buoy. Averaging better than 10 knots, wind west-southwest at 25 knots, we dropped the Holiday Inn on St. Catharine's Head below the horizon before I'd had time for lunch. It was by now rough enough to dull the appetite.

If Amy decided to lurk in southern waters much longer, ten hours would see *Streamer* being tested in 60-knot winds. Should WWV report Amy hooking south, I'd have at least 70 miles of sea room if I should be caught in her center and have to heave to. If she moved northeast, as forecast, I figured I'd have ideal sailing in her wake. I might even set some sort of solo record from Bermuda to Gloucester.

"A year from now," as I'd said to Larry at the club, "when I'm coming to the end of the single-handed race, I might well be caught out in the 1976 equivalent of Amy. I'd be tired after two thousand miles of racing and much less ready to cope than rested as I am now."

So it was not with dread, but with anticipation, that I regarded the murky horizon stretching across the north. Great pillars of slate-gray cloud spiraled vertically like smoke from a faraway forest fire. I was reminded of those Bikini photos of the mushroom cloud. Awe-inspiring, majestic, but on such a scale there was no guessing how near or far.

By 2:45 the wind had piped up enough to warrant a second reef in the main. While winching down the jiffy-reefing lines, luffing into the wind, I noted the wind-speed needle hovering at 40. It could have been overreading. By 4:15, with the log showing me 30 miles north of Bermuda, I dropped the main. We continued to scuttle north under staysail alone at a steady eight knots. Seas were building. The sky seemed prematurely dark.

At twilight I got conflicting reports on Amy. The eight-minutes-past-the-hour WWV coordinates placed her center 350 miles northeast of my position. The Bermuda forecast was less comforting, showing her about where she'd been reported at the time of my departure and still dawdling northeast at less than the 10-knot speed that would indicate her commitment to a northerly course. But neither forecast seemed alarming. I was gaining a mile of sea room every seven minutes. While it was tumbly enough to make dry crackers all the dinner I wanted, *Streamer* seemed to be enjoying the ride with no strain.

We rushed on through the starless night. At 2:08 A.M., July 2, WWV said Amy's center was 400 miles north. The log said we'd put the first 100 miles of the 600 from The Spit to Chatham beneath our keels. No need to sleep the first night out. I stood at the helm until first light, noting the mounting seas, the strengthening wind, our greater speed, and wondered how sharp those guys really were way out in Fort Collins, Colorado, who read off the storm reports. It seemed increasingly clear to me that *Streamer* was traveling north faster than Amy and might soon be locked in an embarrassing embrace.

The staysail, 305 square feet of 10-ounce Dacron, was now providing the motive power to thrust 14,000 pounds of vessel on a beam reach, without benefit of surfing, at a steady 12 knots. When a particularly heavy gust accelerated us to 15 knots, I felt it prudent to rest. I'd been almost steadily on the helm for seventeen hours. Concentration was needed to play the following seas without risking a broach. My attention had begun to wander for lack of sleep.

So, at 4:15 A.M., after reviewing what Mike McMullen had told me about his 1972 hurricane experience in *Three Cheers,* our smaller, elder sister, I warily rounded up into the wind. Mike reported that he'd been running off under bare poles at 12 knots in enormous seas. Unused to tris, he had feared pitchpoling and decided lying ahull would be safer. He had dreaded the moment of rounding up. Dick Newick believes the fear was groundless because of the ever-enlarging buoyancy of *Three Cheers's* big wing deck. But Dick concedes Mike was there and he wasn't.

With no wish just then to test *Streamer's* ability to remain upright against intensifying centrifugal force, I slowed down as best I could by sheeting the staysail flat, waiting for the nearest thing to a lull, that is, any moment below 50 knots of wind, to coincide with a propitious absence of advancing comber, and brought her into the wind. Smoothly, as if shooting a mooring, she slowed her mad rush.

My big ears provide me with a portable anemometer. When I face into a gale and they flatten back like a rabbit's, it's time for caution. This morning I could rotate my head and jibe them like spinnakers — the most wind I'd been in ever. The wind gauge was locked at 60, its maximum.

Except during the occasional super wave that would catch the windward outrigger just wrong and shake the whole boat, *Streamer* cocked her bow 30 degrees to the wind. I sheeted the staysail clew slightly to windward, lashed the wheel down hard against the stop, and pulled up the big daggerboard so that it protruded only a few inches below the keel. The log showed 2 knots forward progress. I estimated we were making leeway at about 3 knots. The combination should provide not more than a mile an hour of easting off the rhumb line. The next day's sextant position showed it might have been nearer two miles an hour, or 26 miles for the thirteen hours *Streamer* remained hove to. But with nothing to the east between us and Casablanca, why worry?

I slept fitfully. With sunrise the seas seem to get bigger rather than smaller. First the windward, then the leeward, outrigger would take the buffet of breaking seas. The jostling made it noisy below. I poked my head out the companionway, shielded by a small canvas dodger, for a quick scan. Inadvertently I let my morning coffee get scooped right out of the mug by the suction of the wind passing over the cockpit. I considered going on deck to take pictures but delayed it. At about five-minute intervals a breaking wave would dump six inches of water into the cockpit. Going on deck meant suiting up, harness and all.

Clouds denied a noon sight, but dead reckoning showed us 155 miles north and a bit east of Bermuda. I could hear WWV on the Brookes & Gatehouse shortwave receiver only at night. The Bendix couldn't pick up Bermuda, but all signs said Amy was leaving rather than approaching. I slept for four hours, then snacked, puttered, flipped through *Playboy, The New Yorker, Newsweek, Oui, Scientific American, Viva, Yachting World.* As the afternoon wore on, I became more and more impatient to get moving north. I daydreamed how, with a full racing crew, I might have kept going the whole time to record a 300-mile or more noon-to-noon performance.

At 5:00 P.M., though the wind gauge was still locked at 60, it seemed more like 40. So I suited up and went on deck. Up staysail. At 7:00 P.M. up two-reefed main. She held her course with only a lanyard lashed to the wheel to offset a light weather helm induced by locking the boom just about amidships. At midnight a northbound ship passed two miles to the east. The log said we were 200 miles from Bermuda.

Dawn brought the usual storm aftermath; blue sky, cooler air, and a sharp westerly breeze. By leaving her reefed, I held the speed down to 8 knots, slow enough to self-steer without the Aries. I was sleeping soundly when the noise of a plane waked me at 11:25 A.M. A four-prop navy plane was circling low. On his third pass, I thought he caught my wave before he flew off toward Bermuda. Larry told me later that the plane reported *Gulf Streamer's* presence but that no crew was visible. This worried him and Tom, preparing to leave Hamilton.

The noon Bermuda newscast spoke of three yachts overdue: one en route to Bermuda, later reported safe; *Meridian,* the Piver-designed trimaran that had left Bermuda June 26 for Norfolk and was later found capsized 200 miles east of Cape Hatteras; and a northbound ketch that I'd seen leave Sunday just before the first hurricane warnings. All hands were plucked off her by a Russian cruise ship just before she sank.

At 2:45 P.M. the navy was back flying figure eights above me. How to convey I was "A-okay"? There's nothing in the signal manuals to cover this message.

Arms upthrust, fingers in the victory V's, I gave the Nixon wave. But back they came. I tried the British casual pose — lean against the mast and lift a mug of cheer. Still the plane circled. I grabbed our biggest Yankee flag. Grabbing one corner in my teeth, I held it out with my left arm, raised my right arm in the Boy Scout salute and stood at attention. Navy got the message, gave me a wing-waggle and headed for Bermuda.

The foggy morning of Saturday, July 5, with the Nantucket light vessel 38 miles to the north, in flat calm, I turned on the diesel. We'd traveled 560 miles in ninety-six hours, well beyond the qualifying requirement. *Gulf Streamer* had been storm-blooded. Her only needed repair: a new bulb in the port light.

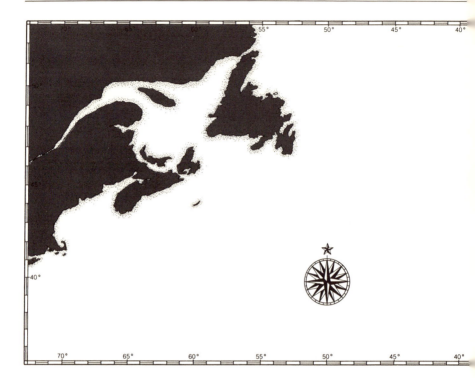

10

5:30 A.M. Sunrise at 5:00. *Moxie*, under full sail, is making 7 to 8 knots on starboard tack, heading southwest into a 10-knot westerly straight out of the White Mountains.

Yesterday afternoon the BBC threw a chill into us. Right in the middle of a newscast, the announcer broke in with "Storm warning. Force Ten winds will blow in the eastern North Atlantic for three to four hours this afternoon at . . ." and he gave the coordinates a bit to the north of where we are, right where the French seem to be.

Then this morning's detailed race forecast opened with "No storms." So I guess the scare is over. But I wonder how *VSD* and *Paul Ricard* made out.

8:00 A.M. A lovely sunny Sunday. The wind has backed more into the southwest. Since we've dropped down to 44° north latitude, only 60 miles north of our aiming point at the southeast tip of the Grand Bank, I tacked to port. It seems the favored tack to Newport. The breeze is so shifty I'll sit in the hatch where I can write and tweak the Autohelm at the same time.

1:00 P.M. Everything's coming up roses today. A ship set me straight

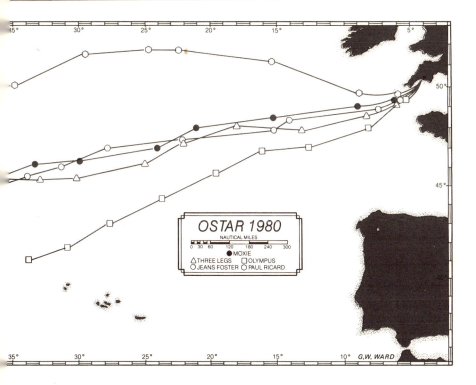

OSTAR 1980
NAUTICAL MILES
0 30 60   120   180   240   300
● MOXIE
△ THREE LEGS   □ OLYMPUS
○ JEANS FOSTER ○ PAUL RICARD

G.W. WARD

on my DR latitude just as a header persuaded me to tack to port. Now we're making 9 knots directly for Newport in only 12 knots of wind. No seas. Sparkly. Warm. Real June.

Our noon position, "Real Noon for Day 8," shows us almost as far west as the dot on the chart for "Ideal Noon Day 10" that I plotted in my race plan last August. Don't say a word. Speed-made-good for the trip is still averaging more than 8 knots, 8.02, in fact, and being improved right now. *Moxie* is a super boat!

But, dear me, this is Nick Keig weather. He must be hard on my heels. The 3:00 P.M. report may show he's passed *Kriter VI* and *VSD* if they got hit by the Force 10. Nick has stayed south with me and right behind him is the indefatigable Walter. So let's get cracking.

8:00 P.M. Sundown. I set up the hand camera on a bracket on the cockpit seat to try filming a happy hour à seul. I suspect nothing will show of me above the belt. I laid out an impressive meal. A horrible cabbage salad and a Scottish tinfoil-wrapped, vacuum-packed beef goulash. Our spaniel, Oliver, would have snubbed it.

But having snacked on nuts and fruit all day, I'm not hungry. Fresh

Bill Homewood's **Third Turtle.** *His cameras furnished blood-chilling storm footage for the film.* (Norman Fortier)

food is about gone. I've still lots of eggs and the sausage from Nick Clifton's sponsor, Fleury Michon, is sensational. I suppose I could get by on orange juice and mountain pack. My muscles feel really flexible from the built-in yoga regimen required to move in and out of the cabin dozens of times a day.

How I'd like to know what the other filmers are up to! Call the roll: monohulls — Judy Lawson, Francis Stokes, Warren Luhrs, Jerry Cartwright. A merry, diverse, competent quartet. Then the tris: Walter Greene, Bill Homewood, Tom Grossman, and me. "American Challenge" is the film's working title. Sounds okay.

Walter must have the bit in his teeth by now, coming up fast. Have I paid too little heed to this adverse current that seems to have been checking our westward progress since dawn? We're going through the water dandy, about 9 to 10 knots at an apparent wind angle from 32 to 38 degrees. But three afternoon sun lines plot disappointingly far behind the DR. We were spoiled by that glorious five and a half days of reaching.

Looking at my weather map, I don't see how any front-runner can have significantly better wind than I. I'm still glad I skewed south. To have been up north for yesterday's Force 10 could have been disastrous.

No OSTAR news on the BBC this afternoon. Guess the Sunday crew were never told about us. Millions of listeners to Europe 1, the French station co-sponsoring OSTAR, know just where we all are while none of us has a clue as to the whereabouts of any boat but his own. As a leader, I'm lucky to know where I am in relation to a few, but they're not necessarily the ones closest to me. There's that long list of entries whose Argos transmitters have failed, Phil Steggall among them. According to the pilot chart, I should now be slanting northwest across the main shipping lane from New York to England. Yet I've seen only one Greek ship today. The VHF crackles often with intership talk, suggesting I'm near the traffic.

What with filming, trying to catch four weather forecasts, bucket-bathing, and "futering" (Martin Read's word for "puttering futilely"), this day, which started at 4:00 A.M. and now concludes sixteen hours later, has simply flown by. The life agrees with me. Just so long as I'm too busy to brood over how much I miss my chick. What fun if I can get to Newport sooner than twenty days and really surprise her!

Love Sustains the Soloist

A vital ingredient for doing well in this race is having the perfect wife.

Anne must have been about ten, and I eight, when first we met in the early twenties. Her parents, the Sam Warrens of 261 Marlborough Street, Boston, were old friends of my parents. Once a year they would drive their three children out to Dedham for Sunday lunch and "to play with the Welds."

Both Anne and her older sister, Helen, wore the dark blue serge bloomers, midi-blouses, long brown stockings and sneakers that were the day-school uniform of the period. Despite teeth bands and two tight braids for her long blonde hair, Anne struck me as extraordinarily beautiful and especially kind and tolerant of her younger brother's friend. Ten years later Sam and I were rooming together as freshmen in the Harvard Yard and many was the weekend I spent at the Warrens.

Envy of Anne's many suitors among the upper classmen battled my shyness. When she took a trip to China and India during my senior year, I used to peek at her letters to Sam, prepared to learn the worst, that she was engaged.

On April 17, 1936, somehow emboldened, I invited her to the Modern Arts Ball at the Copley Plaza. A Friday night, white-tie party with champagne and Ruby Newman's full orchestra, it danced on till 3:00 A.M. Dawn had come to the Back Bay when our taxi — I'd urged the driver to take us on a circuitous route — pulled up at 261. Moments later, standing in the front hall, I knew we were engaged.

We married February 6, 1937, almost six months to the day after I started work at the *Chicago Daily News*. My father, bless him, had ruled I should hold down a job for six months before any wedding. To this day, however, it's not February 6 we celebrate, but April 18, the engagement.

I can still evoke the euphoria that had me soaring throughout that Patriot's Day weekend of my last year at Harvard. As undergraduate head of the Porcellian Club, I had that Saturday to preside at a luncheon to which many alumni traditionally came. Anne's uncle, former Maine Governor Tudor Gardiner, sat on my right as the graduate head. Once or

Marriage to Anne in King's Chapel, Boston, February 6, 1937. (Photo by Joe Dixon, Boston American)

twice he seemed to eye me quizzically as if he sensed something other than wine had made my eyes shine, my cheeks flush.

Married to my mother-in-law's sister Margaret, Uncle Tudor always said Anne was his favorite niece. The Gardiners gave the bridal dinner at their Beacon Street house. After all the toasts, Uncle T took us aside for his advice to young marrieds: "Let not things temporal move us greatly; never be afraid of pleasure."

Anne at the helm of Gulf Streamer *on passage from Madeira to St. Croix, December 11, 1974, my sixtieth birthday.* (Forbes Perkins)

In our forty-four years of marriage, his two mottoes have served us well. He was killed at the age of sixty-one when the light plane he had learned to fly at fifty crashed in a thunderstorm while he was returning from a World War I regimental reunion.

"It's not only that Anne's so good-looking," my father often said in our private exchanges, "she's got so darned much sense." He even paid his only daughter-in-law the ultimate compliment: "If anything happened to Kay, your Anne's the one woman I could imagine wanting to marry."

My mother, whose antennae are legendary for their capacity to foretell the success or failure of a marital match, still recalls her trip to Rome in 1931 with Mary, first of my five sisters. They saw quite a bit of Anne and her mother, who were there too.

"My heavens, I love that Anne," my mother confided to her eldest. "Do you suppose she and Philip might ever get together?"

"Come on, Mom," came the scornful response from my beloved Mame. "That little squirt. Why, Anne Warren wouldn't look at him." Both were jubilant when five years later I told them of my good luck.

Today's young marrieds wonder that there's never been an angry word between us. The only bodily harm done one to the other was to the bridge of my nose as we departed the three-day fifteenth reunion in

Moxie's *cockpit viewed from below.* (Christopher Knight)

Cambridge of the Class of 1936. I must have prolonged my farewells too boisterously at the curbside. Anne finally grabbed my necktie and hauled me into the car, bumping my nose against the jamb.

No matter that half the world separated us through my World War II years in Burma. We were never really apart. Throughout the 1944 campaign with Merrill's Marauders, when all our supplies came by parachute and mail at best once a fortnight, I had a letter for every day. In each envelope were a note, a bouillon packet, and a clipped dispatch from *The New York Times* by Tillman Durdin telling how the Burma campaign progressed. With news from home, I had flavoring for my rice. I also had the big picture more clearly than anyone but Colonel Hunter, our field commander. I could lecture my squad leaders on the Stilwell strategy. My seminars even drew majors from battalion HQ, all thanks to my angel's smartness.

By grace of Anne's family reserves, I was able to dare the transition from general news reporter to proprietor of my own daily newspapers. A good hunk of her un-trusteed funds, along with all my savings and a loan from my mother, made it possible for me to buy a 35-percent interest in the *Gloucester Daily Times* in October 1948. The agonizing interval before I could buy the rest of the stock in January 1952 would have caused most wives to lose faith. Hers never wavered.

It's been the same with my sailing. Though more content on land with her dogs and flowers, she nevertheless makes the best of it aboard, never panics, always uses her head in a crisis. The first full night at sea for both of us, following the start at Cowes of the 1970 Crystal Trophy in *Trumpeter*, found us at dawn down by Wolf Rock Light. The steering cable broke, we broached under spinnaker, broke several battens, and as the shackle holding the topping lift to the boom end shook loose, it managed to bounce off and smash the speedometer dial. Murphy's Law at work.

As Bob Harris, Bill Dunlop, and I tidied up in the near-gale, Anne remained quietly below. When at last we had to drop out and head into Falmouth under jury-rigged steering, I had time to ask her what she was reading.

"*The Yachtsman's Medical Companion*," came her calm response. "I supposed the mast would come down next. I wanted to be ready if one of you got hurt."

Through three Round Britain races, it's Anne who has coordinated the pit stops successively for *Trumpeter*, *Gulf Streamer*, and *Rogue Wave*. Making friends and buying food and drying clothes in Crosshaven,

Barra, Lerwick, and Lowestoft have become her ever-cheerful routine. She equally charmed the French at Saint-Malo and Pointe à Pitre, at the start and finish of the Route du Rhum. I could rely on her to do it right at Newport.

She cocks her head when asked, "Do you ever sail?"

"Oh, yes. I sailed on *Gulf Streamer* from Madeira to Saint Croix. Phil and I have taken lots of short trips alone. But I prefer cruising to racing." She was the only grandmother on the 1978 Crystal Trophy.

Her friends marvel that my solos don't worry her more. Her intelligence has assessed the risks. She concludes that a man is safer alone at sea than driving home sleepy to Gloucester from a men's dinner in Boston.

Race reports warned her *Moxie* might finish Monday, June 23. She rendezvoused with Dick Newick and *Rogue Wave* at Goat Island, Newport, Sunday afternoon, rallied the family, kept everyone calm all day Monday and Tuesday. My five sisters marveled at her composure while responding to questions from the international yachting press. They agree with my mother that I'm the luckiest guy alive.

11.

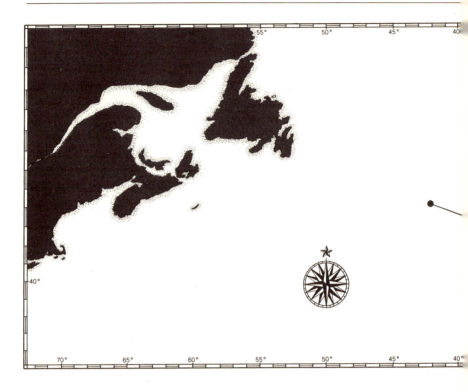

3:00 A.M. A little before midnight I spoke with the skipper of the British ship *Strategist*, passing close by, heading east. I asked him if he'd seen any other OSTAR entries. "Negative," thanks be.

It's foggy but I don't want to run the batteries down too far by leaving the navigation lights on. I'll stay on deck till dawn and write up my journal by flashlight. Solar juice may be under ration today.

It's blowing only about 12 knots from the southwest. We're close-hauled doing an easy 8 knots. It's a good time to catch up. Some of the topics to cover: A series of thumbnails on other competitors that I could use to spice my film chatter; an imaginary cassette on first hearing the Nantucket Light vessel beacon because it may be dark when it happens; explore the phrase "Lindbergh Syndrome" to explain the lure of the OSTAR (hint: "Lucky" Lindy was a meticulous planner); how to become the Jacques Yves Cousteau of wind energy, especially for ocean transport, using OSTAR recognition as the microphone; a talk to the Naval Architects Conference on the need for attention to improved rig.

6:30. The barometer has been falling rapidly. Postpone above.

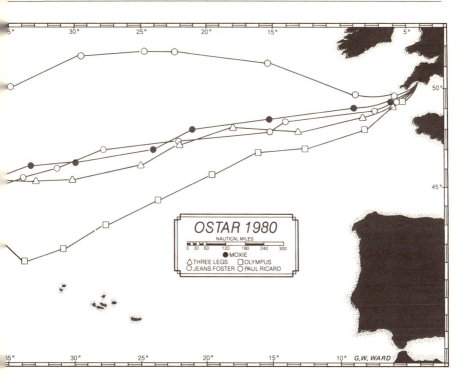

Then and for the next nine hours it was a battle. The fourth gale of the race had arrived. Three times I went on deck to shorten sail, each time blessing the Stoway mast for the time and energy it saved. By 10:00 A.M. in order to hold our speed below 8 knots, I was down to a half-rolled-up staysail and a scrap of main. Any faster and the poor boat comes off a big wave, and there are more all the time, with such a shuddering smash that I fear for the shrouds and their chainplates where they join the deck.

I don't worry about hulls and cross arms, she's so strongly built, just so long as I don't abuse her. She's like a good horse cantering over hummocks. So long as she isn't pressed into a gallop, she'll take it fine. But as a ride it's some different from *Rogue Wave's*. She'd be powering right through this stuff, whereas little, light ol' *Moxie* tosses her head and twists her ass real frisky-like. I bloody well have to hold on downstairs or I get thrown on my can into the pipe berth. Easy to get hurt, too.

Boy, am I glad I don't have any reason to go forward. I just don't see how those young fellas cope with going up into the bow to make all

117

those jib changes. They get soaking wet each time, run the risk of getting tossed overboard. Give me my roller-furlers.

10:45. Shocking news on the BBC, following Sunday's silence. *Moxie* has taken the lead over *VSD*. He didn't say by how many miles. Walter is third, Nick fourth. Only 83 boats left in the race. Did the Force 10 take its toll?

At 3:00 P.M. I noticed the first sign of wear and tear, a fraying of the outhaul line that pulls the clew, the back corner of the mainsail, taut along the boom. Nothing for it but to roll up all the main inside the mast and jog along into the 30-plus southwester at 3 to 4 knots under staysail alone. It took me twenty minutes to sew a messenger, a light line for hauling a heavier, on to one end of it, pull it through, then sew a replacement to the messenger and pull that through. Lucky I caught it in time, for it would have been much more time-consuming to have to fish a new line through the boom from scratch.

It's the sort of warning that makes one wary. I snapped on to the jack line and went forward to give a good look aloft from the bow. It's on hands and knees in this weather. She really bucks. I sat on the boom to watch for minutes the grace with which she took these big waves. Many boats her size would be heaving to in these conditions.

It's too rough below to try heating anything on the burner. One of the final beers out of the cockpit locker has been tossed about so that it spurts all over when I pull the tab. A few saltines and an apple is about all I care to eat. I doze off for a bit but one of those smashers shudders me awake. When I try to sleep in this stuff in a wing bunk, the slap of the waves against the undersurface can bounce the mattress up five inches. It often gives me The Spastic Nightmare: I'm walking along a crowded sidewalk and have lost all muscular control. I lurch and careen. People think I'm drunk. I have to cling to a friend to avoid knocking people over. I wake feeling sorry for all cripples and drunks.

At 8:00 P.M. I note the barometer has started to rise again. It's still blowing 30 knots from the west-southwest, but the evening sky shows some pink to the west. Another low is on its way to Scotland.

THE PRACTICAL LONE VOYAGER

My parents blessed me with genes suited to the demands of the OSTAR.

"Do you smoke?" my father was asked by his new Boston internist,

Dr. Ivy DeFriez, when he had a checkup after his seventieth birthday.

"Only about a dozen cigars a day."

"Do you drink?"

"Yes. About a pint to a quart of bourbon a day."

He'd just retired to his native Massachusetts from New York after a working lifetime, first as a cotton merchant, later as a commodity broker. He chafed that he was no longer playing fifty-four holes of golf of a Saturday. Not even at eighty-nine can my mother be made to take a nap. She takes after my grandmother Saltonstall, like my grandfather Weld a high expender of energy. Ancestry counts more than jogging to prepare a man to endure physical stress.

A long voyage refreshes, rather than tires, me. I eat less, drink less, and sleep less. I'll lose ten to fifteen pounds this three weeks. The constant going up and down the narrow ladder from cockpit to cabin flexes every muscle. The whole adventure is better for me than a fortnight at Elizabeth Arden's camp. Every healthy person ought to try it to see how it tones the skin and sharpens the senses.

Thirty years ago, I'd wind up Monday mornings with a sore back from chopping wood. Dr. Gene Record, a Harvard high-hurdler in the thirties, gave me a series of simple exercises designed to "build an intrinsic corset of muscle" around my vertebrae. Daily I lie on the floor or the cabin top and spend seven minutes doing leg lifts, sit-ups, shoulder and buttock squeezes. I haven't needed an osteopath since Gene prescribed. When not sailing, I play tennis two or three times a week, winter and summer.

A while ago we found an Indian yoga teacher who was willing to come to the house and give lessons to all the family on the lawn. About all that's stayed with me of Shri's drill are neck rolls and deep breathing. These help keep me awake on a long night watch.

Solo sailing, like living alone, brings out a bit of the "old maid" in one, a tendency to indulge crotchets. My whimsy on this race has been to see how quickly I can perform routine chores and functions. A glass of orange juice starts the day about 3:00 A.M. It sends me straight to the bucket where I kill two birds by shaving with my battery-powered Norelco. (Safety note for soloists: never pump ship at the rail. Too easy to bear out the Coast Guard statistic that they find most drowned males fell overboard with flies unbuttoned. Use a plastic, quart-size container.)

Two slices of toast scorched on the galley's one-burner propane camping stove, eaten with honey, no butter, and a mug of black coffee sustain me till I've plotted the 8:30 sun line. Then I'm ready for bouillon and saltines. For lunch, after the noon sight, I'll have a tuna and mayonnaise sandwich on dark bread. A glass of sherry helps induce a nap. A cup of tea and a ginger cookie wake me. About an hour before sundown, I enjoy a happy hour with crackers and cheese washed down with a double bourbon and water. Dinner depends on how rough it is. In a chop, soup and a sandwich with a glass of wine suffice. My more elaborate cuisine, in the first week with stores still fresh, produced steak, lettuce, and tomatoes every night. Later I scrambled eggs or chopped an onion to liven a canned meat from Walnut Acres.

For the hours of darkness, about 9:30 P.M. to 3:30 A.M., I snack on raisins, peanuts, "trail mix" from my son-in-law's health-food store, dates, granola, sunflower seeds. We've always managed on our boats to do without a refrigerator, even cruising in the Caribbean. It's surprising how quickly guests adjust to a gin and tonic without ice. For teaching an American to prefer warm beer, there's no better training center than the bar of the Royal Western. In the fortnight before the start, I spent so much time there that Colonel Jack Odling-Smee, the race committee chairman, said I was getting "field officer's gut."

At Plymouth, I divided my stores into three basic boxes, each with the whole range from fruit juice to chocolate bars. Oranges, apples, and grapefruit hung in a basket and lasted till Newport. Shopping for the race took Anne and me only a couple of hours the day before the start.

One duffle holds all my clothing. Nights on the North Atlantic, even in June, stay down at 50 degrees. Next to the skin, I wear underpants and a cotton polo shirt. I carry enough for a daily change. Over these I pull on a two-piece suit of Helly-Hansen underwear. This Norwegian blessing is woven from some mystery combination of woolen yarn and acrylic. The inside surface has a nap like sealskin, the outside has the texture of a football jersey. No matter how wet it gets, so long as you move about, it never feels wet. It warms up inside like a scuba-diver's wet suit. After this come two Shetland sweaters. Then the two-piece Helly-Hansen yellow oilskins favored by Gloucester fishermen with no pockets to fill with seawater. The front bib of the trousers comes up to the armpits, providing a secondary shield if a wave penetrates the snaps of the jacket. In the foulest weather, I pull over these a knee-length, Shetland fisherman's oilskin smock with hood. I bought it in Lerwick on the 1974 Round Britain.

By now, if I've forgotten to change out of moccasins, I'm so trussed up I can scarcely reach down to pull on my knee-high Top-Sider boots.

Wriggling into my safety harness reminds me of the circus fat lady struggling into her brassiere. Experts say 20 percent of the body's heat loss is through the scalp. I wear a wool toque that can be pulled down under the chin. After making a log entry, I'm ready to go on deck. Having adjusted the Autohelm, following a check of our course, I pull on wool gloves, then over these, black rubber fishcutters' gloves. So accoutered, I'll stay warm till dawn provided every half hour I jog in place and beat my chest. It's a lot of work, dressing warmly, but shivering is hateful.

Too much sleep, like too much food, can be self-defeating. "Sleep's a habit you can learn to break," I've heard it said and I almost believe it. To keep healthy on this race, sleep discipline is as important as keeping the bowels open and the body clean. It's the one department where the elderly have a clear advantage. I need less sleep than Walter Greene.

I've been averaging four to five hours in twenty-four, usually in three installments a day. An hour in mid-morning, an hour after lunch, two hours at twilight. At least that's the theory. Crises interfere with the schedule and some nights I have to cheat. But I try never to sleep in the dark with ships about.

The trick is to sharpen the desire for sleep so that it descends instantly when summoned. If you go without sleep the first thirty-six hours of a race, as you must leaving from Saint-Malo or Plymouth because of all the traffic, you find you can drop off in less than a minute after your head hits the bunk. I command instant slumber by reciting the Lord's Prayer while breathing yoga-style. By "trespasses," I'm out. One hour later, wakened by my timer, having had the efficient 70 percent of the sleep period, says the literature, I rise refreshed. I suspect the reason one can't follow this routine ashore is that we all live surrounded by so many noises. *Moxie* makes music to dream by as she warbles on her way.

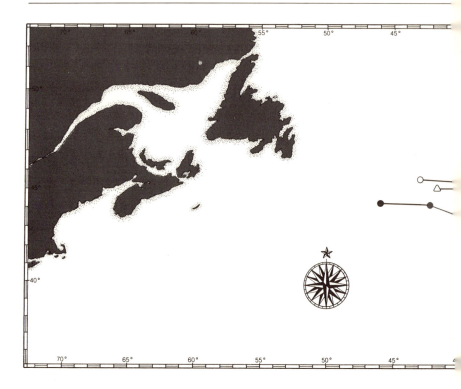

12

4:00 A.M. With 1,951 miles on the log, I figure my DR leaves us with about 1,152 miles to Brenton Reef, six to eight days, placing our arrival between Tuesday, June 24, and Thursday, June 26. The fog is thick, visibility about 600 yards. Everything is dank and clammy. I wouldn't be surprised to hear Spencer Tracy — remember him and Freddie Bartholomew in *Captains Courageous?* — hail me from the deck of the *We're Here.*

9:45. Now I have a new worry, Jaworski in *Spaniel II*, probably the strongest monohull in the race and with a tough skipper. Polish, he probably knows his Conrad. The BBC has him only 84 miles behind me, but the position they give for me, 44.25° north by 43.91° west, is actually where my DR had me yesterday afternoon, so possibly he's not that close. It spoke of the storm inflicting damage through the fleet, *VSD* among the victims. There have been so many Argos failures they're now concluding each report with an appeal for us to report our positions "daily by whatever means." Among those with failed transmitters are Judy Lawson and Warren Luhrs, two of our filmers, and Phil Steggall. He's another worry.

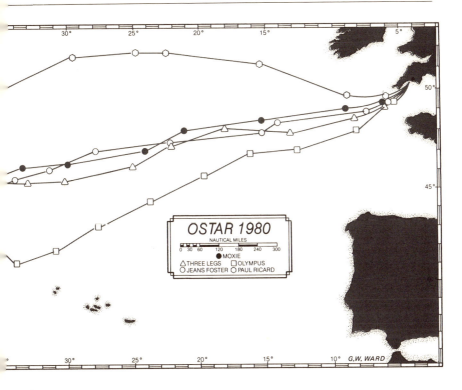

OSTAR 1980

NAUTICAL MILES

0 30 60   120   180   240   300

● MOXIE
△ THREE LEGS   □ OLYMPUS
○ JEANS FOSTER   ○ PAUL RICARD

G.W. WARD

3:00 P.M. We've just been blessed by Aeolus with the most fortuitous wind shift, from southwest to northwest, making starboard the favored tack, and allowing us to lay a course of 270 degrees magnetic, just perfect for sneaking under the Grand Bank. Now the BBC says I'm leading Jaworski by 181 miles.

Soon the breeze had fallen enough to call for the reacher, which we carried for about four hours. Then inexplicably, the Autohelm blew a fuse and I had to drop the big sail. At the 4:00 P.M. rendezvous on the ham band, I could just hear Art Zolot calling for *Moxie*, but he couldn't hear me.

HOIST BY MY OWN HALYARD

I had to replace the blown fuse for the Autohelm just now and I had to change the outhaul yesterday. These have been *Moxie's* only demands for hosunry so far this race. What a contrast with 1972. Then

Judy Lawson, first American woman to enter the OSTAR. After she lost her mast, her camera produced the most dramatic moment in the film. (Christopher Knight)

Trumpeter presented me with a new list of demands every morning. The memory of the eighth day still haunts me.

I needed to tighten the backstays. Instead of turnbuckles, *Trumpeter* had rope lanyards that passed back and forth six times through big butterfly shackles at the chainplates. First I had to slack the rod-furling jib to relieve the forward tension on the mast. As I eased it, I looked aloft and froze. The wire of the port backstay had begun to strand. If I didn't replace it, the mast would soon topple when we went on to port tack.

To meet this crisis, I wrote:

Port Runner: Replacement alternatives

A. Self up-haul: 1. Drop old shroud, replace with makeshift of short-ened spare headstay; 2. shorten the original by cutting off the stranded bit and replacing the Norse terminal; 3. go back up mast and swap. (If it breezes up, this can be postponed.) 4. While aloft, check to see if we have an epidemic of frayed wire where Norse fittings have been crimped to the ends.

B. Carry on warily on starboard tack. If and when we must tack to port, use the spare jib halyard to back up the stranding shroud.

C. Do nothing. Simply sweat it out, whenever on port tack, all the way to Newport.

D. Put into Flores where I could find someone to help with a replace-ment.

Because the thing I wanted least to do in all the world was go up the mast, I procrastinated. I fiddled with the life-raft lashings and tightened all the bolts in the self-steering. But there was really no alternative to going up.

First I assembled a pile on deck: two jumar grips, bosun's chair, spare headstay of 1x19 wire, a 150-foot coil of quarter-inch terylene line, wire for fastening shackles, wire clippers, and a light line with which to lower the frayed shroud. While Mike McMullen's fiancée, Lizzie Good-enough, served Anne and me a delicious lunch aboard *Binkie II*, Mike had introduced me to the jumar, a mountaineering device for climbing up ropes to escape a crevasse.

"Hoist a block and tackle to the masthead," Mike explained. "Attach the bosun's chair to its bottom block and get in it. Tie the bottom end of the jumar's six-foot strop to the chair and attach the device itself to the downhaul of the tackle. Attach a sail bag to a leg so the downhaul can flake into it. Hoist yourself to the top of the mast by pulling down on the downhaul, while one hand slides the jumar up the rope. If you lose hold of the rope, the jumar will automatically grip and it will be im-possible to fall."

Demonstrating, he made it look easy. "Don't forget the sail bag. You must be careful not to let the downhaul rope snag on the deck. You could tie yourself up there," he warned. I bought a pair of jumars. They looked like hand-exercising grips. I prayed I'd never need to use them.

Now, here was I trying to recall Mike's drill. Legs spread on the cabin top, I steadied myself against the boat's oscillation. The sea might be glassy but there was swell enough to move the masthead through a ten-foot arc. To hang on up there would have tested me in my prime.

At fifty-seven . . . ? Well, Ahab was fifty-eight when he chased Moby Dick.

To cushion me from bruises, I'd put on my long Norwegian under-pants under my shorts with the handy thigh pockets. Top-Sider moc-casins and a wool hat completed the look of Superman without the cloak. I buckled into my safety harness and passed a heavy length of shock cord through its straps to hug me to the mast and make me less of a human yo-yo. Recalling Mike's warning, I tied a sail bag to the bosun's chair.

I practiced stuffing the downhaul line into it. Then I inventoried my tools. A holster held knife, screwdriver, wire cutters, and pliers. In one pocket I put two big shackles, wire for binding shackle pins, two spare clevis pins, three cotter pins. The extras were to allow for my butterfin-gers.

Dangling there 400 miles from Spain, 600 miles from Flores in the Azores, trussed up like a phone-company lineman in a blizzard, I had tentatively raised myself a few feet off the deck when I looked astern. There, not 400 yards away, a boat had appeared. Too much work to climb out of this rig to get a camera. I gawked. A tunny fisherman from Portugal? She was about 60 feet long, pale blue, with two long poles sticking out from each side of her deck house.

The two men aboard stared at me as they motored past at about 3 knots, so close I could see the gap in the teeth of the younger. I waved casually as if hanging from the masthead was routine. They waved but said nothing. On the transom I could read *Christmas*. I'd heard ship-to-ship talk in French on the marine band that morning. Why wasn't she named "Noel"?

A mile ahead they halted. To fish, I suppose. Or to wait for me to get in trouble. Or did they dismiss my behavior as a yachter's eccentricity? Studying *Tartarin de Tarascon* in school, I'd enjoyed the humor of Al-phonse Daudet's villager going off to slay a lion in the veld of southern France. Now I felt just as absurd as I resumed the assault, desperate and intent.

My first hoisting rope was so stiff it wouldn't run freely through the blocks of my three-part tackle. Before I'd hoisted myself halfway to the spreaders, my arms were aching so that I had to return to the deck.

Next I tried using a storm jib sheet. It was softer, less prone to kink, but it was only 100 feet long, only enough for two parts mechanical ad-vantage. When I was halfway up to the spreaders for a second time, my arms told me I'd never make it all the way. Back on deck, I took a drink of water, for now I was sweating hard. I stared at the fraying shroud and wondered if its eighteen remaining strands might not get us to Newport. Yet I knew that 1x19 stainless, once one wire has broken, will go like a run in a stocking.

"How about the spanker sheet?" I asked aloud.

Forward to the forepeak. Out with it. It was at least 150 feet long. Back to the mast. No hesitation now. When hoisted with the main halyard to the point 40 feet aloft where I'd be working, it proved to be long enough for three parts. Cautiously, like an ant on a flower stalk, I ascended. I had to grip the mast with all the strength in my knees to prevent the swell from swinging me about. The shock cord helped. Socks inside the long underwear at each knee absorbed some of the blows.

I rested at the spreaders, remembering to tuck the lengthening tail of the hoisting line into the sail bag. The replacement shroud hung at my left hip as laboriously I ascended the second twenty feet. At last I was up to where I could dismantle the old one. My right leg, thrust downward in the jumar loop, took my weight. I could use both hands to pull the cotter pin with the pliers. It came free more easily than I'd expected. To give myself a downhaul for the halyard of the rod-furling jib, I lashed the two together.

When the pin for the replacement was in position, I breathed easier. Now to tackle the twists in the rod-jib halyard so it could be tautened enough to take some of the sag out of the jib. I became so intent on the task of separating the jib rod from the halyard that I failed to notice my hoisting line escaping from the sail bag. When finally I dropped the jib, its upper swivel hit the deck with a thud that left a dent I could see from aloft. At last I was ready to come down.

But just as Mike had warned, the swaying of the mast had activated the end of the hoisting line, now lying on the cabin top, so that it had managed to cleat itself around two winches at the foot of the mast. No matter how much I tweaked and jiggled it from aloft, it remained fast. I was hoist by my own halyard. To try to wiggle out of the bosun's chair and have it slip up under my arms could leave me twisting at the masthead like the victim of a lynching.

Now I sweated. To try jumping into the nets between the cross arms occurred to me as an alternative to sliding down the mast like a fire laddie. There were now two tunny boats a mile to the west. Could *Christmas* be planning a salvage job? It was misty now and twilight had arrived. Had I really been aloft so many hours? I smothered a moment of panic. The mast danced in one of its dervish oscillations that threw me around like a mitten in a puppy's jaws. I was scared.

"Come now," I said aloud. "This is ridiculous." It's not all that far to slide if you keep a good grip with your knees on the mast and your hands on the halyard. Out of the chair and on our way.

To get out of the chair wasn't so easy. If it slipped over my hips and up under my armpits, I'd be trapped with my arms above my head like a sailor at the flogging post. Cotton-mouthed and panting, I took my weight on my right arm so that with my left hand I could back off the shackle pin joining the chair to the hoist. Now it was free and fell away. I still had to free my right foot from the jumar loop. If I lost control, I'd hang by my right instep, ignominiously to die from blood to the head.

For one breath-stopping moment, I held on with just my left arm and my knees while with my right hand I shook off the loop. Then I lost no time sliding down to the spreaders.

The second slide to the deck was positively bracing. I got on my hands and knees and kissed the cabin top. It was getting dark and the ship was a mess. The calm that mercifully had lasted throughout my ordeal had yielded to a light westerly. I yanked on the damaged shroud and down came the jib halyard. One home free. Next a tug on the bosun's chair hoist, after unsnarling it, and down came the main halyard. Hallelujah. Get sail on and scram out of here. I felt under observation by the two fishermen now lying to the east. It had been inept to forget Mike's warning against allowing the hoist to snag at deck level.

Up main, up storm jib. I'd not delay to drag a bigger jib out of the forepeak. Tired, bruised, and thirsty, I wanted to flee the scene. I mixed a heavy bourbon and made this triumphant log entry: "I went up the mast." I supposed it would have seemed like nothing much to a younger man but I felt good about the shroud. Tomorrow would be time enough to shorten it to proper length. The rod jib could wait. After a quick cup of soup, I hit the bunk. I slept till after midnight when I awoke to an excruciating cramp in my left thigh, result of hours with the leg clamped around the mast. Two quinine tablets drove it away.

The euphoria that comes with simply being alive surged over me. I hadn't felt this way since the night following that morning in March 1944 under Japanese machine guns at Shaduzup in northern Burma.

13.

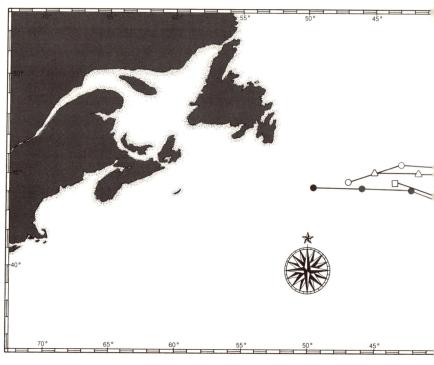

(FROM THE FILM SOUND TRACK)

10:30 A.M. *The spinnaker run we've been on across the Grand Banks this morning in thick fog is the first mildly imprudent thing I've done so far this voyage. Averaging 10 knots. Visibility about 500 yards. I suppose if something loomed up ahead I could reach for the Autohelm, give it a tweak, and dodge it. But the risk is absolutely necessary if I'm to keep that* Spaniel *from yapping at my heels. He's too close there, only 181 miles last night.*

In another hour, I'll know where he was this morning. Jaworski's a tough guy. He's probably got his boat working great. Bet he's got his spinnaker up. Wonder if he's getting into this peasoup.

Forecast says sunny for this afternoon, which should clean off the fog and give me a chance at a sun line. The last two days the only thing I've had to go by is dead reckoning and the BBC broadcasts of my somewhat dated Argos satellite positions. Anyhow, we're getting there. Less than 1,000 miles now. Probably the most interesting thousand miles of all.

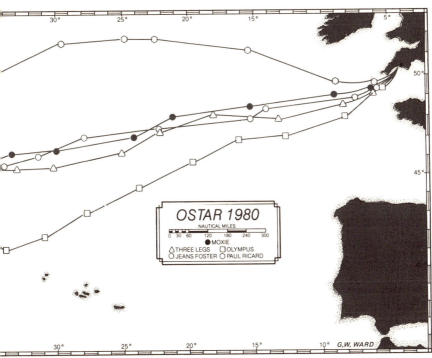

1:30 P.M. *Well, now, this must be one of the most extraordinary afternoon sails of my life. Putting it into the calculator, we just did 22 miles in one hour and 35 minutes. That's a 14-knot average. That means most of the time we're doing nearer to 17 knots. Spooky this being on the Grand Banks. The depth gauge shows only 60 meters of water below us. It's foggy as I guess the camera shows. Lots of birds with us here, no seas, wind from the southwest. Absolutely perfect reaching conditions for a boat like* Moxie. *I don't feel we're too imprudent. We have the DROM, the radar warner, and I've hoisted the radar reflector. It just would be nice to see something. . . ." (Here the film shows me stretching out on the cockpit seat and falling instantly to sleep.)*

As well I might have, for the log shows I was up at 1:00 A.M. fussing with a jammed furling line in the drum of the roll-up jib, caused by a bad rope-to-wire splice. At 4:15 I'd braved hoisting the spinnaker at first light, always a workout, and then had come word that Walter had passed Jaworski and that both of them had gained another eight miles on me. Once I got caught aback while down below trying to respond to Art Zolot's weather call, for the first time coming in loud and clear.

It was interesting to note that when the ship lay dead in the water, the true wind was only 15 knots. When I was below, the speed of the boat had made it sound and feel like a near-gale. While it was exhilarating, it was exhausting, too. I tried to control my anxiety over possible collision with a fisherman by doing deep yoga breathing in the cockpit, meantime staring into the mist. I was coming on to swimming seabirds so fast they flew off squawking.

After six hours of this mad pace — the speed rose frequently to 21 in the puffs, once to 27 — my nerves could stand no more. I rolled in enough jib to slow us to 10 knots and went below for a cup of tea and a nap. The DROM beeped and flashed me awake. I went on deck and there in the lifting fog, about a quarter mile to windward, lay two medium-sized draggers, rolling in the sea. As I flashed by, their crews were on the far side hauling in nets. They didn't act as if they'd seen me though I waved and tried to raise them on the VHF.

I celebrated our having just knocked off 56 miles in four hours by scrambling four eggs with Julia Child's very own wrist motion. I felt content, confident. Not many had had a better afternoon than I. Halifax commercial radio was coming in strong. And what do you suppose was on? Readings from *Lady Chatterley's Lover.*

... TO THE RUSSIANS: POST-CAPSIZE KINETICS

Meade Gougeon cautioned me on the 1977 Tradewinds Race, after we had averaged more than 20 knots crossing from the St. Kitts–Statia passage to the finish at St. Martin, that "a boat like *Rogue Wave,* no matter how strong we build her, can be sailed to pieces. Given the right conditions this boat will just go faster and faster. The loads the rig puts on the hull will build up geometrically. With very little warning, she'll just disintegrate." This had to be equally true of *Moxie,* and my awareness of the possibility, as much as the fear of collision, prompted me not to overdo on our sprint over the Grand Banks.

However, of all the hazards of the course, it was capsize to which I'd given most attention in pre-race preparation. *Gulf Streamer's* loss produced at least one gain. The capsize skeleton was brought out of the multihull closet. Before my calamity, the danger of flipping a trimaran, like a teen-age daughter's possible exposure to pregnancy, had mostly been discussed in hushed tones. Now all multihull gatherings talked about how to prevent it and how to cope if it happened.

My first action, after expressing gratitude to Captain Stapleford and crew (with a special word for Michael Emslie, the watch officer whose alertness had picked up the blip of our reflector on his ship's radar screen), was to mount a salvage effort from Vineyard Haven with Dick Newick. We asked the tugboat *Whitefoot* to stand by with scuba gear to aid us in righting *Streamer* if our air search succeeded. Tim Flynn, our charter pilot, a veteran at policing these waters against violators of the fishing rules, had packed into his twin-engine Piper two vital pieces of equipment: a loran set, for continuous position checks, and an infrared thermometer to tell us when we were over the Gulf Stream.

As we neared the search zone, 315 miles southeast of Nantucket, the thermometer showed the surface water to be 25 degrees Centigrade (77°F). Miles-long necklaces of Sargasso weed reminiscent of the yellow-orange lines on a macadam road, marked the course of the Stream. Like a heavenly echo of the great ocean river itself, a double-lane skyway of cottony cloud stretched left and right to infinity. Its underside magically reflected the pale gold in which the afternoon sun bathed the ocean beneath.

"Did you ever see anything more beautiful?" I rhapsodized to Dick over the noise of the engines. It was the closest to viewing the Pearly Gates I'm ever likely to get.

On the loran chart for North America East Coast, Cape Race to Cape Henry, Dick had penciled an "A" at 38° 56' north by 64° 06' west to mark the point where Bill Stephens and I had been plucked off the upturned hulls four days before. We could look down on the Stream's axis and see its water texture contrasting as clearly with the main body of the ocean as if we were flying over a gravel road through a sandy desert. Tim commenced to fly a pattern of overlapping rectangles, trending northward as advised by the experts at Woods Hole. Each time we left the Stream the thermometer would drop five degrees. We could look down and see the hard edge of the current.

Dick looked off to the right, I to the left, straining to descry *Streamer's* blue bottoms and white under-bunk surfaces, which I cursed myself for not having painted distress orange. After three hours and several false hopes of sighting, our dwindling fuel supply demanded we head downwind for Halifax, right back to where the *Federal Bermuda* had landed me Monday morning. We took off again at 8:00 next morning, only to return because the nose wheel wouldn't retract. Tim said its extra drag would reduce the time we could search. When we could find no mechanic to fix it, we topped off the tanks and took off again. More fruitless rectangles. Once I spotted an orange fishing buoy from quite a distance.

We gave up and flew against a sharp headwind for the Vineyard. The nose wheel slowed our progress enough so that our fuel got us only as far as Nantucket. I confess to acute nerves watching the emergency fuel gauge sink closer and closer to E. If we had to ditch, the flimsy, token life raft would never float us in the style to which I'd become accustomed.

Back home it was a little like living in a ghost-ridden house. Every time the phone rang, we expected to hear the Coast Guard Rescue Center in Boston relaying news of another sighting of *Streamer* by a ship. On May 21, the British freighter *Brimnes*, 180 miles north of Bermuda; May 29, the Italian motor vessel *Americana*, 300 miles northeast of Bermuda; June 8, the Russian freighter *Magintogorsk*, 200 miles farther east; July 15, a second Soviet sighting.

Captain Corrado Bardessi delayed the *Americana* while a boat was lowered to allow his mate to investigate. Recovered and sent me were some notebooks, the rusted rescue beacons and the Brooks & Gatehouse RDF compass, preceded by a letter: "I come from an island of seagoing people along the Dalmatian coast. I come from a family where all the men went to sea as captains, commodores, admirals, shipowners of the majestic sail ships trading from the South Pacific to Europe around Cape Horn. So I am in a position of well understanding what it meant to you, the loss of the beautiful *Gulf Streamer*. What we did is in the best tradition of seafarers; investigate and offer assistance in case of an SOS situation."

On June 2, three days before the OSTAR start, I cabled Lloyd Foster: "Seeking forestall needless involvement, tell skippers capsized *Gulf Streamer* boarded from Italian ship May 29, north 38 west 61, hulls drifted northeast 200 miles previous 8 days, no need competitors waste time or energy investigating further. Fast passages all."

In September, Anne and I boarded the *Viking Northstar* at Piraeus for a cruise through the Dardanelles to the Black Sea to view Greek antiquities. Varna, Odessa, Yalta, Sochi now blend into a drab memory of obese, sun-tanning comrades, sulking in queues. Odessa could have been exciting. When, on September 7, we walked down the Potemkin steps to the waterfront, we might have seen *Gulf Streamer* being lifted on to the dock from a freighter. This possibility we discovered when we returned home to find a letter from Lloyd Foster. He wrote that a Soviet-watcher in the London Foreign Office had spotted an item in the September 13 issue of *Nedelya* (The Week), a Soviet "news" magazine, about *Streamer's* salvage. I found the publication in Harvard's Widener Library and asked my classmate, Robert Lee Wolff, professor of Slavic history, to translate. A postage-stamp-size cut of the boat showed the aft section of the port outrigger had broken off. The item told how the *Nikolai Ananiev*, proceeding eastbound, had found her at a point 1,000 miles northeast of our capsize. At Lisbon she'd been transferred to the *Biryusa*, which took her to Odessa.

With the help of Ambassador Henry Cabot Lodge, a Beverly friend and my most influential access to the State Department, I was able to send via the Moscow diplomatic pouch a letter to the editor. A prompt reply from Jack F. Matlock, our chargé d'affaires, said: "Your letter has been forwarded to the Chief Editor of *Nedelya*, Mr. V. A. Arkhangel'sky. A copy was also sent to the Minister of the Maritime Fleet, Timorey Guzhenko, asking that appreciation be extended to the crew of the *Nikolai Ananiev*. Good luck in your efforts to encourage Soviet participation in the 1980 races."

Results were disappointing. Maritime law said technically the boat still belonged to me. But the salvager didn't have to release it until I'd reimbursed him for the costs, which he could set higher than I'd conceivably be willing to pay. If the Soviets didn't choose to follow the form, so what. I had an indubitable casualty loss for my tax return, which, since I had no insurance, would recompense me for half the loss. However, I was still curious to know how well the hulls had survived being wracked by seas through May, June, July, and part of August. Had cracks appeared in the cross arms? Had the mast stayed in place?

In July 1977, Dick Newick got a letter from his Russian pen pal, Igor Pertestiuke, a trimaran buff. It enclosed eighteen glossy 8 x 10 prints showing several Russians working on *Streamer's* rehabilitation. Winches had been removed. The stern of the port outrigger was being rebuilt. Then, a year later, Charles Chiodi, publisher of *Multihulls*, got more pictures from Igor. The boat was back in the water. Her new skipper, standing on the Odessa Sailing Club's float, natty in Bermuda shorts and a visored cap, held a briefcase in one hand and with the other pointed to her new mast and boom. All original winches appeared to be back in place.

Gulf Streamer *under repair at Odessa after a Soviet ship salvaged her in mid-Atlantic.*

I wrote *Katera I Jachti* ("Motorboats and Yachts") an open letter. I urged that *Gulf Stream*, her new name, enter the 1980 OSTAR. I offered to fly over to help tune her. No reply. So much for my effort to reverse the cooling of détente.

For months after *Streamer's* loss, I tracked down every lead that came my way as to what caused rogue waves and how one could avoid future encounters with them. I found no warnings in the literature of yachting against entering the Stream too soon after a gale had whipped it. There were lots of stories of tankers splitting in two as the result of being caught on top of freak waves off South Africa. There the warm water of the Agulhas Current meets the polar stream. Like two football lines colliding, it can cause epic turbulence.

Dr. Philip J. Richardson of the Woods Hole Oceanographic Institution helped most. He showed me satellite photos of the Stream before and after April 27, taking what he termed "a great leap northward." Its northern edge showed as a shadow, shaped like a tiger's fang, right at the point where we'd upset. He speaks of the Gulf Stream being "the Atlantic ocean's aorta." He measures with transponders, mounted on buoys scattered in the path of the Stream and linked to the same Argos

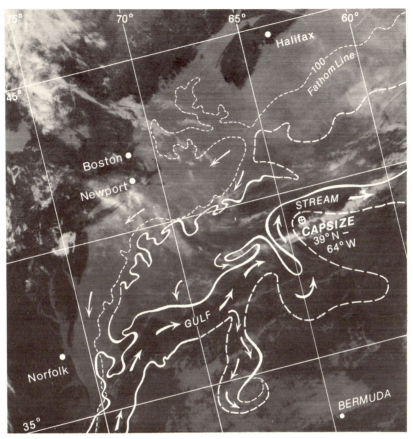

At the point where a rogue wave capsized Gulf Streamer, *this satellite photo and chart show the Gulf Stream taking a "great leap northward."* (Photo courtesy NOAA; chart by Samuel Bryant)

satellite monitoring this OSTAR, the great rings of water (they're called eddies) that he terms the "supernovae of the sea."

Our rogue wave, I concluded, had resulted from three forces colliding at 120 degrees to one another — one, the surge to the northeast that thirty-six hours of southwesterly gale had built up; two, the 4-knot thrust of the Stream lashing back to the northwest like a giant firehose after the hydrant has been suddenly opened; third, the surface waves freshly kicked up by the cold, 30-knot northwester that had blown in behind the passage of the low pressure center. Like giant hands scraping up a cone of sand, the three elements squeezed up a pyramid of water 40 feet high right beneath my bunk. It set the boat on a sidewise skid. Like a skier who loses control while traversing an icy slope, "an edge caught" — that is, the lower outrigger got pushed under water. The weight of the mast was enough to topple us over.

On December 30, 1976, the 19,000-ton tanker *Grand Zenith*, thirty-eight crewmen aboard, reported she was 100 miles south of Halifax bucking heavy winds and strong seas. It was her last message. After a prolonged air-sea search, the Coast Guard recovered two life preservers stenciled with her name, a brown trunk, two planks, and a mattress at a position less than 100 miles from our capsize. Maybe lightning can strike twice in the same place. I've been telling my friends, if caught in the aftermath of a gale near the Stream, try to stay out of it until the surge subsides. If sailing to Europe except in summer, go north or south of the Stream. Going west you'd naturally try to stay out of it because of the adverse current.

The recent record reveals this was not safeguard enough, at least in the early months of the year. In April 1979, Olivier de Kersauson, attempting to break the schooner *Atlantic*'s eastbound record, watched one of *Kriter IV*'s aluminum outriggers break off in a storm. He kept the tri from capsizing long enough to accept rescue for himself and crew from a ship standing by, but he had to abandon his 70-foot craft. Soon after that, Alain Gliksman lost *Three Legs II*, which he'd bought from Nick Keig for the Route du Rhum, while sailing from Bermuda to New York preparatory to his assault on the Atlantic record. Then in March 1980, Eugene Riguidel, making the third French assault by tri on the record, capsized *VSD* even before he'd reached the Stream. Enlisting the help of a French warship, he recovered her and managed to have her refitted in time for the OSTAR.

Two other entries were less fortunate. Yves Le Cornec, a perky twenty-year-old Frenchman soloing Walter Greene's original *A Capella* to Plymouth from Marblehead, capsized and lost her. Finally, Rory Nugent, sailing alone in his 1,200-pound proa, *Godiva Choclateer*, from Martha's Vineyard, got caught aback north of the Azores. Before he could release his sheets, his two-hulled vessel rolled over. Their emergency beacons brought rescue within two days. But the impact of the five calamities had been sobering.

On the agenda for the symposium put on by the British Multihull Ocean Cruising and Racing Association at Plymouth the weekend before the 1980 race, quite understandably, there was considerable attention to safety. Rory, who'd been deposited in Lisbon by his rescuers, flew in just in time to address the group on his experience. This prompted the OSTAR skippers in the audience to hold a second symposium the next morning in the cockpit of Nick Keig's trimaran, the biggest one in the fleet. Among those in attendance, there were several with experience in coping upside-down:

Nick Keig, who had flipped his Iroquois catamaran in 1972 racing in the Irish sea;

Nick Clifton, who had overturned between Nantucket and Bermuda in his small trimaran, *Azulao,* returning to England after the OSTAR in April 1977;

Walter Greene, who for the good of the art and the advancement of science, had deliberately capsized his brand-new tri with the aid of a boatyard crane in Maine in October, so that he could test the theory of self-righting;

Riguidel, Nugent, and Weld. Among the undipped skippers were Tom Ryan, Bill Doelger, Rob James, Roger Forkert, Bill Homewood, and Paul Rodgers. Damian Laughlin, builder of Mike Birch's boat, Dick Newick, and the film team filled out the crowd of eager seminarians.

Cockpit conference on capsize prevention and procedure. (Christopher Knight)

Discussion began over what to do with the Argos transmitter following capsize. It had an emergency switch to signal distress. I'd asked to have mine bolted on the cabin top just forward of the cabin hatch. Keig pointed out that this would leave me with such a deep underwater swim that I'd never be able to hold my breath long enough to release the catch clamping it to its base. Right off the conference had benefited me. I would ask the Argos technicians to move it to the afterdeck. Here it would be much easier to reach if the boat inverted. Right side up, it was shielded from waves by the after cross arm.

We moved on to communications. To keep the portable VHF radio dry, pack it with the flares. Who had bought helium balloons? This new gadget to call attention from a spotter plane hadn't yet reached America. I argued for my little kite. Orange paint. A second radar reflector. "Can't have too many flares," everyone agreed.

Greene reminded us that it was futile to fire flares at a ship after it had come abeam. "They only look ahead." Rob James, a British merchant seaman and veteran of two Whitbread Round the World races, concurred. "The watch is likely to be looking off the leeward wing of the bridge," he said. This made it pointless to try to attract attention if you lay to windward. I reminded the group that the Baileys had been passed by seven ships and the Robertsons by nine before they'd been picked up. Both examples involved couples whose keel boats had sunk after hitting whales in the Pacific.

We asked Rory to recommend a sequence of actions. "Get into your survival suit." It could be assumed we each carried one of these loose-fitting, unsinkable rubber coveralls with hood, two-finger mittens, and feet. I had one lashed to the afterdeck and a second in the cabin. Once armed against hypothermia, one should concentrate on retrieving essentials before they sank or floated away. Stuff them in a sail bag tied to the hull. Oranges should be a priority grab because they provide liquid nourishment. In stowing for a voyage, put lanyards on the most important items — like the emergency water jug and cutting tools — and hitch them to the boat.

"Use snap hooks," Greene advised. "Bowlines are too hard to untie."

I had a saw, drill, hammer, and chisel, taped to a block of Styrofoam, inside a waterproof bag, lashed to the afterdeck beside the sea anchor, to use for cutting my way in from the outside. Down in the cabin, next to the emergency beacon, was another set ready to cut a hole, if need be, from inside to the open air.

Life rafts gave us much to talk about. "They're going to kill you because the darned water's too cold," Greene said. Then, slapping the orange vinyl bag holding a rolled-up survival suit, "If you don't have this thing on, you're going to die." His vehemence had been sparked by talking with Le Cornec, who, to avoid freezing, had stood for two days in his raft before rescue.

Keig made the point that "rafts are designed for monos that sink" and therefore need a painter that parts under strain, a disadvantage to the multihull survivor able to remain with the buoyant habitat of his upturned craft. Clifton advised packing a 60-foot length of half-inch nylon line to supplement the raft's too easily parted, 30-foot painter.

What food to stow in one's calamity locker? I recited my stock — peanut butter, honey, fig newtons, peanuts, a pint of rum. "You're going to put on weight, Phil," Keig cracked. Homewood recommended the concentrated dextrose candy mountaineers carry and told of a local campers' store that stocked it. Doelger asked about vitamins. Clifton urged taking two anti-seasick tablets immediately to forestall dehydration.

"Boredom was a big obstacle," Rory interjected. I plumped for the *Works of Shakespeare* to meet it. Newick offered his clients wax statues of himself into which they could stick pins. Clifton recommended a routine for efficient solo watch-keeping. "It's important to keep as good a lookout as possible. Scan the horizon for five minutes. Then sleep like this [demonstrating the fetal position] for ten minutes."

"Right," from Homewood. "Keep your heart warm."

Rory explained how he'd prolonged the life of the battery powering his beacon by keeping it warm and dry inside his survival suit. It was still pulsing on the fifth day.

We ended with a useful exchange on capsize prevention. When it blows too hard to keep sailing on course, is it better to heave to? That is to say, point the boat as close as possible to the direction from which wind and waves are coming while trailing a sea anchor from the bow. Or was it better to run off before the waves "under bare poles" while towing warps to slow the boat down? The latter stratagem would most likely cause you to lose ground on the race. But with the bow to the waves, there was the danger in some tris of doing a back somersault while slipping backward. Testing the alternatives with *Moxie*, Tom and I had decided I should put out my sea anchor, also known as a drogue. It's a canvas cone with a hole at the point. Its rim is kept rigid by a stainless wire circlet five feet in diameter. It was folded and lashed to the afterdeck, ready for the anchor line that would lead through a snatch block, or pulley, in the bow to prevent chafe when, like a parachute, it took the strain of the faster drifting boat.

It had been a fruitful hour and a half. Not only had it given the trimaran group a sense of community and a confidence that nourished us all, but it had given each of us some solid tips. As soon as I got aboard *Moxie*, I tested the zippers on my survival suits, found them sticky with salt. I rubbed the teeth with beeswax from the sail repair kit. I checked over every item in the calamity locker in the cockpit. Since Newick had told us, "All my boats are going to float with the bow well down," I reassessed the narrow, empty space under the afterdeck. It should be the driest spot for living upside down. At a shop for divers, I bought a waterproof flashlight to squirrel here and a diver's heavy sheath knife to strap to my leg if conditions got really bad. If all other tools disappeared, I could cut my way through the wood with this.

I think we'd all felt the magic of talking about something so that it would never happen.

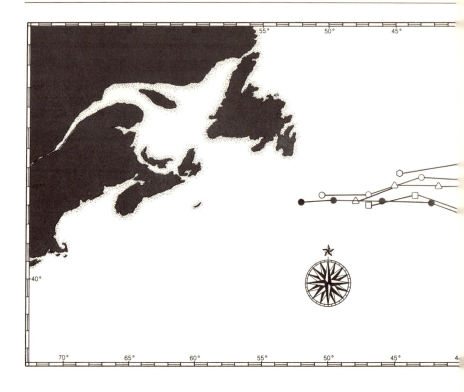

14

6:30 A.M. *After yesterday afternoon's exciting sleighride at 14 knots, the wind just gave out. We've been puttering along at about 3 knots for hours. I'll get the spinnaker up now. You can see all the lines, like patriotic spaghetti, red, white, and blue.*

A good thing happened during yesterday's sprint. We got through to Art Zolot. I could hear him fine. He asked me to come in fast with "Moxie, Moxie, Moxie, I read you, Art." This I did and he responded: "I'm going to contact Bob Rice for forecasts from now on." So our weather plan operates at last.

11:30. *I've been trying to film a greeting committee of porpoises down from Nova Scotia. They were here in force a moment ago. You can see it's still foggy Grand Banks weather although we're well across the Banks. The BBC just said, "It looks like an American win," giving Moxie's position as 44.5° north by 51.8° west, with 800 miles to go and*

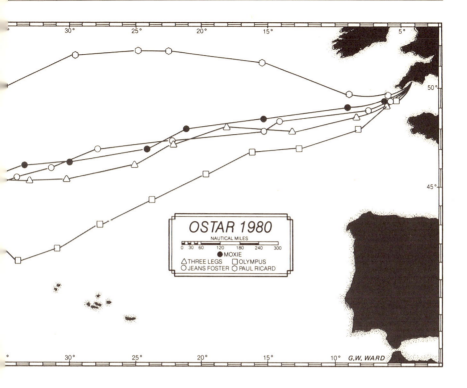

OSTAR 1980
NAUTICAL MILES
0 30 60   120   180   240   300
● MOXIE
△ THREE LEGS □ OLYMPUS
○ JEANS FOSTER ○ PAUL RICARD

G.W. WARD

*"clear of his rivals by . . ." then static interfered with the
number of miles by which they say I lead. Only ten miles
separate the three boats fighting for second place — Walter
Greene, Nick Keig, and Jaworski. Then the fascinating foot-
note: "Paul Ricard is well behind the pack. Pajot says he
may put into Saint John's for repairs."*

*I've now deduced that the broadcasts, to avoid revealing
tactically useful information to the competitors, deliberately
lag in the position reports. I'm at least 50 miles further west
than they say. But so, of course, are the others. With those
three at my heels, the race isn't over till we cross the line.
They're three great sailors.*

*Spinnaker's up. We're jogging along at about 8 knots. I'm
still on Cloud Nine over yesterday's 14-knot average for four
hours.*

4:30 P.M. Busy afternoon. The wind veered southwest after noon and
I had to douse the spinnaker. The squeezer, thank heavens, helped me

get it down fine. I had the reacher up for four hours, and ghosted along in the mist at 7 knots with just a whisper of wake. Then I switched to the genoa as it breezed up. We hit 18 knots in 12 knots of wind.

8:00 P.M. Bob Rice's first weather report, tailor-made for our position, has been most helpful. It gave me fair warning of this low that has just moved through. It was wild for a bit as the wind rose to 38 knots. I'm jogging along now at 6 knots under a tiny bit of main and half the staysail.

How I Lost the Route du Rhum

Rogue Wave should have won the Route du Rhum, the first French transatlantic solo, raced in November 1978 from Saint-Malo on the Brittany coast to Pointe à Pitre on Guadeloupe. She was the fastest boat in the fleet of thirty and in the first twenty-four hours built up a comfortable lead.

But I was guilty of two stupidities. First, I failed to heed basic rigging rule No. 1: "Regard as suspect any bit of rig or gear in use for the first time." Second, I succumbed to some French gamesmanship that I should have known enough to ignore. Writing in *Voiles et Voiliers* before the race, Eugene Riguidel, skipper of *VSD*, predicted, "Weld, having capsized his trimaran once, will 'lever le pied,'" that's to say, take his foot off the accelerator in the clinches. Then *Figaro* said of *Rogue*, "a superior vessel but given her 64-year-old skipper, the caution of age will not be able to combat the power of 'jeunesse française' confronting it."

The gear error concerned the newly designed batten-pocket-enders in my new mainsail. Until I went geriatric with my Stoway mast, I had loudly advocated the efficacy of full-length battens. They greatly helped to still the flogging of the main when reefing in a squall and they retained some shape in the sail when the boat rolled about on the ocean swell in very light air. Their disadvantage lay in the inability of anyone yet to design a good way to prevent their chafing the luff of the sail where they pressed it against the back of the mast.

Then Bob O'Connor, Marblehead sailmaker, hit on using the gooseneck fitting of a dinghy boom as the ready-made stainless-steel universal joint we'd been seeking. He mortised them into the Tufnol cheeks bolted to the forward ends of the four upper batten pockets. I brought the new sail with me to England, where I'd left *Rogue* for the summer after the Round Britain, and experimentally raised it in the Plymouth dock before sailing for France. It seemed to drop easily enough without battens. But the only chance to lower the sail with battens in place came as we rounded up in light air at the crowded Saint-Malo lock entrance eight days before the start. I'd counted on being able to test-sail during that week, but once inside we were not allowed to leave the lock.

Most of the time it blew hard over the stern so that raising the sail at the dock would have been risky. I proudly demonstrated the swivel-in-any-direction capability of the goosenecks to a dozen "multi-coquers," including Eric Tabarly, "Le Maître" of French sailing, who was not entered in this race. No one suggested the obvious — to assure they'd slide easily in the groove of the mast by slobbering them with Vaseline.

"You seem so relaxed," people commented. "No worries?" I furrowed my brow but couldn't think of one.

Came dusk, Monday, November 6, the second night of the race. Blowing out one of the two single-luff spinnakers the first night, while threading my way through the ship traffic off Ushant, had dampened some of my machismo. But I wished to hold my lead. I was determined to refute Riguidel and not reef prematurely. As dark came on, it became more certain we were moving into a gale. The barograph was dropping fast, with clouds and rain and freshening southwest wind. This had to be the low Bob Rice forecast in our phone call to Bedford the night before the start. "If you can get behind it and ride the northeast winds on its back side, you'll have it made," Bob had advised.

At 10:00 P.M., I must have passed through the low's center, for the wind dropped. I even considered rolling out some jib, but prudence prevailed. Wearing oilies and a wool hat, with my harness buckled on, I lay down on the starboard settee foward to catnap. My bunk was too bumpy for sleep. To rest before the inevitable hassle with reefing seemed wise. A crash awakened me from a twenty-minute doze. By the dim light of the kerosene lamp, I looked aft to see the chart-table books strewn about. When we ski-jump at 12 knots off a big wave, hard on the wind, this happens. I sensed trouble.

On deck the wind needle showed 40 knots plus. The rain stung. One or two reefs? Automatically I tautened the topping lift, eased the main sheet, unhooked the autopilot, and manually rounded up. Lashing the wheel hard-down, I let off the wire on the main halyard winch, watched it run out, then halt. Shining aloft one of the disposable flashlights I can hold in my teeth, I could see the headboard might be stuck. Clutching at the handier of the tack reefing lines, I hauled, then winched down on the luff of the main. "Oh, bloody, bloody," I muttered. "The goose-necks must be binding."

The flogging of the main and staysail now sounded like rapid enemy rifle fire. I tamed the staysail as best I could by winching down hard on both sheets, but I couldn't take time to lower it. I looked aloft. Horrors. Just below the masthead a black triangle of sky, clearly defined by the lighter tones of mast and sail, appeared. I crawled forward to pull with all my weight on the front edge of the sail. I couldn't budge it. Head back, the light in my teeth, I saw the top batten, made of incredibly strong carbon fiber, bent into a tight ring between the cap shroud and the mast. I jibed to free it. The jibe worked but the maneuver gave the staysail such a whack that two seams let go near the head and in seconds it had shivered to tatters.

I ran forward to drop it and get stops around it. Meantime, the luff slides along the front edge of the main were letting go one after another, domino-fashion. I rounded up again just as the main hit the water. The headboard slides had broken free so now the halyard ran off the winch to the bitter end. It became a race to save the halyard. The luminous dial showed the wind gusting to 50. It took all my strength and painstaking use of winches and sundry lengths of line to get the head of that main back aboard, even though we were only drifting at about 3 knots, sideways to the building seas.

Mouth sticky-dry, Helly-Hansen underwear drenched with sweat, I was panting like a cross-country runner before I'd tamed the monster. I'd have welcomed aboard some of *Figaro's* jeunesse. All but spent, I furled that sail in unseamanlike bunches, observing that it was damaged beyond my limits to repair at sea. All four dinghy goosenecks had sheared, all the luff slides were damaged. I would have to switch to the old main when the gale passed. I stuffed the ripped staysail down the hatch and allowed myself an hour's sleep before hanking on its backup.

The panic party started at 10:30 P.M. We weren't back on course till four in the morning. I must have drifted 15 miles back toward Ushant. Good-bye lead! It wasn't until twilight Tuesday that I got the old main in place and partially fitted with battens. Twice thereafter, damaged batten-pocket-enders required dropping the sail for refit. When I recapitulated the disaster, I figured it cost me 402 miles: on Days 2 and 3, I made good only 130 miles, instead of 300, a loss of 170; Days 4 through 11, mainsail inefficiency cost me 20 miles a day for another 160; on Day 12, I dropped the main for twenty-four hours for repairs, reducing speed under headsails alone by 3 knots, for another 72 miles.

Route du Rhum award ceremonies at Pointe à Pitre, Guadeloupe. Mike Birch, center, caught Michel Malinovsky in the sprint to the finish to win by 98 seconds. (J. B. Thomas)

So much for postmortems. All the same, *Rogue* arrived at the northeast tip of Guadeloupe on the dawn of November 28, only two hours behind Mike Birch and the French monohuller Michel Malinovsky. Mike, sailing Walter Greene's *A Capella*, was in a 98-second photo finish. But as Dick Newick warned us all, Mike Birch "just never makes a mistake."

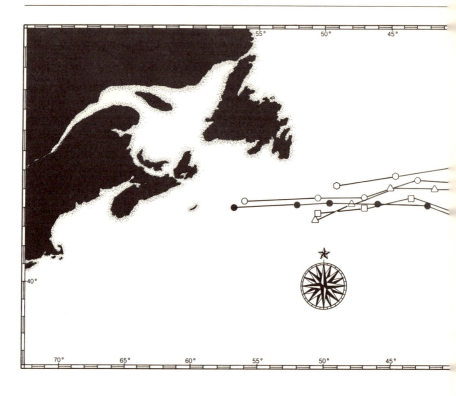

15

8:00 A.M. Thick fog notwithstanding, *Moxie* barrels along at 12 knots under staysail and reefed main with 27 knots over the masthead at an apparent wind angle of 67 degrees. Seas easy. Super. We'll be in Monday evening at this rate.

The BBC has conceded the race to us and now talks of our breaking Colas's 1972 record of 20 days, 13 hours. That I can accept but I sure can't yet count out Walter or Nick. They may push harder than I. Last night, I could have carried on at 20 knots into the dark and fog but I felt chicken and slowed to 15, then down to 10, as the wind and seas mounted. In a neck-and-neck situation, what would I do? I lean toward caution. Riguidel was right. "Lever le pied." I don't want another capsize.

I just ate the last banana. I've still got some fresh British bread. There's enough food aboard for another round-trip solo. Should I throw some of it over the side? I lightened the water burden yesterday with a sponge bath. I'm using less than a half-gallon a day, so when the sun comes out, I'll have a fresh-water bucket bath and a shampoo.

Bob Rice's first forecast, relayed yesterday by Art Zolot, warned of

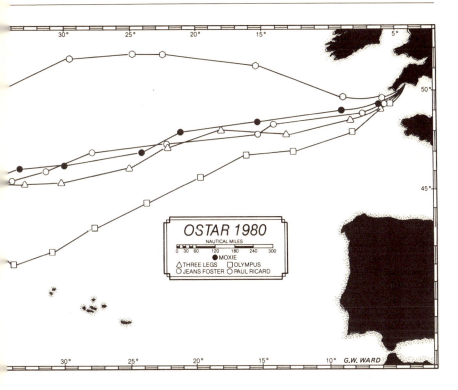

this "small low." Now Portsmouth, Virginia, has added an OSTAR special following its regular offshore analysis. It spoke of a cold front over Newport at noon today moving east. The solar panels, even in this fog, have in two hours brought the batteries up to 11 volts from a perilously low 9 volts last night.

(FROM THE FILM SOUND TRACK)

3:00 P.M. *We heard Art Zolot again with a report saying we're on a collision course with another small low. It's great to be in contact. He says they're saying in Newport to expect* Moxie *on Monday — sixteen days, four days ahead of Colas's record. Cross fingers. Seems to be a little wind shift here. Should we tack?*

4:30. *Oh, criminey, I hope we haven't been boarded by end-of-the-voyage gremlins, like the last day on the* Route du Rhum. *Just as I tacked after getting my weather forecast, I'd gone over to starboard to get south again as we were being headed. Lo and behold, I came on deck to find the jib halyard*

had fallen down. The wire had stranded right at the point
where it exits the mast. Now I've got to pull a new halyard
through the inside of the mast with a messenger. . . .

5:05. *I guess there's something spooky about the end of the*
voyage. It makes me nervous to have people assuming I've
broken Colas's record. It's like talking about a guy pitching a
no-hitter when he's still in the seventh inning. I shall assume
nothing till Brenton Reef. At least the fog has gone. But my
sleeping bag is so damp I wear my oilies to bed.

ME AND MY MESSENGER

"Well, if you're that helpless, I don't see how you're allowed off
alone," said Nick Keig, in disbelief of my claim to being a three-
dimensional paraplegic.

Nick, who built *Three Legs* with his own hands, was rafted beside us
in the Milbay Dock. He can't understand why bosunry challenges give
me the blues. Unlike Walter Greene, Mike Birch, and so many others
among the competition, my capacity to mend what's wrong falters all
too often.

I'm saved from disaster only by adherence to Dick Newick's formula
for coping with clients like me. His acronym for it is KISS — keep it
simple, stupid. By eschewing an engine and all plumbing, by allowing
only the minimum of wiring, by using the best of everything — Barient
winches, Hood furlers, Schaeffer blocks, Marlowe line — we planned
that *Moxie* would make few demands on Weld-the-Shipwright. The
steering cables lead across the open deck to a husky Edson quadrant at
the stern in a straightforward way that even I could understand.

Alas, there's always wear and tear and that's what got to the jib halyard this fourteenth day of the race. I guess the jib had been winched
an inch too taut so that the thimble, fitted onto the end of the wire, had
been pressing against the sheave, or turning pulley, at the top of the
mast, in a way to fatigue, and eventually sever, its seven strands of
nineteen wires each.

This left me at the end of Week 2 with my first major bosunry crisis,
to replace a halyard, a simple chore to most, but to me intellectually
demanding. The wind was dead ahead at 3 knots and falling. It couldn't
have happened at a time to cause less damage to our race standing. First
I needed a quick nap. I'd been hard at it, working the ship, since 3:00 in
the morning. Thirteen hours later with no respite, I'd a right to feel

tired. Fifteen minutes of sleep and a hot cup of tea renewed me. But nervous about goofing it — a false step could mean either no jib or a trip up the mast — I talked through every move out loud.

"Remember what Tom said Walter said about having all those knots where the messenger's tied off at the deck. 'Make it hard to undo, so you'll have time to think what you're doing and not louse it up.' "

"Messenger" is the word sailors use for any light line to be left in position through the inside of a boom or mast against the day when a heavier line, like a halyard or an outhaul replacement, needs to be reeved, or threaded through, an otherwise too long or narrow aperture. Leaving Plymouth, *Moxie* had two messengers in place — one for the jib's spare halyard, one for the spinnaker's.

To the tune of "Me and My Shadow" I hummed:

> Me and my messenger's
> Goin' to make it
> Somehow all alone . . .

Then fortissimo, from my newspapering subconscious: "Don't shoot the messenger."

With the end of the rope tail of the replacement in my lap and the correct end of the light messenger in my left hand, I took a heavy sail needle and thread in my right and commenced to sew the two together. I'd watched Joan Greene do this very chore on *Rogue* three years before at New London before going out to beat *Spirit of America* in a 35-knot northeaster. I can play the sedulous ape. I'd observed the dozens of stitches she'd pushed through with sailmaker's palm before she judged the linkage strong enough. When I could pull one line against the other with all my strength, I felt it safe to haul the new halyard aloft.

Joy. It passed over the masthead sheave smooth as a snake. On the downward passage, it checked at the upper spreaders. Panic. Steadying myself against the mast, I put my whole weight on the messenger and let it move about inside the mast with the motion of the ship. Double joy. After two agonizing minutes, it descended. A repeat performance at the lower spreaders. Then complete success.

Massively content, I stowed my sewing kit and repaired to the cockpit for a large bourbon and water with which to salute a gorgeous sunset. Anyone who says booze isn't good for you just hasn't lived.

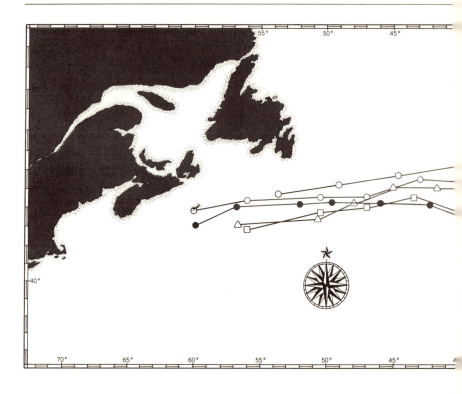

16

5:10 A.M. A suggestion for the Royal Western and the BBC from "Citizen Fixit." At the end of the 0330 weather report, as the race proceeds and the breadth of the forecast area diminishes, could not the unused time be devoted to a longer list of racers and their positions for the benefit of those still racing?

9:45. A point to make if there's a press conference. Breaking the record has been in the cards. While all of you have been concentrating on the same old Twelve-Meter thing, a nostalgic exercise in driving stagecoaches, the real advances in yachting have been taking place in preparation for the OSTAR, here in New England, in France, and in the UK. The widely beneficial object — to make it easy for lots of people to sail a boat short-handed across the Atlantic in as few days as possible — has been achieved.

Much has been learned since my friend, the late, admirable Alain Colas, set the record in 1972 in *Pen Duick IV*. Had he not been lost with his ship in 1978, he would have entered this year's OSTAR with a boat

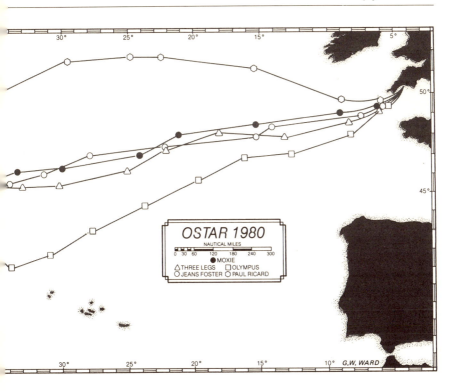

OSTAR 1980
NAUTICAL MILES
0   30 60   120   180   240   300
● MOXIE
△ THREE LEGS   □ OLYMPUS
○ JEANS FOSTER   ○ PAUL RICARD

G.W. WARD

conforming to the new maximum length. Alain, even with only one good leg, would have been here at dawn Saturday in time for Frank Page to file his story of the race for Sunday's London *Observer*.

In 1976, my friend Mike McMullen exuberantly predicted that theoretically a tri as fast as *Three Cheers* could finish in fifteen days. Given this year's conditions and his competitive nature, Mike might well have done it in a *Three Cheers II* or a *Binkie III*. All of us who used electric autopilots should remember that it was Mike, acting as the racing member of the race committee, who in 1975 lobbied for the change in the rules permitting these devices. For my faithful Autohelm, I blessed Mike six times a day.

(Post-race note: At the Sheraton press conference following the finish, it helped to have these paragraphs to read from the log. I had generous letters from Mike's parents, Colin and Gill, who have become close friends, and touching cables from Lizzie McMullen's parents and from Alain's widow, Theura, and brother, Jeff.)

Alain Colas and the author pose with the Lord Mayor and his lady at Plymouth festivities before the 1974 Round Britain Race. (Western Morning News Company, Ltd.)

The late Mike McMullen, lost with Three Cheers on the 1976 OSTAR, provided an élan to short-handed ocean racing that will long survive him.

(FROM THE FILM SOUND TRACK)

10:00. *In four more hours we finish the second week. I never thought a fortnight ago we'd be just about abeam of Halifax, well on our way to the last sixth of the race. We've got about 460 miles to go. Maybe 500. I'm uncertain because it has been so hard to get a decent sun line. You can see the sun up there, now and then just peeking through. But you just don't get a sharp horizon. The Argos position from the BBC helps even if it is twelve hours late.*

Just now as I was trying for a sight, the Autohelm seemed to get tired. Moxie slewed off course to the right, then back up to the left. Otto just couldn't cope. So I'm doing a little hand-helming now to rest the batteries. It favors going to the right a bit. If she gets off course, it takes quite a bit of strength to get her back on track. We're doing 17, 18 knots. Absolutely effortless. Newport, here we come! Hot diggety damn!

3:15 P.M. *We're just about through the cold front they talked about on Portsmouth weather. I missed Art's latest broadcast. Dammit, too much static. Seven foggy days and no decent horizon has me uneasy about our dead-reckoning position. If I can get one more sight before dark, I'll be more confident. We're down at the latitude of Newport, maybe even below. I may have overstood the mark. We're coming up on Georges Bank. It's breezed up to 35 knots over the deck. I've had to put two and a half reefs in the main, roll up all the jib, and reef the staysail.*

The BBC just placed us about where we were this morning. Nick Keig's second. Only fourteen miles separate him from Mike Birch and Walter. Jaworski's Argos is out so we don't know where he is. Cripes, this is his weather. I wouldn't be surprised to find Spaniel right up here. Last I heard, I was only 130 miles ahead of him.

It's supposed to come in northwest. They're saying I'll be in on Monday. Well, this is Saturday afternoon. Got to go some to get there Monday. We're bound to have some flat-ass calms on Sunday . . .

JOY OF SAILING

People assume if you do well in the OSTAR, you've sailed all your life. True, I started young, but there have been big gaps. I first capsized on July 4, 1921, at age six, off West Chop, Martha's Vineyard, where we spent part of each summer with our grandmother Saltonstall. I had been asked to crew in the holiday Dog boat race by a smashing blonde of nine, Judy Adams. The Dog boat was a heavy dory with a demountable mast and a leg-of-mutton sail. Ours was red and rolled over gently when a gust caught the skipper inattentive. Bill Cox, fleet champ, later to win fame as a Twelve-Meter coach, rescued us.

Most summers we spent at Indian Neck, Wareham, at the head of Buzzards Bay, in the reclusive enclave created by my grandfather, General Stephen M. Weld. It backed on Bourne's Cove, shallow, muddy, and a safe place for my sister Mary and me to learn to sail in a pair of flat-bottom skiffs, *The Rat* and the *David*. Before we were allowed to sail outside alone, my father made us pass his swimming test: five eighths of a mile in to the shore from Little Bird Island.

We graduated to the *Black Maria*, a Cape Cod baby knockabout, a centerboard sloop, and were urged into racing. Saturdays we set off early, Mary and I with one or the other's friend for a third, on a two-hour beat against the prevailing southwester to the Beverly Yacht Club, then located on the point by Bird Island Light. The girls would come in to the chowder lunch soaking wet, conscious of the contrast between their dank locks and the appearance of the girls from Marion, who'd only had to come downwind from the harbor in their Herreshoff Twelves and Fifteens.

My father couldn't stand the knockabout's savage weather helm and traded us up to a Fifteen the summer I was fourteen. *Vixen* was one of the original fleet of eight that my father remembered were towed over from Bristol, Rhode Island, in 1897. With their shallow keels, centerboards, and sporty expanse of gaff-rigged mainsail, they made the perfect boat to race in warm Buzzards Bay, where it didn't matter how wet you got in July and August. Dad was sentimental about her. On November 9, 1912, he'd sailed his bride over to West Chop from Wareham in his Fifteen before a three-reef northeaster. My mother has never expatiated on the joys of this honeymoon voyage.

"It was so cold," my father told me, "I had to sneak a pee into the bailer to warm my hands. My fingers were so numb I couldn't uncleat the halyards."

Physical discomfort never deflected his enthusiasm if he was doing what amused him — salmon-fishing, quail-shooting, golf in the rain or sailing *The Rat* by himself against a 20-knot sou'wester. He cared little for the niceties of yachting, didn't buy the magazines or care much about light-air tactics. But he taught me and my five sisters not to panic in a capsize and to believe that lots of wind was to be relished, not feared.

I became adept enough at sailing the Fifteen to fly the spinnaker alone, but I never did well racing. Day-long "cruises" to Naushon and back with my sister Rosie were more to my taste. The only real boyhood cruise I ever took was aboard my grandfather's big, comfortable catboat, the *56*, named for the 56th Massachusetts Regiment, which he commanded in the Civil War. For several summers after his death, my step-grandmother, whom we called "Aunt Edie," kept the boat in commission under the surveillance of Ben Savary, a marvelous jack-of-all-sea-trades. Ben dug clams, hauled and repaired boats, harvested scallops and oysters, and generally led the good life of a hard-working Cape Cod Yankee. A special treat arranged for me the summer I was twelve was to have Ben sail me to West Chop for the night, then to Cuttyhunk for the second night. He had a marvelous ringing voice and generally conversed loud enough to be heard well out to sea. But when I got seasick on the run home, he was all concern and sympathy. He was an admirable man in every way.

Three years later I cruised in a Herreshoff Twelve with Donnie Cutler and two other teams of two in Twelves from Marion to New Bedford, where we promptly tied up at the town wharf to explore the fleshpots on a sunny afternoon. We smoked English Ovals madly, pored over copies of *Captain Billy's Whiz Bang*, and took in a double feature. Not the maritime regimen our parents imagined.

Between 1932 when I entered Harvard and 1945 when I got out of the army, I scarcely stepped in a boat. Then in June 1946 and for a number of years thereafter, four of my closest friends and I chartered a succession of cruising auxiliaries in which to sail down to New London to watch the Harvard-Yale crew race. The aim was conviviality, the adventures hilarious, or at least we thought so. We — Joe Richardson, Anne's brother Sam, John Storey, Charlie Woodard, and I — called ourselves The Bird Club. The name derived from John's having once headed up the Milton Academy ornithologists. "Associate Birds" filled out the crew.

My annual responsibility was to bring a laundry bag full of used tennis balls and a worn-out racket with which to loft gentle lobs onto the decks of passing yachts by way of making friendly overtures. We never harmed a soul; we enlarged our Yale acquaintanceship and strengthened our Harvard ties enormously, or so we all agreed. One year Eliot Dalton launched a ball in a 300-foot parabola onto the conning tower of the nuclear sub *Nautilus*. The skipper acknowledged the feat over the bullhorn with "Good shot. But don't try it again." Our motto, "Who says martinis and sea water don't mix?" represents the club's contribution to the lore of the sea.

In 1955 we bought our house on Dolliver's Neck. It overlooks Gloucester harbor and Freshwater Cove, so named because it was here that Samuel Champlain filled his water kegs at a spring in 1607. It gave us the ideal mooring for our Thistle, a mahogany, cold-molded 17-foot version of the International 14 dinghy. It planed at 10 knots or more and there were then New England fleets with whom to join for the occasional regatta. Our preparation was always far too casual, our racing knowledge too slender, for us ever to move up from the back of the fleet except once in a blow at Marblehead when everyone but us dropped out to save their gear. Simply by finishing we won.

Then in June 1960, while in Paris on a "working sabbatical" as publisher of the European edition of the *New York Herald Tribune*, I avidly read the dispatches to the London *Observer* by Francis Chichester, who was engaged in winning the first OSTAR. He planted an idea. "Look at this fifty-eight-year-old drinking champagne in mid-Atlantic to celebrate a good week's run. What fun," I thought. Here was a sport where the accretion of wisdom could offset diminishing physical power. On the tennis court, I was not getting faster in coming to the net.

Back in Gloucester, I began to collect books about sailing and bought a fiberglass Thistle so as to be more competitive. Doug MacGregor, the Thistle champion and local dealer, sized us up as good multihull prospects. For his own racing, he'd just switched to the Tiger Cat, a daysailer designed by Bob Harris that had won the *Yachting* One-of-a-Kind regatta. Doug took us for a demonstration sail on Boston harbor on a

Opposite: *The Thistle, our introduction to high-performance sailing.* (Bill Lane)

day with little wind. The 17-foot catamaran's ability to accelerate in the slightest puff captivated us then and there with the lure of the multi-hull.

He advised us to buy a Pacific Cat, slightly more powerful than the Tiger, the design of Carter Pyle, a surfer from Newport Beach, California. I called Harry Sindle, his East Coast builder, down in New Jersey, who intrigued me over the phone with this immortal line: "Once you've multi-ed a season, you'll never mono again." Accompanied by my fourth and youngest daughter, Helen, I trailered P-19 back to Gloucester from Barnegat Bay without ever having seen a P-cat in the water.

Come Sunday we took her out, Helen and I and Annie, our next older daughter, to follow after the 210s racing off the Eastern Point breakwater. Many pleasure craft were homing on Gloucester because at 2:00 P.M. the Cardinal was to bless the Italian fishing fleet in the inner harbor. We crossed the yacht club starting line a minute after the 210 gun. Within three minutes we'd sailed through the fleet on a reach at, perhaps, 14 knots, though it seemed then like 25. Then a gust caught me before I could release the main sheet and we capsized gently within sight of those lunching at the house.

One of the big Coast Guard cutters from Boston was in attendance to police the spectator fleet. She sent two frogmen to our rescue in a launch that towed us ignominiously to the mooring, wiser in the ways of multihulls.

But the exhilarating responsiveness of the catamaran had us hooked. We bought a second P-cat so we could enjoy family match-sailing. We persuaded four others in the yacht club to join us and the following summer had some great racing. We gave our pair horsey names — *Pegasus* and *Phaeton* — because of the equine manner in which they'd gallop when one headed up into the wind after a dead run before it. The curve of the mainsail roach, stretched taut by the full-length battens, reminded us of the horses' manes on a Parthenon frieze.

Always to want "a little more boat" seems to be a yachter's weakness. The urge rose in me in September 1966 at King's Point, Long Island, scene of the First World's Multihull Championships. Bill Plante, executive editor of Essex County newspapers, had agreed to crew for me in *Phaeton*, attracted by the chance to meet Arthur Piver. Arthur, the

Opposite: *The Pacific catamaran, the boat that showed us the joy of multihull speed. (Gordon Abbott)*

Bill Plante and Charlie Powers help to assemble the cross tubes and hulls of the 32-foot, trailerable catamaran, Poseidon's Chariot. (Bill Lane)

With the Phil Cronins, père et fils, on Leonardo the Tornado, showing the complex rig controls to make a catamaran go faster. (Bart Piscatello)

Daughter Helen bravely conceals her distaste for crewing on the frostbite dinghy at Marblehead. (Boston Globe)

San Francisco evangelist of the trimaran movement, had captured Bill's imagination with his books on how to home-build at minimum cost a family cruising boat. He'd gone on to build a Nugget in his own backyard, with his own two hands. A man with Bill's talent with a typewriter has no right to be so competent with tools.

A black nor'wester blew so hard the second day they canceled the races. But *Wildwind*, a D-class catamaran from Long Beach, California — that's to say, no more than 500 square feet of sail, with hulls 32 feet long — ventured out with a reef in the main to cover the measured

167

mile off City Island at speeds clocked as high as 28 knots. Bobbing along at 15 in *Phaeton*, I became enraptured by the aura of imperturbable power exuded by *Wildwind* as she cantered through our lee.

"Bill, I've just got to have one," I confessed as the cold autumn spray stung our cheeks. That night over steaks, I learned from Jay Johnson, one of her crew, that his Glascraft Company, makers of a device for spraying chopped fiberglass, would deliver a production model of *Wildwind* for $8,000. The next August, Anne and I took delivery at the Long Beach Yacht Club float from Jay, two nights before the opening of the Second World Multihull Championships. Because *Wildwind* had captured all the important trophies, defense of them had moved to exuberant California. We stayed in a motel filled with traders attending the convention of the Matchbook Cover Collectors of America.

Two days of speed trials against electric timers and two days of racing in a mixed fleet of smaller cats and two small tris barely acquainted us with our new toy. We finished second to the champ, but we had experienced the giddy thrill of flying a hull in competition. The uninhibited enthusiasm of the Californians caught up in the multihull movement encouraged the belief that the ballasted "monomaran," the "lead mine," the "heeler-keeler" — all terms of opprobrium hurled about through the week by our small band of disciples in defiance of the hundreds upon hundreds of conventional craft filling every slip in square miles of marina — would soon be obsolete. In my naiveté, I envisioned the D-class cat as a new class that would sweep past the Solings in membership, just as they could on the water.

However, by the next spring, the only other D in the east was *Bull Roarer*. Bill and I trailed down to Rowayton, Connecticut, for a weekend of match racing. On the way home, the trailer fishtailed and overturned in the middle of the Sunday turnpike traffic. The station wagon escaped upsetting only because the hitch broke free. This "capsize" still marks the most hazardous incident in my multihull career. Furthermore, the accident required ordering a new mast and extensive repairs to the bolts holding in place the cross tubes that joined the hulls.

To fill in an otherwise lost summer, I bought a Tornado, the hot new class with the promise of being the first multihull to achieve Olympic status. We called her *Leonardo* because the delicacy and spare logic of her rig reminded us of a da Vinci sketch. I'd been frostbiting, that is, sailing dinghies on every winter Sunday that it blew less than 17 knots, regardless of temperature, to learn something of starting tactics and the rules for rounding racing marks. This helped me to work up to the

The Chariot *could claim to be "fastest" but she was also the "wettest" boat on the* coast. (Edwin Hills)

middle of the Tornado fleet in a couple of regattas. I tasted the joy of competitive sailing for the first time in my life. All the same, the D-cat, while she had been repaired for the 1969 season and now had *Poseidon's Chariot*, painted in big letters on her flanks, still had no one to race.

"Being the richest kid in town has always been a lonely business," I wrote for that summer's issue of the *Harvard Bulletin*.

Owning the fastest sailboat around presents the same need for playing fantasy games. No matter how hard you try to be a regular fellow, play-mates treat you with suspicion. Suspicion? In some quarters, downright segregationist contumely describes the attitude better. Read for example, the sailing instructions for the 17th Patton Bowl Regatta conducted off Gloucester in June: "ELIGIBILITY — all entries shall be conventional, single-hulled inboard auxiliary yachts, suitable for off-shore racing." [Note: five years later, cruising multis were invited.]

To a multi-huller, the phraseology stings like "white Anglo Saxon Prot-estants only need apply" in a want ad. But the Patton Bowl bespeaks a gay event. It brings out 70 of the finest cruisers from among the local fleets. We couldn't bear to stay away. On a laughing diamond of a Sunday morning, the event's second day, we lurched across the trampoline of *Po-seidon's Chariot*, slipped from our Freshwater Cove mooring and trotted for the starting line off Eastern Point breakwater. We would make believe we'd been invited to play. The crew comprised Bill Plante and his 18-year-old son, Billy. Owner of the trimaran *Triad*, Bill qualifies as a partner in the crime of enjoying unconventional boats.

At 0950, between the starting guns for Classes B and C, we pretended the enlightened Manchester Yacht Club had instituted a special gun for multi-hulls in the spirit of Phillips Exeter Academy taking in the first ghetto black and thus making boarding school history. We crossed the line on a broad reach at a stately 15 knots in a 12-knot nor'wester, hugging the whistler buoy to be as far from disapproving eyes on the committee boat as possible. The *Chariot* — two 32' x 2' wide hulls, held together by three 16-foot cross members of aluminum tubing — can be, if it breezes up, about as unobtrusive as the Roan Stallion at Sunnybrook Farm.

Sensitive to any charge of interference, we lurked at a distance, well to leeward to avoid back-winding anyone. On the last leg back to Manches-ter, the breeze freshened as we came nearer shore. So did the temptation to show off. But we held to a hand gallop. At Gale's Point, the finish, John T. Bethell, Bulletin editor, hailed us. He seemed disappointed we hadn't made good a winter-day promise to cross the line towing a topless balle-rina on skis.

Homing to Gloucester, whip-flicked by dark offshore gusts, we full-galloped the six-mile reach in twenty minutes. An ideal slant of wind for another of our solitary games — "chase the stink pot." This involves sneaking up on a wake-making power boat, busy with beer drinkers out of Lynn, then surfing past them on their very own wake and shouting "Hiya, baby!" Unnerving for the skipper if none aboard has spotted us coming from astern.

Here we give our crew the Buckminster Fuller treatment: "Those un-aware people are needlessly consuming our dwindling supply of fossil fuel, polluting the air, damaging their eardrums. To achieve relaxation, we need only use today's output of solar energy, mixed with a pinch of lunar gravity." Those familiar with his "Operating Manual for Spaceship Earth" know that Bucky just has to be pro-multi. The Fuller goal of greater performance per pound leaves the *Chariot,* at 1,400 pounds all up, way out front for hydrodynamic design efficiency.

Still and all, on long trips she was austere. On a reach home from Wareham, through the Cape Cod Canal, and across Massachusetts Bay to Gloucester, one gray sou'west day in August 1969, her dolphin-striker, a V-shaped strap of stainless steel affixed beneath the forward tube to take the thrust of the mast, was scooping gallons over the trampoline. Anne, my son, Phip, and his wife, Elizabeth, made up the crew. Every time we'd close-reach, the speed would rise to more than 15 knots, and for all but the helmsman, sitting far aft, the spray, as if from a firehose nozzle, drenched the luckless passengers. The 45-mile passage, with no land in sight, cooled even my enthusiasm for D-cat cruising.

"Never again," Anne announced. "We've got to have some shelter." She recalled the comforts of our March cruise in the Virgin Islands aboard Dick Newick's 38-foot trimaran *Trial.* Her two-berth main cabin and solid cockpit seemed utter luxury compared to the *Chariot.*

Launching of Trumpeter, *June 6, 1970, at Sandwich, Kent. The aluminum tubes eventually cracked from metal fatigue.* (Philip S. Weld)

We decided to fly to England in September, look into the Round Britain Race set for the coming June, and try to decide whether it was a cat or a tri we wanted for cruising. We'd become so doctrinaire the thought of a monohull never occurred to us.

California might consider itself the multihull day-sailing capital, but no question, or so I thought, the south of England was the center for offshore expertise. Here we'd find the men who had designed and built the oceangoing cats and tris that I'd read about in *Multihull International*. We began with Reg White at Sailcraft Ltd. in Brightlingsea. The foremost cat helmsman in the world, Reg built Tornados and the 30-foot Iroquois cruising cats that had done so well in the 1966 Round Britain. He suggested we get an Apache, a 40-foot version just designed by Rod MacAlpine Downie for Mike Butterfield, a London attorney, for which the mold was already finished.

"She'll be the boat to beat in the Round Britain," Reg said. "You can have the second one off the mold in time for the Crystal Trophy. It starts June tenth." We were tempted.

Next we drove to Sandwich in Kent to talk with Derek Kelsall. His trimaran *Toria* had won the 1966 Round Britain. As *Gancia Girl* (the British were on to beverage sponsors ahead of the French), she had done well in the 1968 OSTAR. His yard on the River Stour had pioneered big boat construction in fiberglass-and-foam sandwich. Here the conventional ketch *Sir Thomas Lipton*, the 1968 OSTAR winner, had been built for Geoffrey Williams.

"For the Round Britain, Derek, which should it be — cat or tri?"

"Tri, no question." Derek marshaled much the same arguments we'd heard from Dick Newick in St. Croix. Greater stability, equal speed, slightly better windward ability. Conceded to the cat: more living space for the same length.

We traveled to Poole in Dorset to go aboard *Trifle*, the 44-foot tri Derek had designed with General Ralph Farrant. In the 4-knot tide that swept past her mooring, she seemed to glide nervously about like a great swan feeding. Even without sail, she felt like the fastest boat in Britain, which she was. We flew back with Derek's sketch for a tri 40 feet on the waterline and capable of winning the Round Britain. To my question: "And would she be capable of crossing the Atlantic?" "Why certainly," said Derek, who after all had crossed in thirty-nine days in the 1966 OSTAR in his home-built Piver 34-footer.

Looking down on the Atlantic from the plane, with Derek's contract still to be signed in my pocket, I didn't yet believe I'd ever cross it in my own boat. But the voyaging urge was taking hold. The trip had tilted me to tris. As soon as I got home, I mailed a check to Kent and I was off on the intoxicating dalliance that was to keep me charged for more than ten years.

WHAT!
ANOTHER TRIMARAN?

Following the capsize of *Gulf Streamer* on April 27, 1976, I had many hours to brood upon the demerits of multihulls. *Trumpeter*, while great fun and beautiful to look at, had revealed structural weaknesses. To correct them had meant adding weight with extra tubes in the cross arms and these had slowed her down. *Gulf Streamer*, in the eyes of the world, had played me false no matter how much I protested that she was the victim of a fluke. Hadn't I had a bellyful of this multihull nonsense? Did you ever consider buying a proper boat? No one had quite the temerity to ask it, but this became the unspoken question.

I really tried to open my mind to the virtues of the ballasted boat. I sailed aboard some good ones: a Concordia yawl, Bob Derektor's *Wild Goose*, and a Marco Polo. I flew to Sausalito to consider buying the late George Kiskaddon's beautiful schooner *New World*. She had the speed the others lacked, but I could never single-hand her and this was a requisite.

Throughout the summer the agony was compounded by the disappearance of *Three Cheers*, another Newick tri, with Mike McMullen aboard, and by the torment his parents were suffering. Partly offsetting the dismay this loss occasioned were the triumphs of two 31-footers from Newick's drawing board: *Third Turtle*, skippered by Mike Birch, sailed to an astonishing OSTAR third place, and *Friends* to eighth by Walter Greene. These performances demonstrated, at least to my satisfaction, the seaworthiness of Newick trimarans.

Then, to focus my thinking, I drew up this table, weighting it rather in favor of monohulls:

HIGH-PERFORMANCE, OFF-SHORE
SAILING YACHTS COMPARED

The Buoyant Trimaran

FOR

1. Unballasted, hence unsinkable
2. Doesn't heel or roll, hence less tiring
3. Easier helming because of good downwind tracking
4. Shallow draft opens up cruising grounds and mooring areas
5. Light overall weight permits use of lighter gear, less sail area, smaller engines
6. Consistent speed permits small crews to make long passages in fewer days
7. Heaves to comfortably
8. Sprinting speed exhilarates

AGAINST

1. But it can capsize
2. Harder to find dock space
3. Harder to find a railway wide enough for hauling
4. Poor weight carriers so fewer amenities
5. Few chances to race
6. More costly to build
7. More difficult to resell
8. Still unaccepted by most establishments

The Ballasted Single Hull

FOR

1. Can survive 360-degree flip if well-designed
2. Easy to find docking
3. Easy to haul out
4. Less weight-sensitive
5. More room below for amenities
6. Much better racing
7. More builders to choose among
8. Better resale values
9. Accepted by establishments

AGAINST

1. Can sink — whales, collisions
2. Heeling and rolling can be fatiguing
3. Helming harder off the wind
4. Deeper draft denies some cruising areas, demands deeper moorings
5. Overall weight demands heavier gear for bigger headsails, more engine for powering in calms
6. Limited to hull speed unless manned for racing, means slower passages when short-handing

But in my heart, I knew it had to be yet another trimaran. Voyaging at speed becomes addictive. Once you've knocked off a week of 220-mile days, there's just no going back to a 150-mile average. L. Francis Herreshoff said it all: "The enjoyment of sailing is in direct ratio to the speed." Having seen the light in the eyes of friends aboard *Gulf Streamer* when the speed needle pushed 20 knots, how could I do other than re-create her?

Meade (left) and Jan Gougeon, two of the three brothers who built Rogue Wave. (Sanders of Bay City, Michigan)

But where to build? No boatyard in New England seemed either eager or ready to tackle the job. So Dick Newick and I flew to Bay City, Michigan, to talk to the Gougeons, and that's how we came to build, this time in wood. During the building of *Streamer*, Alan Vaitses had more than once bewailed the passing of the wooden yacht as a feasible alternative to the glass and foam sandwich — "the frozen snot" that Newick reminded me was the phrase his idol, L. Francis Herreshoff, used to describe fiberglass. The experts seemed to agree that wood is too expensive to maintain. Who was I to argue?

Then, as I beat the bushes from Maine to California for custom boat builders, the term "WEST system" kept recurring. "Wood epoxy-saturated technique" formed the acronym that Meade Gougeon had trademarked. He and brother Jan, a world-class iceboating champ, had attended the Multihull Symposium at Toronto in June where I had been asked to describe my capsize. We renewed acquaintance after the banquet but I was still too wedded to the thrifty notion of reusing the hull molds for *Streamer* to contemplate rebuilding in other than glass and Airex foam.

This fixation faded within two hours of entering the Gougeon shed on the Saginaw River. No matter the material. These were people with whom Dick could communicate by phone without the need for computer printouts filled with stress calculations. The shop exuded competence. If they liked wood, wood couldn't be all bad.

Having suffered through one-off gestations in Pasadena with the D-cat, in Kent with *Trumpeter*, and at Mattapoisett with *Streamer*, I have an inner radar screen that flashes warning blips upon my entering shops whose proprietors are clearly over their heads. No blips at Bay City. The floor was swept every noontime; power tools hung on orderly pegboards; competent secretaries were mailing customers' bills for resin orders on time. Over forty years in newspaper publishing had taught me to tell two minutes after entering a print shop whether or not it's solvent. Boat by boat, I was acquiring the same instinct for shipyards. This time it felt right. Within twenty-four hours we had our letter of agreement: Weld to buy all gear and materials, Gougeon's to supply all the labor. After 9,700 man-hours, the yard rate, including overhead and profit, would drop to just the out-of-pocket costs for labor. This way neither side could be hurt if things went slower than expected.

We had only one crisis and this was not of our making. In December, just when the two outriggers had been completed and the planking of the main hull had started, I had a call from Frank Page at the *Observer*. Had I heard that the OSTAR race committee had set a new upper-size limit of 56 feet overall? I exploded. The British race would lose its glamour to the French, now they were simply encouraging unsafe, little boats, I spluttered. We spent an agonizing weekend wondering if we could lop two feet off the bow and two feet off the stern to comply. Then a second call told us the maximum waterline length was to be 46 feet. There was no way to cut eleven feet out of the keel. I was destined to own a racer-cruiser, ideal for OSTAR competition but illegal.

Never mind. She'd do for the two-handed British races. I'd singlehand with the French. If I wished to enter the 1980 OSTAR, I'd have to build something smaller. At that moment *Moxie*'s birth was too remote to contemplate. I simply felt bitter disappointment that the race committee had overreacted to the timorous bureaucracy. I could sympathize with their having the spooks over Colas in *Club Med* ramming her 236 feet through a fisherman. But why a rule barring the boat in which Tabarly had just scored a magnificent victory?

Anne wets the stem of Rogue Wave, *Bay City, Michgan, August 6, 1977.* (Sanders of Bay City, Michigan)

Short of twelve months after lofting her lines, on August 6, 1977, a husky crane lifted *Rogue Wave* from the yard's slip-side lawn into the Saginaw. The interposed scale indicated she comprised 9,789 pounds of wood and glue. Meade and Jan had said the year before, after seeing Newick's penciled changes on the old plans for *Streamer*, that the new version in wood should weigh in "at something less than 10,000 pounds for the basic boat [i.e., at least 2,000 pounds less than the foam sandwich] and she'll be a lot stiffer."

"Stiff" to buoyant people means "of rigid structure," not in the sense of a heeler-keeler where stiffness means ability to weather gusts without tipping so soon and spilling wind prematurely from the sails. We sought stiffness that would prevent the main hull from curling up like a Persian slipper when the hydraulic ram tightened the backstay to reduce the sag in the jib's luff. From their own racing experience — going 70 miles per hour on a 35-pound iceboat on Lake Huron or ghosting to a win on their superlight trimaran at the One-of-a-Kind regatta in Florida — Meade and Jan knew better than anyone living how important it was to achieve lightness with strength.

Unlike your usual builder who takes on a tri with the suspicion that the client is as kooky as the design, the Gougeons understood why I wanted to go to sea again in *Streamer's* equivalent. Meade's office, part lab, gave me confidence in wood. Bits of ash, gaboon, and mahogany, coated in diverse epoxy resin mixes, soak in a small vat beneath his drawing board. In the corner, a hydraulic ram stands ready to measure the pounds of pressure required to break a sample. This was engineering I could understand.

During the winter and spring I visited Bay City six times to observe progress and to discuss slight modifications in Dick's revised drawings. Jan, then aged thirty-two, the shop foreman, directed a team of six to eight — Jim and Jim, Larry, Craig, Robert, Dan, Bill, and Tom — none of whom was as old as he. Craig, Jan, and Jim Gardner were building their own tris on weekends; Larry was rebuilding my old D-cat. They cared. Every bit and piece glued into the sculpture that was to become *Rogue Wave* showed the devotion of craftsmen seeking perfection. Meade estimated for Ty Knoy of the *Bay City Times* on the shakedown sail that the boat represented 50,000 to 70,000 pieces of wood of at least nine species. "That's a reconstituted forest," I said.

He explained that the WEST system, by keeping out the moisture, "encapsulating the wood surface by creating a barrier of epoxy through which no significant amount of air or water can pass," preserves the advantages of wood — stiffness, light weight, and resistance to fatigue — over all other boat-building materials.

Rogue's frames are of five-ply Brunzeel mahogany; the stringers (the mile of strips running the length of each hull at 18-inch intervals from keel to deck), of Sitka spruce; the double-diagonal cold-molded topsides, ¼-inch mahogany and five-ply gaboon; the keel, 6-inch-thick mahogany; cockpit sole, teak; bulkheads, fir; here and there birch or cedar have been used to fit the species to the task. There's even a strip of ebony on either side of the bottom of the daggerboard slot for extra hardness. Except for a few stainless screws here and there, the whole boat is held together with hundreds of thousands of bronze staples and gallons of epoxy glue. The RAF's Mosquito bombers were built this way in World War II.

Streamer's mast height had been established at 52 feet because the mainsail size this called for would be about the maximum I could lift alone even after it was neatly folded. Experience showed I could handle another four feet. Combined with an 18-inch longer boom, this would give us one-sixth more working sail area. To offset the added heeling

Rogue Wave *winning the 1978 Round the Isle of Wight Race.* (Beken of Cowes, Ltd.)

effect of a 56-foot mast, Dick extended the overall beam from 31 feet 6 inches to 33 feet.

The design of *Streamer's* cockpit had resulted in an unwanted notch in the center hull's main beam. This "weakened the girder" and reduced our ability to cinch down the backstay. In the altered design, the sheer, or main rib, stiffening the topsides of the central hull, formed one continuous plane the whole 60 feet from stem to transom. Meade predicted it would permit putting 5,000 pounds of tension on the headstay and Jan was forever saying "to win races you got to have headstay tension." This change so improved our ability to sail close to the wind, by reducing the sag in the luff of the jib, that we were able to tack inside 87 degrees true wind.

As for the lines, Dick provided more fullness in the after third of the main hull to support more payload on long voyages, and he added breadth in the main bow at the sheerline and gave a bluffer shape to the outrigger bows to provide more buoyancy in case we encounter another rogue wave.

Nothing like second-time-around to allow for greater convenience, safety, and damage control. Concerning the last, Dick settled on a brilliant rudder solution. The rudder-skeg combination pivots on a ⅞ths pin through the slot in the transom. A "break-away" piece of wood prevents the assembly from floating up. If we hit bottom hard, the rudder swings up, crushing the ¼-inch-thick holddown. To pull the rudder back down, there's a lanyard to lead to a winch. We carry spare crush planks.

Likewise with the main daggerboard. A replaceable crush box has been inserted behind the board to absorb the blow of grounding at speed. (Once after hitting a ledge, it took a diver with a pneumatic chisel to cut *Steamer's* board free from the aft lip of its slot.) To save weight, we chose to use a 50-pound centerboard in place of the 100-pound forward daggerboard that consumed much of the forepeak space on *Streamer*. A dividend is a roomier sail locker. Another bonus in stowage came by moving the rudder aft. Where all we had before was a heavy box, we now have a lazarette for the inflatable dinghy, docking lines, and fenders. Propane bottles for cooking now rest in the starboard, central cross arm. The change in cockpit design gave us four seat lockers for gear. It also made it possible to double the width of the aft cabin — from 4 feet 6 inches to 9 feet. Now Anne and I have a really wide double berth, our own offshore head, many cubic feet of dry, under-bunk recesses, and shelves for books galore.

To position sheet winches handy to the helm becomes a critical concern for the solo ocean racer. (Bill Lane)

Perhaps the most controversial improvement came with the "non-plumbing." While we must carry a portable head to be legal, we go ashore in marinas. For sea duty, we have our "all-purpose orifices." These oval holes, dimensioned as in the best back-country privy, hang over the water in the wings. One sits like Rodin's *Thinker*, stern bare to the breezes and high enough above the water to produce the bidet effect only in gales. The hoots of derision from land-oriented inspectors inspired by this non-apparatus have been drowned out by the happy exclamations of users: no odors, no plug-ups, nothing to clean. A modern miracle.

The non-sink, or "off-shore Disposall" also pierces the overhang. Near the two-burner stove, it's an eight-inch hole closed by a Benmar translucent port. Except in a seaway, it stays open for ventilation, food scraps, taking water temperature, you name it. It's ever so much easier to keep the galley clean than with the more fashionable two-compartment stainless sink. All hands help to wash dishes using buckets in the cockpit instead of leaving it to one slavey below.

On deck and aloft, rig and gear virtually duplicate *Streamer*'s well-tested arrangements. Winch locations aim at easy solo sailing. We improved the method for controlling the traveler car and we gave it a $1,400 titanium track, a luxury but worth every dollar because of the ease with which the car slides. We went from wire to rod shrouds and installed three hydraulic rams to control mast bend.

To sum up, *Rogue* is a stronger, lighter, stiffer vessel than her lost sister. Weighing 16 percent less with 16 percent more sail, she's faster and can point higher. Below decks the lustrous varnish sheen of her bulkheads caused Alan Vaitses to exclaim, "It's like being in a grand piano." The sounds of water on hull are far more restful, too.

"Tribute to Poseidon," our first choice for a name, seemed overly solemn. Anne came up with *Rogue Wave*. Charlton Ogburn, Jr., author of *The Marauders* and closest friend from my infantry days in Burma, said it all in a letter: "Naming the new boat *Rogue Wave* strikes me as marvelous — an impudent hand of friendship and forgiveness offered to old Neptune. I'm sure he'll roar with appreciative laughter."

With Jim Dirk, a key man in the construction, Anne's cousin Bayard Warren, and our grandson Arthur Hodges, we brought her through twenty-eight locks from the Great Lakes to the St. Lawrence. At Quebec, Anne and Arthur left and Jan came aboard to give himself a taste of saltwater cruising. We made such rapid time to Nova Scotia we had two days' leeway on our schedule. We used them to sail up through the

Bras d'Or Lakes. I said to Jan, as we passed north of Sable Island in the fog, "This should be good practice for us for the OSTAR." When we crossed the Gulf of Maine in a light sou'wester, we logged 75 miles in four hours. Anyone who can duplicate that in 1980 will probably win the race, I thought to myself.

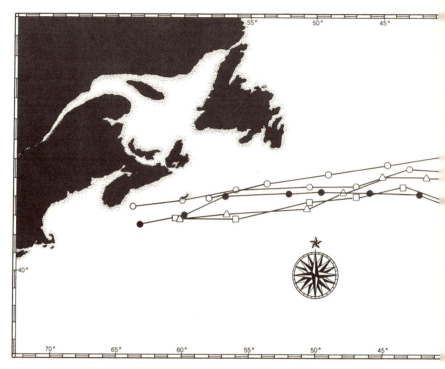

17

7:00 A.M. I woke up to agonized thoughts of *Spaniel*, whereabouts unknown because of his failed Argos, making hay upwind for Brenton Reef. In fact, with my navigational error, he may already be the silent, lurking leader. He eats up the headwinds that were giving us trouble yesterday going through that cold front. And with those three pirates on their trimarans, Birch, Greene, and Keig, three of the toughest competitors going, working themselves to the bone to close the gap on me, I don't for one minute feel this race is in the bag.

To compound the position problem, the circuit board for the speedometer-odometer went haywire last night. At midnight, just as I was taking a mileage reading, it jumped from 946 to 000. Then when I checked it at 0400 after my longest sleep of the trip, it had advanced only to 009 and quit. Fortunately I have a dial-type backup that I wired up to one of the batteries. It runs off the same through-hull impeller as the original. I'm feeling like the Boy Edison.

As soon as the sun had climbed to ten degrees above the horizon, I took the first of what I planned, if cloud cover permitted, as a series of sights, one hour apart, by which I could nail down where we are. As I was working the almanac and tables, the DROM beeped and blinked.

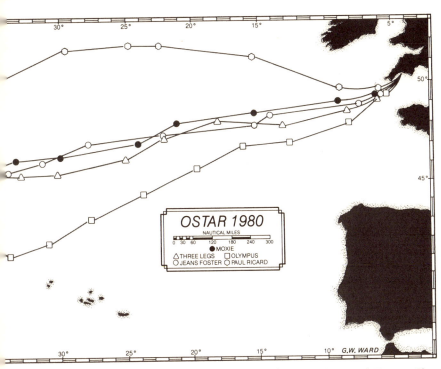

I hustled out to be greeted by the friendly orange shape of *Texaco Clipper.* Her radio officer gave me our position; 42° 37' north by 63° 36' west, 67 miles northeast of my DR and 357 miles to Newport. I asked him to report me to the New York Coast Guard as the BBC has been urging us all to do since the Argos failures multiplied. I forgot to correct the BBC prediction that we'd finish Monday.

(FROM THE FILM SOUND TRACK)

10:00. *Wish I had a crystal ball. Here we are sailing 320 degrees; the desired course is 277; that's a 43-degree difference. It's a tossup whether I'm better off on port or starboard tack.*

Here it is Sunday and for some crazy reason the BBC Sunday sportcaster doesn't mention the OSTAR. Monday through Saturday, it's faithful three times a day. Noon, late afternoon and evening. I've listened to American radio stations. Not a word. We don't exist. Strange because it's not a bad story — an aging Yank fighting it out to the finish against a young Yank, a Brit, a Canadian, and a Pole.

We're coming on to Georges Bank. If I were to tack, I'd be going 45 degrees away from the straight line to Newport. The wind is dead ahead. Freshening nicely now. We're doing 8 knots in about 10 knots of wind. Jaworski won't be doing much better, not as well in this light stuff. Oh, man, it's still a hoss race.

I can't think of anything different to do. I've got the jib drawing perfect. The main looks good. I can point up just a bit and foot just a little bit more, but it isn't necessarily getting me to Newport any quicker. Fascinating business. I could go up into the Gulf of Maine too far and get tanked.

1:00 P.M. It's too dern cold to take an outdoor bath but I'm going to give myself a shampoo on camera. My Route du Rhum performance made such a hit on French TV that I seem to be known as "Monsieur Shampoo-ing." I'll use this extra fresh water that I'd otherwise dump over the side to lighten load. We've got 20 gallons more than we need. . . . We've got warm water here . . . plenty of cold water . . . oh, boy, that feels good after two weeks of no shampoo. Whoosh! Wash all that salt right outa my hair. Ah, mmm, good . . . clean the saucepan too. Now for a final rinse.

7:00. The late Sunday BBC "Sports Roundup" said: "There seems no doubt the sixty-five-year-old American, Philip Weld in Moxie, will win the OSTAR. But a dramatic change to light headwinds will mean he will not arrive sooner than Tuesday A.M." Well, Moxie won't claim victory until she crosses the line. I remember too well the Round Britain in 1978 when Nick Keig came ghosting up in a flat calm and beat us out for second in the last hour. No word of Spaniel, of course, so I'm wary.

We're making 7 knots in less than 5 knots of wind thanks to my having changed to the light genoa. It raised our speed at least 2 knots. I only delayed making the shift for two hours. Generally speaking, my conscience is clear on shirking. I have tacked on every wind shift, mapped every weather forecast, trimmed sheets constantly, brought the board up and down to suit the wind angle; computed and recomputed the desired course (easy with the calculator); and changed head-

sails when I should. Tom would want to shoot me if I hadn't gotten out the light-air genny.

We're on soundings now. The fathometer is registering. Must be Brown's Bank. The moon's out. It's rosy in the west. Most lovely evening of the voyage. A fishing boat, the Kevin O., came up close to wave but failed to come on the VHF. I'd just cooked up another mess of eggs that Julia would be proud of. With toast from the last of the English bread, had a bit of mould to cut away, guava jelly, red wine, and some of Nick Clifton's sausage, none can say we don't have it good aboard here.

What do you bet Nick's off Bermuda now. It would be just like him to come up lickety split in that proa and beat me in to Newport. [I learned only at the finish that Nick had run on a floating timber, broken off his rudder, and capsized when caught aback. He was picked up promptly.]

WHY NAME HER MOXIE?

"Naming the new boat" has always been a family game. The P-cats, *Pegasus* and *Phaeton*, from the stable of Greek mythology; *Leonardo* for the Tornado catamaran; *Trumpeter* for the swan, fastest flying among all the birds of America, chosen quite coincidentally with the publication of E. B. White's delightful story of Louis, *The Trumpet of the Swan*; and *Poseidon's Chariot*, the D-cat, most literary of all. It was inspired by a passage from Robert Fitzgerald's translation of the *Iliad*:

> . . . into his chariot's shafts
> he backed his racing team with golden manes,
> . . . in laughter
> whitecaps parted, and the team full tilt
> airily drew unwetted the axle-tree . . .

During the 1973 Bermuda race, I'd chosen the name *Gulf Streamer* while crossing the Stream on an afternoon filled with rain squalls and deep blue sky. After the capsize, Anne exorcized the event by picking *Rogue Wave*. Each of our names has sought to express the boat's elemental force and beauty. So how come *Moxie* for the newest and most delicate of the lot? An abstract noun. Slang. A word unknown in Europe. A commercial product! There's the point. It came about like this.

I was sailing *Rogue Wave* to England in May 1978 with Allerton "Ats" Cushman and Michael Bryan-Brown. One afternoon Ats and I were

*Allerton "Ats" Cush-
man, who produced the
name "Moxie" while
crossing to England on
Rogue Wave in
May 1978.*

discussing my entry in the French solo race due to start November 6 from Saint-Malo for Guadeloupe.

"I'll be about the only guy in the Route du Rhum without a sponsor. I want to feel like one of the boys."

"So what will you name your new boat for the OSTAR?"

"Help me. Come up with a good name for a mock sponsor."

Ats pondered throughout his three-hour trick at the helm and greeted my return to the deck: "I've got your sponsor. MOXIE. It's got everything. Product. Double entendre. A synonym for courage."

He sold it to me then and there. We reminisced about the drugstore soda fountains of our youth where the bitter-tasting syrup of crushed gentian root was mixed with cracked ice and carbonated water, and sometimes served as a "Moxie float," with a scoop of vanilla ice cream. It outsold all soft drinks in New England. The Moxie-mobile visited Wareham every August, maneuvered by a man in a white coat riding a white metal horse which stood on a Pierce Arrow chassis.

"We'll revive the company," said Ats. "Issue stock. Big pr drive. T-shirts. The whole bit."

Back home from the Round Britain, I found in the clips at the *Boston Globe* that Moxie Industries, Inc. still lived. A new owner had bought the name and the formula and had moved the company from Needham, Massachusetts, to Atlanta. I called the office on Peachtree Street to ask President Frank Armstrong if there were any objection to my naming my new OSTAR entry "Moxie." The word came through Miss Carol Crouch, his friendly secretary, that it was okay. I was even promised a bottle of Moxie for the launching.

Then, to get in on the ground floor of a sure thing, I bought 1,100 shares over-the-counter at 3½. When a West German firm, big purveyors of bottled water and concentrated foods, gained control of the company, I wrote to Mr. Armstrong to suggest that if my *Moxie* brought credit to the name, a corporate contribution to the U.S. Olympic sailing effort would be welcome. His new European bosses, I imagined, knew how much money French sponsors — Paul Ricard, Dubonnet, Kriter, to name just three beverages — were paying to get their product names on ocean-racers' transoms. But no response.

No matter. I'd cast my vote in favor of commercial sponsorship. It's about the only way the youthful and impecunious can afford good boats for this sort of racing. If it works for golf and tennis, why not sailing, too? Besides, the name with a small *m* had made it into American dictionaries after Damon Runyon, in a 1923 short story, wrote of a losing welterweight who'd picked himself up off the floor: "He showed he had plenty of moxie." "The ability to face difficulty with spirit; pluck," says the dictionary.

Moxie comes through unmistakably on radio, especially in Maine, where every grocery store stocks it. The taped voice of Ted Williams, during Red Sox broadcasts over the Portland station, extols Moxie. Before sailing for France, I had printed on orange-tinted paper 500 leaflets reciting the message of the original label.

Distributing these in France, Britain, and Newport led to much hilarity. At La Trinité-sur-mer, I was interviewed on national radio about "my sponsor." I served swallows to the French press from "the only bottle of Moxie in the Common Market," which we'd freighted over in *Moxie*'s hold. They responded with appropriate grimaces and mentioned it in all their stories. My small shareholding became exaggerated to the point where I controlled the company so I could use the name. After the finish, *The New York Times*, the *Boston Globe*, the *Washington Post*, *Sports Illustrated*, *Figaro*, the *Observer*, the yachting journals of six nations, to name only a few, quoted the Moxie label. I doubt that a

Totally unjustified reaction to the flavor of "Beverage Moxie." Tom Benson, left, guardian of race headquarters at Newport. (Boston Globe)

MOXIE

Beverage Moxie Nerve Food
Contains not a drop of Medicine, Poison, Stimulant or Alcohol. But is a simple sugarcane-like plant grown near the Equator and farther south, was lately accidentally discovered by Lieut. Moxie and has proved itself to be the only harmless nerve food known that can recover brain and nervous exhaustion; loss of manhood, imbecility and helplessness. It has recovered paralysis, softening of the brain, locomotor ataxia, and insanity when caused by nervous exhaustion. It gives a durable solid strength, and makes you eat voraciously; takes away the tired, sleepy, lifeless feeling like magic, removes fatigue from mental and physical overwork at once, will not interfere with action of vegetable medicines.

Bottled Moxie, devised by Dr. Augustin Thompson of Union, Maine, in 1876, bore this label.

The leaflet we distributed by the hundreds before the OSTAR.

commercial product for which a boat had been named ever got more mentions in print and on the air in such a short time.

Mac Bell, my son-in-law, who owns a hi-fi and health-food store in Gloucester, The Glass Sailboat, had orange T-shirts printed showing *Moxie*, bow-on, across the chest and the old label in full on the back. All the family wore them at Newport to welcome me. When Mac got home, he called Atlanta to chide the ad manager for failure to exploit the Newport opportunity. This elicited a package of Moxie goodies via UPS: a Styrofoam clock painted with a wood grain, a golf cap, a belt buckle, a shoulder patch, and a ball-point pen. Finally there came a letter from Frank Armstrong, reproduced on page 192.

MOXIE INDUSTRIES, INC.
5775-B PEACHTREE DUNWOODY ROAD, N.E. • SUITE 110 • ATLANTA, GEORGIA 30342 • 404/256-4611
CABLE ADDRESS: MOXIE ATLANTA, GEORGIA — TWX 810-751-3582

July 21, 1980

Mr. Phillip Weld
Dolliversneck
Gloucester, Massachusetts 01930

Dear Phillip:

First, let me add my congratulations (along with the thousands of others you have already received) on your victory on the MOXIE.

Some of the comments in the news stories were, in fact, a fair represen-tation of the taste of Moxie. I guess our reaction is that "I don't care what you say about Moxie as long as you say it". You will be interested to know that we tried to change Moxie to a more palatable drink years ago and our sales in New England dropped about 50% until we put the old drink back. (The current drink.)

The reason I am writing to you, however, is that I noticed that you recently bought 1100 shares of Moxie stock and I wanted to thank you for this. We sincerely appreciate your trust and we are going to work very hard to make your Moxie equity grow.

Sincerely,

Frank Armstrong
Chairman of the Board

FAA/sm

Unfortunately for the growth of my equity, the stock has fallen to 2½. There's been no Olympic contribution forthcoming from Atlanta. Nonetheless, it has been a happy name; witness the gracious couplet in *The New Yorker*'s 1980 Christmas greetings by Roger Angell:

> Ring out, wild bells, from here to Biloxi
> For Philip Weld and the good ship Moxie!

18.

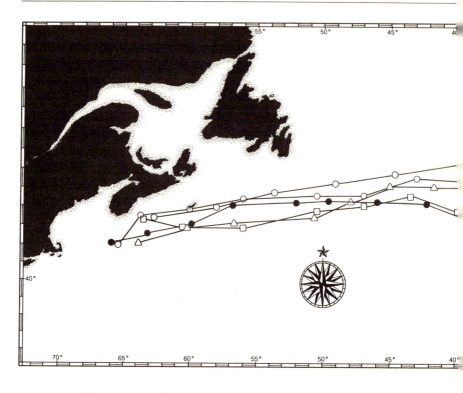

2:30 A.M. We just sailed past three fishing boats as I slept. At 4 knots, we wouldn't have hurt them much, but I should be more careful, I suppose.

7:30. A big trawler just dragged through our wake. New and handsome. She didn't respond to my VHF call.

12:00. The light genoa is a delight. The least riffle on the glassy surface and *Moxie* accelerates to between 6 and 8 knots.

Many excitements. The noise of a plane waked me from my morning nap. Canadian Air Force Number 96, on fisheries patrol, circled and buzzed, then came on the VHF to say they'd been told to watch for OSTAR competitors. To my nervous question as to how many they'd spotted, they replied, "You're the first today." Cryptic. I asked them to report my position to Newport and to add that I'd not likely be in before dark Tuesday.

At 9:30, I called home through the Yarmouth, Nova Scotia, marine operator. Even though I'd waited for the sunshine to raise the battery voltage from 8 to 11, I must have been on the edge of the set's range. Just when I'd learned that Anne had left yesterday afternoon for New-

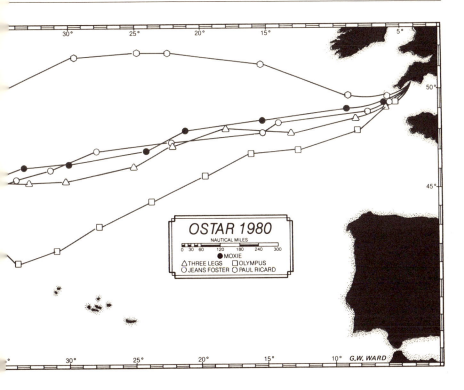

OSTAR 1980
NAUTICAL MILES
0 30 60   120   180   240   300
● MOXIE
△ THREE LEGS □ OLYMPUS
○ JEANS FOSTER ○ PAUL RICARD

G.W. WARD

port, the call "broke up" and I could no longer raise the operator. Even so I felt I'd made contact and it was thrilling. No doubt about it, modern communications have their merits.

After all this, a pod of whales just passed. Busy, busy neighborhood.

3:45 P.M. Panic on the block. I just overheard an arresting conversation between a fishing boat and a lone sailor. I could hear only the fisherman. "So you've sailed all the way from England . . . You're all alone . . . You say you're racing . . . well, good luck to you."

I've been calling around the VHF network trying to find out who it could be. I'm guessing it's Nick Keig, making time in this light air with his tall mast. I think the fisherman is the same one who was being told by a research vessel not to drag too close to a research buoy. This could be the same buoy I passed about 40 miles back. I feel threatened.

American Archer, on her way to England, gave me a detailed forecast, saying that this light southwesterly will persist through tonight. The low to the south is too far away to bring us much wind. Her radio operator, a sympathetic fifty-two-year-old who confided he used to drink beverage Moxie in his youth, tried to find out for me about the competition with no success. He knew all about the race because he'd sailed through the fleet coming westbound two weeks ago. I told him it made me edgy to have a rival so close.

"Well, don't get edgy," he said. "Anyone with your moxie is sure to get wind." That's the first-ever VHF recognition of our name.

He also gave me a position check. We're right on the latitude of Newport. It's now a question of when we should tack. Should we keep on to the south toward Bermuda where there's a low that might be bringing wind well to the north? This will be my strategy: sail on 240 degrees until Sankaty Light on Nantucket bears 330 degrees, then tack for Newport.

(FROM THE FILM SOUND TRACK)

5:15 P.M. *There can't be more than 5 knots of wind. Yet the boat's doing 7. The jib's setting fine, the main's fine. Nothing to throw overboard. I'll just have to sit here in yoga calm and hope to hell I'm not being caught. . . . I'll use the rest of the tea water for a Japanese facial . . . that feels good. I've been nervous as a burglar ever since I heard that solo sailor speak the fishing boat because it just has to be one of my buddies. Nick or Walter or Mike sneaking up in this calm weather, erasing my nice lead just as my nightmares have suggested for the last two years.*

Have I done something dumb? [Note: post-race examination with Bob Rice of the Bedford weather maps showed I was, at this moment, sitting in a "tiny bubble of a high" while those behind had a nice breeze. There was nothing I could have done about it.]

I must say it's like home to be back with Eldredge [holding up a copy of the New England Pilot]. *We'll be using these Pollock Rip tidal charts tomorrow to get past Nantucket in the best fashion. It's the New Englander's bible. I hope some of those sharpies behind me don't have it.*

Now let's turn to London for news of this race . . . "lack of wind is slowing down all the leaders . . . catching up with Philip Weld in Moxie." That broadcast was based on mid-morning information, I believe. It's not as up to date as the conversation I overheard. The BBC said Moxie still leads by 90 miles, Nick second with Mike and Walter close be-

*hind, the three of them no more than 12 miles apart. No
word of Jaworski. Paul Ricard an "unofficial" second.*

*They count on us all being in tomorrow. It's still one hel-
luva ball game. I don't think the race is anywhere near over.
I predict we'll have a photo finish in Newport and I'm not
sure I'm up to the excitement. As for the wind, who knows?
Russian roulette.*

MIRACULOUS COMMUNICATION

Moxie advanced down the track of reflected light from the setting
half-moon dead ahead. A golden cable drew her noiselessly to Newport
over the glassy sea. As I stood in the bow watching a school of dolphin
play "chicken" across the advance of her three bows, the only sound
from the ship was the hum from the air passing across the slit in the aft
side of the mast. I'd not heard this resonance before, perhaps because
the bustle of the water usually obscured it. The boat was truly going
faster than the wind — 5 to 6 knots in a breeze of 4 to 5. But so won-
derfully matched are her hulls to the surface of the sea that each snort
from our gamboling retinue sounded loud as a sneeze at a pause in a
concert.

I counted the lights of seven fishing vessels within two miles. Georges
Bank seemed too busy a place to be safe for sleeping until after daybreak. The best keep-awake entertainment for such a circumstance is to
eavesdrop on the VHF radio. I chose Channel 86, Nantucket Marine
Operator, who was handling a stream of fishing-fleet calls. They were
all short and to the point until Mike, a hand on a New Bedford dragger,
got through to his wife, Brenda, in Moorehead City, North Carolina. At
first I sensed a coolness between the two as if there may have been a
recent tiff to smooth over. But Mike asked all the right questions about
the kids and soon the airways warmed up with endearments inter-
changed between the customary transfer language of "roger and over."

Suddenly Brenda switched from this formalized jargon. The inter-
play began to sound like this: "Mike, I love you — come back."
"Brenda, I love you, too. Come back." The pace quickened. There'd be
lulls when the conversation would revert briefly to family matters. But
for most of fifteen minutes, on this still moonlit night over Georges
Bank, the all-male crews of the fishing fleet were treated to what I can
only describe as audio soft-porn, intercourse by shortwave. No one

197

among the queue of waiting callers broke in on the heavy breathing. It beat baseball scores on "The Voice of America."

"Where will you meet me, Mike? Come back."

"At the New Bedford dock, silly. Come back."

"Oh, I can't hardly wait, come back."

"Me, too, oh, oh — come back."

About then a pause allowed the marine operator to intervene. "If you're nearly through, it's just as well," came the flat Yankee voice. "There's quite a few waitin'."

"Oh, sorry about that," flashed back Mike. "Tell 'em I told you to put theirs on my credit card." Such are the marvels of modern communication.

Back in the days of *Trumpeter's* crossings, all we had for ship-to-ship communication was an oilcloth banner, eight feet long by three feet high, on which had been painted in large letters: "TRUMPETER — Please Report to Lloyd's." The technique was to tie the two right-hand corners to the windward backstay and, grasping the two left corners, stretch the banner taut as a ship passed.

It led to some wild deviations from our course as we attempted to intercept a ship overtaking us or coming toward us from the distance. The successes, except for three reports on the 1972 OSTAR when shipping had been alerted to the race, were so few that I submitted to progress and installed a VHF on *Gulf Streamer*. Few merchantmen have refused to pass along a message home provided I've made it clear they are to call "collect."

On the Route du Rhum, I went from the fifth to the twenty-first day of the race without contacting a ship. At least twice a day, I'd switch on Channel 16 to reiterate: "American sailing yacht *Rogue Wave* calling any ship that can read me. Wish to report my position to the Route du Rhum committee." Never a response till Sunday, November 26; then there came out of the air, "American yacht. Can we help you?" It was the Dutch ship *Farmzum*, en route to Brazil. I asked them to relay my position — 18° north by 56° west — to Lloyd's and then to give me theirs — 18° 23' north by 65° west. "But that's in the Virgin Islands," I protested. "That's 420 miles from here. It can't be."

But indeed we were both right. Two days from the finish a radio miracle had answered my prayers. The VHF line-of-sight signal had bounced off the ionosphere precisely right. My message reached Lloyd's who, by prearrangement, relayed it to David Cooksey in Scot-

David Cooksey, right, with the brothers Bryan-Brown, Mike and Nick, after Rogue Wave *finished first in a fleet of 750 yachts in the Round the Isle of Wight Race, June 1978.* (Jack Heming, Multihull International)

David Cooksey executes a bosunry chore, at Barra in the Hebrides, Round Britain, 1978. (Reg Allen)

land. David, twice my shipmate on the two-handed Round Britain, called Anne in Portland, Oregon, where she was visiting our daughter Helen. She was able to catch a plane to Miami and thence to Guadeloupe in time to greet me at the finish.

Late in the day, after I'd spoken to *Farmzum*, the VHF roused me from a nap. "Rock Wave. Rock Wave. Do you hear?" The Gallic rasp was unmistakably the voice of Olivier de Kersauson, calling from *Kriter IV*, the biggest trimaran in the race.

"This is *Rogue Wave*. Is that you, Olivier?"

"Where are you?"

I gave him my position and asked for his.

"I don't really know."

"Come on, Olivier. Of course you know." He had a $30,000 satellite navigation system aboard.

"Well, I am about . . . fifteen miles from you."

Two months later, Olivier and his beautiful bride, Caroline, took Anne and me to dinner at the most chic dining club in Paris. "Remember that night we talked on the radio? I called because, mysteriously, I felt you were so close I could smell you," said Olivier. "But, I lied to you. I was seventy-five miles behind you." We had laughs and many good drinks on that.

However, the miracle of VHF radio offers no help to the capsized. It needs the power of a storage battery. What's needed then is the hand-crank, emergency transmitter that World War II navy pilots called the "Gibson Girl." War-surplus stores once sold them cheap, but now their equivalents, items big passenger ships carry for each of their lifeboats, cost more than $5,000. It's the only way to talk on 500 megahertz, the frequency that ship's radio officers are required continuously to monitor. No one has been able to tell me why a yachter's model can't be marketed for much less.

To fill this communications gap in my armory of post-capsize goodies, I have packed in the calamity locker no less than three emergency radios. One is a battery-pack, portable VHF that has just enough strength to talk to a ship that I could see. A short conversation would exhaust the sixteen penlight batteries with which I replaced its factory-installed battery. This, I learned, depletes rapidly in storage. Second is a rescue beacon that transmits a beep on the aircraft frequencies and also lets you broadcast and receive voice on 2182, the ship-to-ship emergency frequency, as well as on the aircraft frequencies. Third is a $2,500 aircraft radio for the full range of interplane conversation. I've never tested it at sea. It's not legal for a boat to use it so I'd turn it on only to save a life.

Anyone in need of rescue who has been passed unwittingly by a ship shares my paranoia. What if capsize occurs in reaches of the ocean far from airways or shipping lanes? I equipped *Rogue Wave* with a longboat in the best Captain Bligh tradition. It's 16 feet long, weighs 80 pounds, complete with lateen sail and steering paddle, and fits snugly lashed to the after cabin. With blowup rubber tubes tied port and starboard, it won't capsize. If I got restive, and if I had drifted within 100 miles of land or a shipping lane, I'd have a way to go for help.

In one respect, Captain William Andrews of Beverly, Massachusetts, who sailed solo from Atlantic City to Spain in 1892 in his 15-foot, canvas-sided *Sapolio*, was better off than we moderns. His log records many close-aboard exchanges with sailing ships that couldn't keep to any lane, moved more slowly and posted lookouts. His voyage, celebrating the four hundredth anniversary of Columbus's discovery, was partially sponsored by the makers of the abrasive kitchen soap, Sapolio. To win the name attention, he dropped a trail of bottles enclosing a printed slip that described the boat and its mission and on which he'd record his position. This the finder was to "return by mail with the attached envelope." I know no more jaunty book on solo sailing than *Dangerous Voyages of Captain William Andrews*, edited by Richard Henderson, published by Abercrombie & Fitch, in 1966.

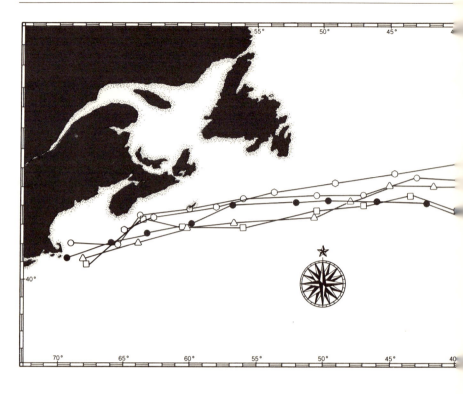

19

The pace of life became so hectic as *Moxie* approached her landfall that I had time only for the ship's log. I kept no journal, did no filming. From twenty-three hastily scrawled hourly entries, I've tried to reconstruct the day.

By 8:00 A.M. the wind had strengthened enough to require replacing the light genoa with the heavier working jib, a sweaty half-hour undertaking. At 8:45 the BBC announcer, in what for him were almost staccato tones, told of the resurrection of Phil Steggall among the race leaders. His *Jeans Foster*, originally called *Friends & Lovers* but later named for a French sponsor, was a seven-eighths'-rig close twin of Walter Greene's tri. Her tall, bendy mast made her, Walter said, the fastest light-air boat in the fleet. Because his Argos had failed, Phil had not surfaced in the news for ten days. Off the air, off my mind. I should have guessed he was the other side of the fisherman's conversation.

A hasty note shows: "within 100 miles — *Moxie*, Steggall, Keig; within 20 miles Steggall, Birch, Greene, fighting it out for Gypsy Moth trophy; *Paul Ricard* somewhere near; Jaworski in Halifax for repairs."

At 1:30 P.M., I called race headquarters in Newport and got Captain

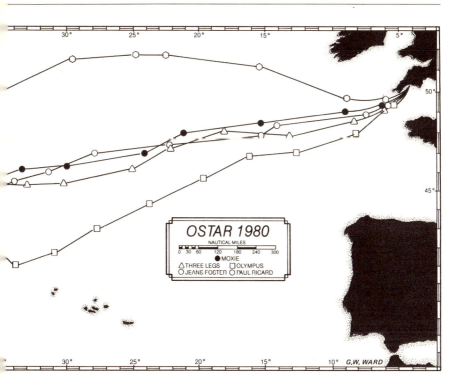

Terence Shaw, retired sailing secretary of the Royal Western and the Mr. Chips of the OSTAR, who had faithfully met us in his Boston whaler at so many Plymouth finishes. He told me the Europe 1 plane had been out all morning without seeing a competitor. I told him my arrival was at least fourteen hours away. At 3:00 a small plane buzzed us. The pilot waved. We were making 8 knots, on port tack, straight for Nantucket.

Haze reduced visibility to less than three miles. Now and then it would lift and I'd almost be sure I could see the gray line of the island's sandy shore. The fathometer read erratically from 20 to 60 feet. The sea's surface had the choppy turbulence of a tide rip. No question we were over The Shoals. By 5:00 the late afternoon sun blocked any chance of seeing the land at any distance. A golden haze concealed America. My DR plot showed us beyond where we should have found the Rose and Crown, the buoy I'd hoped to pick up that marks the northerly end of the shoals.

The freshening southwester carried *Moxie* along at a 10-knot clip, close-hauled, dangerously fast to be crossing these ominous-looking streaks of brown water that every so often bounced the fathometer down to single digits. A mile ahead I spotted a fisherman. I altered course slightly to the north to speak him. Rounding up suddenly under his stern, as I rolled up a loudly flogging jib, the flying-saucer-like spectacle of *Moxie* must have startled him. It took quite a bit of pantomime with the VHF mike clutched in my left hand, the wheel in my right, to get him to come on to Channel 16.

"American sailing yacht *Moxie* just over from England. Could you give me a position, please?"

"You're seven miles from Nantucket. About four miles west of the Rose and Crown." I think she was the *Anthony B.* out of New Bedford. I'd no time to write it down and I remember for sure only that she was dark brown.

"Could you give me a course for Newport?"

"You'd be smart to head south till you clear Davis shoal. Can be real nasty there. Then you'll be safe to head west for Noman's." (He said the name of the little island that flanks Martha's Vineyard to rhyme with yeoman's.) "Newport's just beyond." I thanked him profusely.

Then I raised the daggerboard as high as I could to reduce the danger of hitting the sands and hastened south for two hours at 10 knots along what the chart showed to be a sort of valley between two long fingers of the bottom. I sweated to think what might have happened had I run in too close and damaged the rudder. At 8:15 it was safe to tack for Newport. I'd been taking radio bearings of Nantucket Light vessel, Montauk, and Cape Cod, but I relied more on the look of the surface to guide my turn. When finally the menacing mix of waves at cross-purpose disappeared, I felt free to leave the helm and put in another call to Race HQ.

This time I heard the cheery British voice of Ruth Shaw, the other half of the vigilant watch team. "How many in?" I asked with pounding heart.

"You're the only one to call so far. We're counting on you to be first. Dick Newick's about to leave with Anne and your family to meet you with *Rogue Wave.*"

"Please try to persuade them to wait until first light. It's going to be a long night and I shan't possibly be in before dawn."

Ruth's words comforted me long enough to snatch soup and crackers and cheese and prepare for a nap by rolling in some jib. I really had to rest, having had no sleep for more than twenty-four hours. Landfalls made all alone can be tiring. Before putting my head down, I tried to raise Dick on the VHF. Instead I got *Aperture.*

"*Moxie,* this is *Aperture.* We're out here to take pictures for Hood Sails."

"*Aperture,* this is *Moxie.* Where's your man Phil Steggall?"

"Last we heard he was about five miles behind you."

I leaped on deck, barefoot for the first time the whole race. I hate bruised toes. Out spun the rolled jib. Speed picked up from 6 to 8. I tried hand-helming but kept drowsing off. I needed a nap. Placing the wind-up, one-hour timer under my ear, I lay down at 11:30. I slept right through its rattle and for two dreamless hours beyond.

When groggily I waked, I rushed on deck in nervous alarm. Had I blown the race? I recalled Odysseus' catastrophic approach to Ithaca and his later confession to Aeolus: "mischief aboard and nodding at the tiller . . . a damned drowse did for me." Was this to be the end of my tale? No. *Moxie,* like the faithful mount returning the drunken cowboy, had jogged along dead on course to the finish at a steady 6 to 7 knots. What a boat!

THE JOY OF SINGULARITY

After *Moxie* finished at Newport, various interviewers asked what I found to enjoy in the sport of single-handed ocean racing. The answer I'd been giving for ten years — "what better way at my age to get my name on the sports pages?" — had worn thin. I'd coined a couple of phrases during the race that I hoped would give my questioners something to chew on: "The Lindbergh Syndrome" and "The Joy of Singularity."

The first intended only to suggest the satisfaction of achieving success with painstaking preparation. Ten years of tuning four different boats, the tedious trial and error to select the right rig, the weather study — all of this reminded me of what "Lucky Lindy" (luck, my eye) had gone through to ready the *Spirit of St. Louis* for history's first solo transatlantic flight. Heaven forbid that anyone should think I was equating my little win with his epic feat.

"Singularity" takes more explaining. As a child in Dedham, I sought adventure on my Shetland pony, Bridget. We explored the trails of Rockweld daily. In spring, there was a corridor where blazing orange

With Shetland ponies, Midget and Bridget, Dedham, circa 1924.

Aboard Jessie, right, the chestnut mare who won me a place on the Cate School second Gymkhana Team, pictured here at Carpinteria, California, 1929.

azaleas bloomed on both sides and I could make believe we were escaping a forest fire at the gallop.

At thirteen I was sent for two years to the Cate School in Carpinteria, California. The idea was to interrupt my six years at Milton Academy and thereby gracefully drop a class. I was judged underage and undersize for the class I'd started in. Every one of the forty-seven boys at Cate owned a horse. We cared for them ourselves and used them for gymkhana sports and weekend camping trips. I bought a chestnut mare with $150 given me by my grandmother and named her Jessie because I liked the name.

As the only East Coast boy, it was natural I should join forces with the only Chicagoan, Dodge Freeman. We became the most zealous pair of trail riders in the school. The Californians, more blasé about western concepts, rode to the beach. We two would ride away into the hills every Friday afternoon and not return till Sunday evening chapel. In 1927 and 1928, the dam across the San Ysidro Valley had yet to be built. The area now under water gave us our wilderness only two hours from the school corrals. On long holiday treks, we led a packhorse and I learned after a fashion to throw a diamond hitch.

The yen to be "an explorer" surfaced again in college. I took a trip with Charlie Woodard on a succession of Grace Line steamers up and down the west coast of South America, stopping in Ecuador, Peru, and Chile. On our way home, a young man, Presley Norton, to whom we'd been given a letter of introduction, said: "How would you like to come back next summer and take a trip with me into the Ecuadorean Oriente? It's where the Jibaro Indians live. The ones who shrink human heads. On the headwaters of the Amazon." We made an instant deal. So it was in June 1935, my last college summer, that Eliot Dalton and I traveled steerage aboard the *Santa Cruz* to Guayaquil.

We were met by Perez Franco, half Indian, who wore a shrunken puppy head the size of a small walnut as a boutonniere in the lapel of his white starched suit. Norton had canceled coming with us for family reasons but he had recruited Franco to be our guide. "He's friends with all the Jibaros." We took a train to Cuenca, a bus to Gualaceo, horses from there over the 16,000-foot pass across the Andes to a clearing in the rain forest. There we met our five porters, short, smiling copper-skinned men with Dutch clips, skirts, very sharp machetes, and bamboo plugs through their earlobes. For the next five weeks we walked in mud except for three days when we rushed down the Rio Santiago-Zamora in hollow-log canoes till we were within a couple of days of

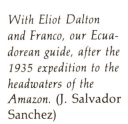

With Eliot Dalton and Franco, our Ecuadorean guide, after the 1935 expedition to the headwaters of the Amazon. (J. Salvador Sanchez)

Iquitos in Peru. Then came the long slog uphill on foot to our starting point. We ate rice, bananas, and monkey meat. The "expedition" proved nothing, but we had a glorious summer that cost about $500 apiece.

Now it's August 1943. I had volunteered a year before to enter the infantry as a private under a program for married men with children that promised honorable discharge if one failed to make it through officer candidate school at Fort Benning, Georgia. I'd made it. Wearing my new second lieutenant's bars, I was waiting at Camp Adair near Corvallis, Oregon, with the other officers and noncoms of the cadre, for what were termed "fillers" for the newly formed 70th Infantry Division. As weeks passed in feckless drills and barracks inspections without troops, I grew restive.

I had found a small sorority house to rent for the summer for Anne and our two children, Phip, five, and Eloise, four, but camp was far from town, the lease ran out with the opening of college, and we were getting desperate. One afternoon the word went out for all officers to report to regimental headquarters before supper. The adjutant read aloud a call for volunteers for "hazardous duty." It specified that those responding should hold three qualifications: experience in the jungle, knowledge of pack animals, and especially good health. It seemed made to order. In my application I cited, of course, my California pack trips and my Amazonian adventure.

When I got home to Anne, I told her the chance of my selection was so remote as not to require a thought. Three days later we were on our way to the port of embarkation at San Francisco. Only years later were we to learn the why of all the hurry. Churchill and Roosevelt had met in Quebec. General Wingate, famed for organizing long-range-penetration columns to operate behind Japanese lines, had been flown from Burma as a British prize exhibit. Intrigued, FDR wanted the American counterpart. Thus was born Merrill's Marauders. While the 70th went to Europe and the Battle of the Bulge, in which my old company commander was killed, I had an old-fashioned rifleman's war in northern Burma that prepared me well for marathon, ocean solo racing.

Whenever the wind speed begins to mount from 30 knots to 40, as the center of a black, foreboding low approaches, my mouth goes dry, my belly muscles tighten, and I forget where I laid down the ratcheting

With son Phip, Barrington, Illinois, 1941.

winch handle. The same symptoms appear that assailed us in Burma when it began to look as if a fire-fight with the enemy was inevitable. I've yet to meet a solo sailor who can honestly say he relishes the approach of a severe gale. I only knew one soldier, Sergeant Al Overby, my rifle platoon's best squad leader, who acted as if he enjoyed the excitement of dodging and returning enemy fire.

Shaduzup, March 28, 1944. A day and a place that, I hope, will forever mark my peak of fear. The routine rotation of risk had chanced to put my unit, 2d Platoon, White Combat Team, at the head of "A" Battalion's single-file column for the stealthy predawn fording of the Mogaung River. On its far bank, a Japanese regimental HQ of unknown strength had bivouacked athwart the main road to the front. My platoon's mission was to establish a roadblock to the north to prevent rein-

With Norman Page at a reunion of Merrill's Marauders in New Hampshire.

forcements from coming to help what we hoped would be the surprised garrison.

It seemed a reasonable plan except that the contour map on which it had been based failed to show a curve in the river just where my platoon had been told to dig in. It meant we had to cross the river a second time before reaching the road. Al and I, in the lead, found ourselves caught in the open riverbed when the shooting started to the south. Above us on the far bank, we could see Japs running to a gun position already alerted to our surprise attack.

My experience of enemy fire was far less than Al's. He had fought at Guadalcanal and had volunteered for this duty, like so many others, on the promise that after one dangerous mission he'd get home leave.

"Let's go, lootenant," he urged, sprinting for the protection of a three-foot-high mound of gravel straight toward the Japs. There he crouched low to pull off shot after shot from his bolt-action Springfield with seeming glee. That he seemed to be engaged in some mad athletic contest struck me forcibly. It did much to still my panic.

Charlton Ogburn's sensitive, accurate book, *The Marauders*, tells that morning's events in full. Of my platoon, Sergeant Olsen died in the

With Sad Sack, the twelve-year-old Kachin orphan who served in the headquarters unit of our Rangers' column, Northern Burma, 1945.

With U Pong, just named village head man, north of Mogok, Burma, 1945.

night of wounds, but Privates Norman Page and Milton Susnjer recovered from theirs. Al and I, though most exposed of all, escaped unscathed. Stilwell judged our battalion's end-run a success. We'd killed a lot of Japs but more important, we'd shamed into action the Chinese general whose regiments had been stalling for months.

That day has provided my solo sailing with perspective. Nothing on the ocean can possibly be as scary as those machine-gun bullets stitching a dotted line beside my feet as I lumbered up the friendly-side bank with Page slung over my shoulder.

Subsequent battles that year and the next, when I commanded a company of native Kachin Rangers, one of the behind-the-lines units of "Detachment 101" of OSS, taught me the value of icy composure in crisis. This schooling helped me greatly to cope with *Gulf Streamer*'s capsize in April 1976. There's usually more time to work out a problem than you imagine. Too hasty a response often makes for still worse trouble.

The infantry taught me other lessons useful to the solo racer such as how to get by happily on very little food, and that uncooked. On a forced march from Shaduzup to Inkangahtawng to relieve "C" Battalion, under siege, we went days without a supply drop by parachute. We had to stretch a K-ration, a packet meant to be one meal, to last us through a day's strenuous climbing. We had to hack our way along a ridge, dense with bamboo, for two days before finding a stream where we could refill our canteens. I used to trickle water into my inflatable pillow, which I'd then strap to my pack. Cups from this reserve could be traded for crackers.

Once you've been really hungry or thirsty for long periods, all other discomforts seem mild. On a well-planned voyage, there's no excuse to want for food or drink. The standard "half a gallon of water per man per day" leaves a margin for wash-ups.

Burma also trained me to snatch a nap on the trail-side during a ten-minute break. I can curl up like a hound dog on the cockpit seat, sleep for a quarter of an hour, then awake refreshed. Being old enough to have gone to war can be a help.

The army taught me that my temperament was better suited to small organizations where responsibility and authority could rest in the individual. Between the two Burma campaigns, I wrote Anne to say that we must aim to buy our own newspaper when the war was over. The idea that it was agreeable to be one's own proprietor was fostered as a "101" unit leader. At one period my company comprised seven different nationalities: Kachins, Karens, Shans, Nagas, Gurkhas, Sikhs, and Chinese. A dozen elephants carried the heavy stuff like mortar shells. It was not an organization for the people back at base to shove around with orders to do the impossible, nor did they try. They trusted us to do our best and we did, among other things, save the British 36th Division from a surprise flank attack north of Mogok that could have been costly.

After the OSTAR finish, I had a letter from Reed Stuart, my dormitory master at Milton Academy fifty-three years ago. "Entrepreneurial instinct was an element of the Weld psyche even then for I recall the partnership which you and Pete Keyes had for polishing shoes. The slogan, 'A better shine for five cents less,' must have been composed by you?" The Forbes House shoeshine concession taught me at the age of twelve the satisfaction from earning money. Pete, later the headmaster of the Westminster School, knew how to keep down the overhead by stretching the Meltonian Cream. Three hours with brush and cloth Saturday mornings from 4:00 to 7:00 filled our pockets with the silver of upper classmen. While our contemporaries made do with a movie, Pete and I bought orchestra seats for the Marilyn Miller musical trying out at the Colonial Theatre.

Another congratulatory note evoked college memories. From Robert Hall, College Park, Georgia, it said: "59 Plympton Street, a great group of men. I am so glad I was with you all in your young days. . . ." Bless his heart, but never was praise less deserved. Robert, tallest and handsomest of several young men from Roxbury who made their way providing little luxuries to affluent Harvard undergraduates, served as factotum of the "rat house" at 59 Plympton Street which eighteen of us sophomores had rented. In 1933, it was still de rigueur for the blades to live in such a rundown tenement rather than move into one of the new houses donated by Mr. Harkness. Roosevelt had brought repeal of Prohibition but the Volstead Act had left its mark. Mild intoxication was not a social breach but virtually a requirement of accepted behavior among the fashionable younger set.

Luckily for me, the law had damped my exuberance the first weekend of my freshman year. The proctor in Massachusetts Hall, then a dormitory, broke up our noisy Sunday evening party. My cousin Leverett Saltonstall Shaw and I rollicked down to the Square for a cooling milkshake. As we left "The Bick," Lev shook open a roll of peanuts. They scattered against the side of a police car just pulling up to the curb. Then, unfortunately giving to the scene the appearance of a junior riot, Lev straight-armed a No Parking sign and knocked it over.

Before we could blink, two Cambridge policemen were marching us down the sidewalk to the old Brattle Street jail, our arms in hammerlocks behind us, our "wait a minute" pleas ignored. All night the subway cars thundered out of the tunnel over our cell. We were driven in the Black Maria at 9:00 A.M. with three down-and-outs, also booked for drunk and disorderly, to Police Court. A probation officer lectured us on the evils of drink and sent us off to classes. About 4:00 P.M. I was walking up from the boathouse after my first tryout for the freshman crew, when I froze. An eight-column headline across the peach-colored front page of the *Boston American* read:

"2 of Senator's Kin Nabbed as Season Opens."

The Hearst stringer had been accurate and on the ball. But we had violated one of the two dicta passed down in those days by worldly upper classmen: "3 C's and a D and keep your name out of the papers." After several painful sessions, Dean Delmar Leighton ruled that because our jailing had occurred so early in our careers, we could be considered unusual enough to escape automatic expulsion. But it would be probation till graduation. This required attendance at every class. Never a cut. In a way, I got off to a good start. I never missed a lecture in four years.

More than once, as a publisher, I had to confront a parent beseeching me to leave out of the paper the name of a son involved with the law. I could honestly tell them: "Look, when I first went to jail Hearst splashed it all over page one. Best thing that ever happened to me."

An autobiographical account should include "life's darkest moment." In September 1945, the army discharged married men with children first. I wanted so much to get back to newspaper work, but in New England, not Chicago, that I grabbed an opening on the *Boston Herald* in the promotion department. Immediately I regretted not having stuck to the plan to be my own proprietor outlined to Anne in my letter from Assam. When Bernard MacQuaid, an old friend from the *Chicago Daily News*, took me to lunch to urge me to join him in starting a new daily paper in Manchester, New Hampshire, I hesitated only over the weekend before giving up my safe job.

Frank Lawlor, general manager of the *Lowell Sun*, for a fee of $1,000, prepared us a pro forma budget. It showed we needed to raise $300,000 to guarantee we could publish for eighteen months. Six months later we had pledges for $240,000, most of it from my family and old friends. Meantime, price controls had ended, the cost of newsprint had doubled, our budget no longer made sense, and I couldn't sleep for worry. So I resigned as president of New Hampshire Daily News, Inc.

My decision dismayed those who had signed on for the venture. Among them was an ebullient, rosy-cheeked, crew-cut ex-navy man, Ben Bradlee, eager to learn reporting. Another future investor-staffer, Blair Clark, asked me to talk with his financial adviser before finally defecting. "You're letting your friends down," argued this respected figure, an old friend of my parents. "Why, Bradlee has even bought a house up there. You're behaving like a shit."

I sat stunned. I could have argued that my terminal-leave money had run out; that I could not betray the trust of those who had pledged funds; that inflation had made our cost estimates obsolete. But the impact of that epithet had made my mouth too dry for speech. I left like a sleepwalker. I slumped down in the nearest seat, a shoeshine chair in the building's lobby. My knees were too weak to keep my feet firmly on the shoe rests. As the polishing rag snapped in annoyance, I made a vow. If ever again I went to raise money for a venture, it would not be from friends but from hard-boiled investors.

I talked my way into a job as "executive assistant" to the lawyer running the failing *Boston Post*, and for two years had a wonderful education in how not to run a newspaper. I discovered a 35-percent interest could be bought for $114,000 in the *Gloucester Daily Times*, a paper of 7,000 circulation published eight miles from our home in Essex. Borrowing some money from my mother and from my wife, and taking what my father had accumulated for me through wise investment, my total wealth, I plunged. Ed Hicken, the publisher, then seventy-two, kept his new minority stockholder at arm's length for two years, but he had to pay good dividends.

For three summers, 1949 to 1951, I published the *Cape Ann Summer Sun*, a free distribution weekly to serve the resort business. It only broke even but it introduced me to Roger W. Babson, Gloucester's wealthiest and most celebrated native son, and the most important man in my business career.

"This is Roger Babson," said the cheery voice. "Some boy has left fifty copies of your paper on my kitchen steps. I enjoy your fine paper but one copy is enough."

I hung up and ran for the yellow jeep with the sign "Make hay while the SUN shines." I doubled as route driver Thursday mornings so I was still wearing army suntans when I arrived at the back door of 12 Hovey Street. The tall, erect man with the trademark white goatee had just

With Paul Kenyon, editor of the Gloucester Daily Times, *1957.*

Dick Brooks, creator of the comic strip "The Jackson Twins" and a Gloucester native, enlivens the "open house" for the new Times *plant, October 1957. Paul Kenyon, right. (Charles Lowe)*

passed his seventy-fourth birthday in 1949. We sat in the kitchen while he cross-questioned me about my newspaper ambitions for an hour. He saw straight off that my *Times* stock, representing more than one third, put me in a strong position to gain control if I could raise the money to buy the remaining 64.6 percent.

There began a friendship that gave me a business education as well as access to the $300,000 loan which I needed to complete the purchase of the *Times* and its sister paper, the *Newburyport Daily News,* in January 1952. "You should own all the voting stock," he said to me in one of our early conversations. This surprised my Boston banking friends who admired his financial wizardry but warned me he'd drive a hard bargain.

"One great thing about a newspaper investment," I said to him. "It's virtually inflation-proof. You just raise ad rates or the price to the reader, or both, to offset the decline in the dollar."

"How about a convertible debenture with an interest rate linked to the newsstand price of the paper? You get three cents from the reader, you pay me three percent." It seemed fair so we went ahead but, thanks to my wise father, with a ceiling on the interest rate of 10 percent. In 1963, twelve years later, a copy of the *Gloucester Times* cost ten cents but by then the bonds had been retired. Their top rate was 7 percent. The whimsy of our arrangement appealed to him.

In 1963, he again lent me money with which to buy the *Beverly Times,* but this time it was on a mortgage at a fixed rate. Essex County News-

Alexander N. Stoddart, my publishing partner for nearly thirty years. (Marilyn S. Myett)

papers, Inc., had prospered. We bought the weekly *Peabody Times* in 1965 and the *Hampton* (New Hampshire) *Union* in 1974. Our enterprise had grown from fewer than 40 employees to more than 225. Then came the capsize in April 1976. Immersion for four and a half days in the Gulf Stream set me to asking what would have happened to my ownership of the papers if Bill and I hadn't been rescued. "To pay death duties, your widow would have had to sell them to the highest bidder," one adviser told me bluntly.

Alex Stoddart, my close friend and business partner for thirty years, agreed this could risk a disagreeable future for the loyal staff. The Jim Ottaway family, whose newspapers form a division of the Dow Jones Company, publishers of *The Wall Street Journal*, seemed to us the most congenial buyers. We sought them out, they liked what we had, we went no further. On February 23, 1978, we sold to them for $10 million. My conscience was clear to enter the Route du Rhum. My pocketbook was ready to take on building a smaller boat than *Rogue Wave* that would be eligible for the OSTAR.

Gloucester Times staff who were with the paper in 1952, when I bought it, gather after the announcement of the paper's sale in 1978. Irene Spinney, Marilyn Myett, John Enos, Everett Tyne, Leonard Davis, George Tobey, Eloise Weld Hodges, Ralph W. Gibbs, Alexander N. Stoddart. (Charles Lowe)

20.

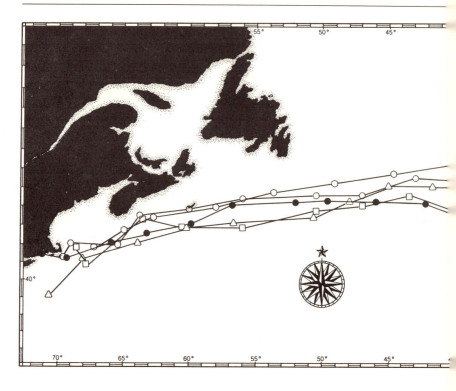

Winner's Delight

(FROM THE FILM SOUND TRACK)

6:30 A.M. *This is positively the last day of the race. We're just coming to the end of eighteen days and I don't know whether I'm leading or not. . . . The big new development yesterday was the appearance of* Jeans Foster *up among the leaders reported by a fishing vessel off Georges. That must have been the sailor I heard talking with a skipper. . . . Phil Steggall has to be among the best sailors in the world. He's got a great boat that he partly built himself, so more power to him.*

I'm deaf and blind as far as other news of the race goes because the batteries are way down and I can't even raise the weather on the VHF, let alone talk to anyone. Having the navigation lights on all last night really drained them. In another hour or two we should be raising Brenton Reef.

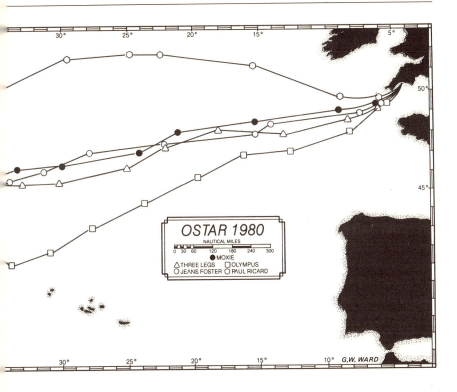

7:00. *Well, here's a plane circling me for better or worse. PRO, the Providence station, just said I was the only one to report in yesterday but that there were two or three others lurking out there. Sheee-it! I wish they'd stop lurking and report themselves.*

It's hard to know whether the race is over or not. Cripe, I don't know. Pretty exciting. All I know is I'm going to take off my Helly-Hansen underwear for the first time in eighteen days and, oh man, is it going to feel good. They say it's going to be record hot weather.

There's a flotilla coming up to greet us. I don't know whether they're going to tell me I'm second, third, or first. [Much background noise of muttering boat engines and shouts of "Hi, Phil!" and "Yea, Moxie!" can be heard.] I'll take a picture of them anyhow. Chris just came alongside. I showed him the big bag of film. Quite a flotilla has gathered as you can see. All pretty heady . . . [The last cassette concludes with the sound of many motors.]

(Photo by Georgiana Silk)

Each time I see the footage Chris shot from his whaler on the last eight miles to the finish, I get wet-eyed watching *Moxie* leap along through the wakes of the powerboats surrounding her. The French press boat had arrived first and it was my Belgian friend, Daniel Charles, calling out, "You are Number One, Phil," who had given me the word I'd been waiting to hear.

Soon *Rogue Wave* bore down on us out of the mist under full sail, looking every bit the stately big sister. A seeming swarm of orange T-shirted figures unfurled a twenty-foot-long orange banner lettered in blue with the message: "First is Beauty-Phil — Moxie Quenches your Phirst." No doubt it was foolhardy to trust so implicitly in the Autohelm when a sudden swerve on my part could have caused a collision. Nevertheless, the excitement had me rushing all over the boat. I dared to go to the stern to lash the American flag to the backstay. When the

Brenton Reef Tower showed through the fog, I went into the pulpit to take my own time crossing the line. But I was careful to wear my safety harness and to clip its tether to a jack line whenever I left the cockpit. This was no time to fall overboard, leaving *Moxie* to finish like a riderless steeplechaser.

Commodore Henry Williams, driving the Royal Western's whaler, ferried Anne across to the port-side net where I could pick her up for a trampoline bounce and a big kiss that landed us on front pages all over the world. Dick took us in tow while Chris filmed, Keith Taylor, covering for the *Boston Globe*, steered, and I gave an interview in French to Europe 1. (Listening in Brussels, my cousin Tootie Grosjean claims she could understand me.)

227

At the entrance to the inner harbor, the New York Yacht Club America's Cup selection committee came as a body to the rail of the official launch to give us a hats-off salute. When we arrived at the Goat Island marina, Ted Turner brought *Courageous* close alongside so Robbie Doyle of Hood Sails could lead his Twelve-Meter crew in hip-hip-horray. Meantime, TV teams and old newspaper friends thronged the float in such numbers that it submerged. Up to my knees in water as I "landed," I became concerned for all the wet shoes and even the hazard of the raft's capsizing.

"This is the most dangerous part of the voyage," I sang out, only half in jest.

Hasty hugs and kisses from the family contingents off both *Red Rover* and *Rogue;* the key to the city and pictorial tile from the mayor of Newport; a big bottle of Moxie from Larry Scahill; and a short drive to the

Sheraton for the press conference. I read off the tributes to Alain Colas
and Mike McMullen as an opener. It helped to have written them out
some days before. Amiable questions followed. I enjoyed every minute.
After years of being on the other end of the collective interview, it was
enormous fun to be the subject.

"AMERICAN CHALLENGE"

A French film company undertook to make a documentary of the Route du Rhum. The producer, Jean Paul Lovichi, brought his projector to our hotel room in Saint-Malo a week before the start to show us a super-8 cassette of Jean Yves Terlain sitting out a storm aboard *British Oxygen*, the big catamaran he had chartered. The boat was breaking apart. You could hear the sundered sections of the aluminum cross tubes grinding their teeth. It was to have been an episode in a film on the 1976 OSTAR that never got made. Lovichi wanted to try again, this time with cameras mounted on five boats, one of them *Rogue Wave*.

The excitement from the immediacy of a solo sailor filming himself in a frightening crisis impressed us. To participate seemed like one more way to heighten enjoyment of the race so I agreed to have a sound camera mounted in the cabin. It focused on the chart table over which hung a small microphone and floodlight. I was also given a waterproof camera for on-deck shots and three dozen film cassettes good for two and a half minutes' shooting.

Every other day I outlined a script that aimed to show my progress using charts as props. To add variety I tried stunts like giving myself a hot fresh-water bucket bath and shampoo on camera. The professionals got magnificent shots of the start and the final six minutes of the one-hour show had breathtaking views of Birch passing Malinowsky just before the finish to win by 98 seconds. But the on-board footage intended to sustain interest in the middle of the race proved disappointing. Equipment problems and lack of skipper interest on the other four boats left Lovichi to draw heavily on my antics to fill out the reel.

He invited Anne and me to Paris for the January Boat Show and the premiere. A preview on national TV had been seen by nearly everyone, it seemed. "Voilà, Monsieur Shampoo-ing" greeted us time and again. It all made for enough fun so that the underwriting of a documentary of the American effort in the 1980 OSTAR seemed a venture with a sporting chance of financial success. Everyone in the know warned me of the high risk, the one in a thousand chance of selling it to commercial TV, the slow trickle of revenues to be expected from public broadcasting, cable TV, and rentals. But none of this scared Chris Knight of the New Film Company in Boston, whose elegant documentaries on environmental issues gave me confidence he'd catch the special quality of the

Christopher Knight filming Moxie's *Newport landing. Jim Mesner with mike; Keith Taylor, editor of* Sail, *in white shirt. (Joyce Zino)*

race. Besides, he was a keen sailor who had twice sailed the Atlantic in his own boat.

Chris began shooting "American Challenge," his working title, in August with the launching of *Moxie.* He chased up and down the coast getting shots of Mike Birch, Walter Greene, Eric Loizeau, Rory Nugent, Tom Grossman, Judy Lawson, and Warren Luhrs building their boats, tuning their rigs, and talking about their motives for competing in this bizarre contest. To test the Plexiglas housing for keeping the on-deck cameras dry, he came down with his wife, Kathy, and son, Max, age three, to join Anne and me at Green Turtle Cay in the Bahamas to sail on *Moxie.*

All these preliminaries paid off when Chris and his filming team arrived in Plymouth two weeks before the start. The skippers trusted him as a knowledgeable sailor who would not place his cameras where they could bother the management of the ship. His final selection of boats comprised four tris: Bill Homewood's, Walter Greene's, Tom Grossman's, and mine; and four monohulls: Judy Lawson's, Jerry Cartwright's, Warren Luhrs's, and Francis Stokes's, all Americans by design. Everyone produced usable footage for the final editing. Only Tom's on-board cameras failed, possibly the result of his collision at the start and resulting scramble.

Chris had fitted the cameras with electronic timers so that they would switch on just after dawn and shoot every four daylight hours thereafter for thirty seconds even if the skipper forgot to do his duty. When a cassette ran out, a tweeter sounded periodic warnings to reload. We came to regard the cameras as more comfort than nuisance, a presence to whom to report progress, frustration, and glee. Walter confided at the finish that the automatic feature had bothered him, too much like "Big Brother," so he fixed his to operate only upon his command.

In October, we had a skippers' party at Dolliver's Neck to show the best of the on-board footage that was not going to make it through Chris's final editing, a painstaking process by which he had had to reduce thirty hours to fifty-seven minutes. At least for those of us in the inner circle it made for five hours of often hilarious entertainment. A high point occurred when Francis Stokes was stopped by the U.S. Coast Guard 200 miles from Newport, ostensibly for a safety inspection, probably for a smuggling check. Suddenly, after many minutes of *Mooneshine's* cockpit solely inhabited by Francis, we see him talking to three men in dark blue uniforms. There follows a shot of Francis alone saying: "Nice fellas. They've handed me a warning saying one of my navigation lights isn't working and that I have an inoperative sanitary device. I wonder what it cost the taxpayers to have this message delivered."

I had tried but failed to immortalize a sight gag that I hoped would be worthy of Joe "Wanna Buy a Duck?" Penner. It was suggested by a talk on the eve of the race with Martin Read while recalling our seasickness when crossing the Bay of Biscay in 1970. He remembered that we had traced the cause to rusting cans of stove gas that had leaked into the bilge. About three days into this race, I felt queasy and traced an equally sick-making odor to a sack of leeks I'd bought in the Plymouth market to go with my steaks. Propane cylinder in the palm of the left hand; decomposing leeks dangling from my right, I went into rehearsal. I had all the right props to lead into the punch line: "Leaky gas or gassy leek. It donna matter. Both make-a you seek." Somehow I couldn't get the timing right to make it to the silver screen.

As this book goes to press it's still too early to tell whether the film will be a financial break-even. But its critical success has been assured by the reception it has won at dozens of benefit showings.* We hope it will flush out some sponsor money for some of the young and impecunious aspirants for future short-handed racing. We believe it will build interest in this sort of sailing among the yachting enthusiasts who will see it at their clubs. It has to have enhanced Chris Knight's reputation as a documentary filmmaker.

---

* At press time, we learned that "American Challenge" will be shown on CBS cable television. It can be rented in 16 mm or bought as a video cassette from the New Film Company Incorporated, 331 Newbury Street, Boston, Massachusetts 02115 (telephone [617] 437–1323).

21

WHERE DO WE GO FROM HERE?

New Englanders, born and raised in the Calvinist tradition, share a quaint weakness. They like to imagine their pleasures are not altogether selfish; that from joyous moments some benefit may trickle down. My self-indulgence for a decade has been four costly trimarans of little utility save for crossing oceans at speed. It eases my conscience to believe that they might have contributed to a better understanding of how to use the wind as an oil-saving source of energy.

So far, the only commercial cargo I can claim ever to have carried was a dozen massive wooden sculptures carved from chunks of St. Croix timber by my friend Arbie Kenny. Son of my closest confidant, author Herbert A. Kenny, Arbie had twice brightened my crossings from Gloucester to Plymouth with his lively wit. To join *Gulf Streamer* for a trip north to Gloucester from St. Martin, he chartered a plane to carry from St. Croix his winter's production — 500 pounds of life-size

With "Arbie" Kenny, sculptor shipmate, en route to England aboard Gulf Streamer, *May 1974.* (Tom Perkins)

heads and child-size statuettes. We stowed them under the after bunk and up in the forepeak. It gave us a sense of accomplishment to be smuggling such exotic freight.

In July 1974, at Lowestoft after the fourth leg of the Round Britain race, Alain Colas joined Mike McMullen and me for a steak dinner in a seaside hotel to discuss the next OSTAR. Alain divulged his grand plan to raise a million dollars to build an enormous schooner. The boldness of his concept left me with only enough breath to ask how he would get the money.

"This will be more than just another racing boat," he answered. "We shall demonstrate the efficiency of a modern sailing rig for ocean commerce. Such a big boat sailed by one man will say something serious to the world."

Both Mike and I were moved by the nobility of his plan. That we three never could pursue the discussion has been a great sadness. First, I capsized en route to the start of the 1976 OSTAR. Then Mike lost his life on that race. At Newport, I went aboard *Club Méditerranée* to offer Alain solace in his disappointment at finishing second to Eric Tabarly. It was no moment to talk of his long-range dream of cargo sail. But had he won, paid off his debts, and been able to show the world how fast this boat could carry passengers or freight with but a handful of crew, the cause of commercial sail might have advanced by years. Alain and his trimaran, now named *Manureva*, disappeared on the Route du Rhum.

As the only survivor of our trio, it's up to me to push the cause. I have tried in various small ways. I backed the building of *SIB* (for "Small is Beautiful"), a simple trimaran designed by Dick Newick and Jim Brown for third-world fishermen. I also invested in U. S. Windpower, Inc., a Massachusetts company newly formed to build 50-kilowatt windmills, which is to say "medium-size." They will stand in arrays of 500 to 1,000 on California mountain passes to generate electricity that will flow directly into the power grid of the big utility companies.

On a chill afternoon in November 1980, I stood with other U. S. Windpower stockholders on the backbone of Crotched Mountain, a 1,000-foot rise in the southern New Hampshire hills. We had climbed there to view the world's first "windmill farm" for the generation of electricity. A research and development array of twenty steel-tube towers, 60 feet tall, supporting 40-kilowatt horizontal axis windmills with a wingspread of 40 feet, had been put up in just a month. A 12-knot breeze set the blades in motion and sent a thrill down my spine. Each unit pumps the energy equivalent of a barrel of oil a day. At 7.5 cents a kilowatt-hour, each will repay its $30,000 installed cost in three to four years. Maintenance is simple. The fuel costs nothing.

A new nuclear or coal plant requires an investment of $4,000 per kilowatt. Norman Moore, the ebullient sixty-three-year-old Californian, who came out of retirement to head up U. S. Windpower, says he can provide a kilowatt for $2,000. He enjoys telling how "six million windmills, each weighing less than a Toyota sedan, and of much less complexity, fewer than one year's U.S. auto output, could replace all the energy we get from imported oil." His evangelism appeals to me.

In August 1979, soon after I launched *Moxie*, I met Lloyd Bergeson, another enthusiast for saving oil. His way was to put sails back on ships. Like Moore, Bergeson had degrees from the Massachusetts Insti-

tute of Technology. Both men had successful business careers behind them to prove they could contain their dreams in the hard net of economic stringency.

Bergeson knows that to attract investors to put money into sail-assist units for commercial ships, he must have a story as attractive as Norman Moore's. They're really working the same side of the street, using windpower to save oil. Bergeson is no gold-earring romantic who sees himself on a square-rigger ordering men up to the ratlines to douse the royals. He built the *Nautilus*, the first nuclear-powered submarine. From this experience, he acquired a fear of nuclear power plants. Unless they are supervised with taut navy discipline, unlikely in a civilian world, he regards them as unsafe. Before the 1973 OPEC crisis, he saw the need to create the LNG (liquid natural gas) fleet. His shipyard built the first of these giant carriers with the bulbous decks.

A keen yachtsman, he took the summer of 1978 to sail his classic Herreshoff sloop single-handed across the Atlantic to visit cousins in Norway. While making that passage, he decided to devote the next chapter of his career to investigating the practicability of reviving commercial sail. Arabian crude oil had already climbed to $30 a barrel when I volunteered to help establish Windship Development Corporation, Inc. It signed a $140,000 contract with the Maritime Administration in Washington (MARAD) to present "the technical and economic rationale for utilizing wind propulsion systems for commercial shipping."

On *Moxie's* eighteen-day sprint to victory in the OSTAR, I savored my investments in Windpower and Windship. I seemed to be getting one good break after another from the weather. I convinced myself that by making these commitments, I had gained special favor with Aeolus. I also reflected that here I was, at sixty-five, making a record westbound passage with no great demand for physical effort. Modern gear, such as my roll-into-the-mast Stoway mainsail and by autopilot powered by batteries charged by photovoltaic displays, provided a metaphor for modern seafaring that should be inspirational, or so I thought.

"If we win," I vowed out loud to *Moxie* more than once, "we'll make 'em listen." I planned to use my moment in the limelight to push the cause of windpower.

Alas, so far I've proved ineffective. Candace Hasey, wearing a cute raspberry-colored sweater, interviewed me the afternoon of the finish at Newport for ABC's "Good Morning America." At my behest, she steered the conversation around to *Moxie's* "good relationship" with Aeolus and my belief in windpower. Two days later, in New York, Tom Brokaw concluded my appearance on NBC's "Today" show with a leading question on sail power. To push the cause, I even submitted to the indignity of appearing with two "imposters" on "To Tell the Truth." All to no profit.

Response has come from youthful romanticists as far away as New Zealand. Many wish to make a living sailing 90-foot schooners in interisland trade in the Pacific. While I wish them well, they will not significantly reduce demand for the planet's precious oil supply. The Bergeson report for MARAD may do just that. Entitled "Wind Propulsion for Ships of the American Merchant Marine," it was submitted after a year's hard work by the Windship team, four brilliant young graduates of MIT in ocean engineering and a pair of old-pro naval architects lured out of retirement to help the cause.

Their work will cool the nostalgic who long for the days when clippers plowed the seas under clouds of canvas. It virtually rules out ships powered by sail alone as too demanding of manpower. It calculates that bulk cargo carriers between 3,000 and 20,000 deadweight tons can be economically provided with wind-assisted propulsion. The smallest vessels in this range could use "cat" rigs with soft sails up to 3,000 square feet in area.

Solid wing sails that could be angled by remote control from the bridge emerge on all counts as the most efficient rig for larger sizes. Ships bigger than 20,000 tons employ engines that become relatively less costly as their power increases. But the bigger the sailing rig the relatively more costly. Hence the upper size limit on sail assistance.

A new 20,000-ton freighter carrying five wing sails with an area a bit less than 30,000 square feet provides the conceptual design for this cost analysis. The investment in the five spars, rising 171 feet above the waterline, and in the gear to rotate them would be no greater than the money that could be saved by equipping the ship with a smaller motor. Windpower will have been substituted for horsepower. The fuel savings in a year's voyaging between, for example, New York and Le Havre, would be 20 to 25 percent, or $300,000, with oil at $32 per barrel. This represents something like 7 percent of total operating costs.

In a summary statement, the report says: "International bunkers presently consume at least 3% of the world petroleum supply. Based on international bunkers only, the world's fleet presently consumes 730 million barrels annually at an average cost or $32/bbl. or $23.4 billion per year."

The figures assume remote control of the wing sails' trim from the bridge with electric-powered devices simple enough so that the normal crew could maintain them. Question: will such a manning plan be received with enthusiasm by officers and crew? Only a working prototype can give the answer.

Working prototype? What an idea! The Royal Western has now raised the upper size limit for the 1984 OSTAR back up to 60 feet. *Rogue Wave* becomes eligible. Harried by the worry of owning two big tris, I have given *Moxie* to the U.S. Naval Academy at Annapolis for the midshipmen's sailing program.

Meantime, back in Bay City, Michigan, the Gougeon Brothers have become the world's leading builders of 60-foot-long windmill blades. On a contract over the past four years with the Department of Energy, they have proved that WEST-system-treated wood stands stress better than aluminum. The techniques they have perfected apply nicely to the fabrication of wing masts so they have not had to neglect their love for fast sailing.

Jan has built himself a new, 25-foot tri to replace *Flicka*, which he capsized and lost sailing back from Bermuda on his OSTAR qualifying 500-miler in June 1979. It carries a swiveling, unstayed wing mast. Its buoyancy will prevent the boat from capsizing beyond 90 degrees so that Jan can attempt self-righting should he have need to. Weekends he and Meade experiment with a main whose full-length battens will be flexible fiber rods, thrust into pockets every three inches, to achieve a perfect aerodynamic foil. As the sail is lowered, it will roll up inside a boxlike boom. It's the Stoway mast principle gone horizontal. It allows easier access if the cloth jams. In a gale, the weight of the furled sail would be nearer to the deck.

"Would it work on *Rogue?*" I asked Meade over the phone.

"Why not? With a wing mast, there's no need for headsails once the wind gets up to ten knots. It would be the ultimate geriatric rig," said Meade. Right away I called Dick Newick.

"Sure, it would work," said Dick. "It should make *Rogue* considerably faster. Now if we were to add foils to the outriggers . . ."

Wind energy. Save the world. Cargo-carrying sail power. Wing mast. Still easier short-handing. No longer a "sexagenarian competent," as one French headline labeled me, it could be: "Septuagenarian braves OSTAR with revolutionary rig." Perhaps, Aeolus, it's too soon to hang up my Top-Siders.

Finishing Order of OSTAR 1980.

Place	Skipper	Nation	Yacht	Class	Time Taken
1	Phil Weld	U.S.A.	*Moxie*	P	17 23 12
2	Nick Keig	Britain	*Three Legs of Mann III*	P	18 06 04
3	Philip Steggall	U.S.A.	*Jeans Foster*	G	18 06 45
4	Mike Birch	Canada	*Olympus Photo*	P	18 07 15
5	Walter Greene	U.S.A.	*Chaussettes Olympia*	G	18 17 29
6	Kazimierz Jaworski	Poland	*Spaniel II*	P	19 13 25
7	Edoardo Austoni	Italy	*Chica Boba II*	P	20 02 30
8	Daniel Gilard	France	*Brittany Ferries*	G	21 00 09*
9	Richard Konkolski	Czechoslovakia	*Nike II*	G	21 06 21
10	Tom Grossman	U.S.A.	*Kriter VII*	P	21 08 01*
11	Wolfgang Wanders	Germany	*Stadt Krefeld*	G	21 14 22
12	Gustaaf Versluys	Belgium	*Tyfoon VI*	G	21 15 01
13	Alain Labbe	France	*Hydrofolie*	G	21 16 41
14	Olivier de Kersauson	France	*Kriter VI*	P	21 20 30*
15	Pierre Sicouri	Italy	*Gui IV Fila*	P	22 02 34
16	Rob James	Britain	*Boatfile*	G	22 22 55
17	Denis Gliksman	France	*France Loisirs*	G	23 10 00
18	Bertie Reed	South Africa	*Voortrekker*	P	23 12 42
19	Eugene Riguidel	France	*VSD*	P	24 01 27*
20	Philippe Fournier	Switzerland	*Haute Nendaz*	G	24 03 05
21	Jean-Pierre Millet	France	*Open Space*	P	25 01 05
22	Victor Sagi	Spain	*Garuda*	P	25 08 23
23	Francis Stokes	U.S.A.	*Mooneshine*	G	25 14 07
24	Dame Naomi James	New Zealand	*Kriter Lady*	P	25 19 12
25	Bill Homewood	U.S.A.	*The Third Turtle*	G	25 20 13
26	Robert Bocinsky	U.S.A.	*Ambergris*	G	26 00 39
27	Jean-Jacques Jaouen	France	*Les Menuires*	G	26 15 21
28	Jerzy Rakowicz	Poland	*Spaniel*	G	26 19 29
29	Jerry Cartwright	U.S.A.	*Le First*	J	26 22 55
30	John Chaundy	Britain	*Free Newspapers*	J	28 00 56
31	Bill Doelger	U.S.A.	*Edith*	G	28 04 10
32	Uno Hylen	Sweden	*Yoldia*	G	28 05 48
33	Desmond Hampton	Britain	*Wild Rival*	G	28 13 44
34	John Charnley	Britain	*Atlantic Harp*	G	29 06 21
35	Ian Radford	Britain	*Jubulisiwe*	J	30 14 38
36	John Oswald	Britain	*Basildon Moonshadow*	G	30 15 30
37	Oscar Debra	Belgium	*Crumpy Nut*	G	30 16 32
38	Richard Clifford	Britain	*Warrior Shamaal*	G	30 16 45
39	Henk Jukkema	Holland	*Victoria*	J	30 18 02
40	Chris Smith	Britain	*Sadler Bluejacket*	J	30 19 20
41	Chris Butler	Britain	*Achillea*	J	30 20 49
42	Kees Roemers	Holland	*Bollemaat IV*	G	30 21 24
43	Angus Primrose	Britain	*Demon of Hamble*	G	30 23 08
44	Roger Forkert	U.S.A.	*Parisien Liberé*	G	31 10 43
45	Guy Bernardin	France	*Ratso II*	G	31 11 45
46	Jim Kyle	U.S.A.	*Dream Weaver*	J	31 23 05
47	Alain Veyron	France	*Cat Marine*	J	32 02 50
48	Don Clark	Britain	*Abacus*	G	32 07 17
49	Thomas Gochberg	U.S.A.	*Mistral*	G	32 18 35
50	Luis Tonizzo	U.S.A.	*Egret*	J	33 05 25
51	Nikolai Djambazov	Bulgaria	*Tangra*	G	34 10 53

Place	Skipper	Nation	Yacht	Class	Time Taken
52	**Wytze van der Zee**	Holland	*Black Pearl*	G	35 11 20
53	**Jose Ugarte**	Spain	*Northwind*	G	36 06 43
54	**Hank van de Weg**	Holland	*Tjisje*	J	36 22 22
55	**Paul Rodgers**	Britain	*Christian Saul II*	G	37 03 11
56	**Wolfgang Quix**	Germany	*Jeantex*	J	38 03 02
57	**Giampaolo Venturin**	Italy	*Cecco*	J	38 08 55
58	**Juan Guiu**	Spain	*Crisan*	G	38 13 43
59	**Jan Verwoerd**	Holland	*Seagull II*	J	38 17 00
60	**Bob Lush**	Canada	*Olympus Sailing*	J	39 01 46
61	**Tony Lush**	U.S.A.	*One Hand Clapping II*	J	39 06 56
62	**Andre de Jong**	Holland	*La Peligrosa*	J	39 16 55
63	**Bob Lengyel**	U.S.A.	*Prodigal*	J	40 06 09
64	**Tom Ryan**	U.S.A.	*Peggy*	G	40 20 16*
65	**Ernest Sonne**	U.S.A.	*Elbe*	G	41 10 45
66	**John Hunt**	U.S.A.	*Crystal Catfish III*	J	41 13 18
67	**John Beharrell**	Britain	*Miscin*	G	42 16 00
68	**Beppe Panada**	Italy	*Mu Lat*	P	42 18 20*
69	**Per Mustelin**	Finland	*Mare Atlantic*	J	42 23 34
70	**William Wallace**	U.S.A.	*Novia*	J	44 10 42
71	**Martin Wills**	Britain	*Casper*	J	46 13 52*
72	**Burg Veenemans**	Holland	*Pytheas II*	P	49 08 16*

* Includes time penalty

Old Navy Lights (Antonios Vassiliades, Greece) and *Jester* (Michael Richey, Britain) finished the course after the time limit expired.

Unofficial competitor
Marc Pajot	France	*Paul Ricard*		18 13 41

Retirements

Miss Dubonnet (Florence Arthaud) Dismasted before start.

Jomada (Simon Hunter) Skipper's injury.

Silke (Hans Schulte) Forestay carried away.

Serta Perfectsleeper (Judith Lawson) Dismasted.

Motorola (Jacques Timsit) Sank.

Maurice Lidchi (Michel Horeau) Structural problems.

Tuesday's Child (Warren Luhrs) Keel problems.

Livery Dole (Peter Phillips) Sank after losing float.

Sea Quest (Mac Smith) Top halyard broken.

Raczynski II (Czeslaw Gogolkiewicz) Dismasted by trawler.

Roundabout (Theo Cockerell) Burnt out in Azores.

Lady Dona (Piet ter Laag) Skipper ill.

Brittany Ferries II (Bernard Pallard) Returned to France.

Mattia III (Antonio Chioatto) Sank.

Gauloises IV (Eric Loizeau) Holed in hull.

Fleury Michon (Nicholas Clifton) Capsized.

Charles Heidsieck (Jean-Claude Parisis) Broken rudder.

Gautier (Jean Yves Terlain) Electrical problems.

Key to Class	Size Limits
P for Pen Duick	56 ft. overall, 46 ft. waterline
G for Gypsy Moth	44 ft. overall, 36 ft. waterline
J for Jester	32 ft. overall, 26 ft. waterline

As I predicted the year before the race, the first six boats to cross the line were trimarans, with the seventh a monohull.

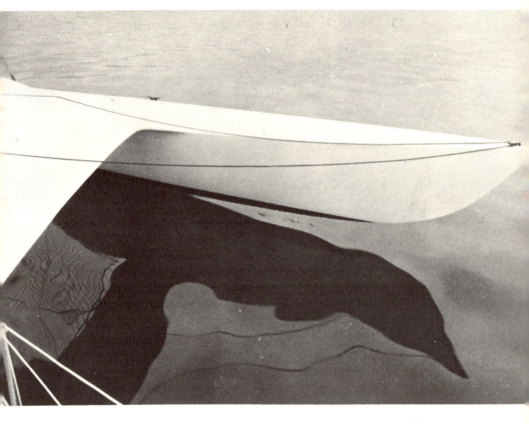

Rogue Wave, *outrigger at rest.* (Bill Lane)

Acknowledgments.

Three old friends, all professional writers whose work I admire — Joseph E. Garland, Herbert A. Kenny, and Charlton Ogburn — urged me to write this book. I shall be forever indebted to them for encouragement and counsel.

Upton B. Brady, Director of the Atlantic Monthly Press, guided my organization of the material with unfailing good judgment and patience. Betsy Pitha of Little, Brown sharpened the manuscript in one hundred helpful ways. Janis Capone labored over the photos and maps until a design emerged that clarifies my tale. How fortunate the writer who falls heir to the handiwork of such talented people. To them my heartfelt thanks.

Philip S. Weld
Gloucester, Mass.
September 14, 1981

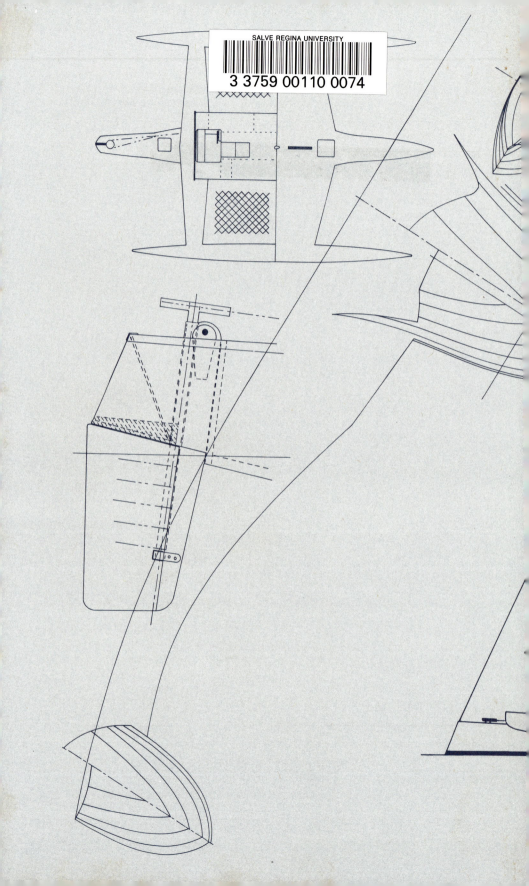